Business Processes:
Operational Solutions for
SAP Implementation

Victor Portougal
University of Auckland, New Zealand

David Sundaram
University of Auckland, New Zealand

IRM Press
Publisher of innovative scholarly and professional
information technology titles in the cyberage
Hershey • London • Melbourne • Singapore

Acquisitions Editor:	Michelle Potter
Development Editor:	Kristin Roth
Senior Managing Editor:	Amanda Appicello
Managing Editor:	Jennifer Neidig
Copy Editor:	Angela Thor
Typesetter:	Sharon Berger
Cover Design:	Lisa Tosheff
Printed at:	Yurchak Printing Inc.

Published in the United States of America by
    IRM Press (an imprint of Idea Group Inc.)
    701 E. Chocolate Avenue, Suite 200
    Hershey PA 17033-1240
    Tel: 717-533-8845
    Fax: 717-533-8661
    E-mail: cust@idea-group.com
    Web site: http://www.irm-press.com

and in the United Kingdom by
    IRM Press (an imprint of Idea Group Inc.)
    3 Henrietta Street
    Covent Garden
    London WC2E 8LU
    Tel: 44 20 7240 0856
    Fax: 44 20 7379 0609
    Web site: http://www.eurospanonline.com

Library of Congress Cataloging-in-Publication Data

Portougal, Victor, 1941-
  Business processes : operational solutions for SAP implementation / Victor Portougal and David Sundaram.
    p. cm.
  Summary: "This book is about Enterprise Resource Planning (ERP) systems implementation, focusing on business operations/processes and information systems to support business operations/processes"-- Provided by publisher.
  Includes bibliographical references and index.
  ISBN 1-59140-979-9 (hardcover) -- ISBN 1-59140-614-5 (softcover) -- ISBN 1-59140-615-3 (ebook)
  1. Management information systems. 2. Industrial management. I. Sundaram, David. II. Title.
  HD30.213.P66 2006
  658.4'038'011--dc22
                     2005023876

British Cataloguing in Publication Data
A Cataloguing in Publication record for this book is available from the British Library.

In Memoriam

Dr. Victor Portougal
(1941-2005)

Victor was a wonderful person who deeply impacted all those whom he touched. His warmth, quick intelligence, hard work, ability to span interdisciplinary boundaries with ease, and great sense of humor will be sorely missed by his family, friends, colleagues, and students. Victor taught me much as I worked closely with him on many projects in the past few years, especially the art of collaborative work. He also sowed the seeds in my mind regarding 'Time as a human construct'. One of the last things he was going to do was teach me to play chess properly (he was the New Zealand Senior Chess Champion in 2002). Unfortunately it was not to be. I will miss him.

David Sundaram

Business Processes:
Operational Solutions for SAP Implementation

Table of Contents

Chapter III
Modelling Business Processes **45**

Chapter IV
Enterprise Systems Implementation Issues **72**

Chapter V
Enterprise Systems Implementation Phases **89**

Chapter VI
Enterprise Systems: The SAP Suite **128**

Preface

This is a book about Enterprise Resource Planning (ERP)/Enterprise Systems (ES) implementation. At the same time, it is also a book about business operations and information systems to support business operations. The question is, why did we decide to unite these three seemingly disparate topics? There are a large number of books treating ERP implementation, operations management, and information systems, separately. At the same time, books dedicated to all three topics applied to practical issues of ERP implementation are scarce. Brady, Monk, and Wagner (2001) say that according to their experience teaching, ERP merely as software did not work. In uniting these three topics in one book, they hope to avoid the problems they encountered, and therefore, better educate the students. They discovered the ERP education was flawed because it was based on the following faulty assumptions:

1. All students understand how businesses and functional areas operate. In fact, many students do not yet have a good grasp of how profit-making organisations operate.

2. All students understand the problems inherent in unintegrated systems. In fact, even the most advanced undergraduate and MBA students do not truly grasp what goes on in real companies, where people in different functional areas must work together to achieve company goals.

3. All students understand how an information system should help business managers make decisions. In fact, some students do not understand this well.

These same assumptions are also applied to ERP/ES implementation team members. When a company decides to implement an ERP system, usually a team is formed consisting of at least two groups of specialists:

Group 1.   Operational staff of the company under implementation; and

Group 2.   System analysts from the software or consulting firm, specialised on ERP implementation.

Sometimes there are other groups like information systems (IS) specialists from the company under implementation, or software professionals from the software company, and this makes the team more inconsistent.

Considering the two basic groups, assumptions 1 and 2 may frequently be incorrect for Group 2, while assumptions 2 and 3 rarely are true for Group 1. For successful implementation, both groups need an understanding that ERP can solve the problems that arise from having unintegrated information systems, for example, that data sharing in real time throughout a company's functional areas is increasing the efficiency of operations, and is helping managers to make better decisions.

Jang and Lim (2004) argue that the use of a commercial Enterprise Resource Planning system is now integrated into Industrial Engineering (IE) curriculum. The ERP system, a business information system that considers all facets of a business, provides an integrated presentation that is needed to educate future managers. It also creates an active-learning environment that uses modern technology. The integration also simulates real employment and addresses educational concerns. Teaching the industry's needs to students, and introducing them to a state-of-the-art ERP/ES system, can foster their future development.

This explains why we think that a book uniting the three above topics is vitally important for implementation specialists as well as for students.

The adoption of Enterprise Resource Planning in the business world may, in fact be the most important development in the corporate use of information technology in the 1990s (Davenport, Harris, & Cantrell, 2004). ERP systems appear to be a dream come true for managers who have longed for an enterprise-wide, integrated, information systems solution. ERP systems are packaged software applications that connect and manage information flows within and across complex organisations, allowing managers to make decisions based on information that truly reflects the current state of their business.

ERP systems also automate complex transaction processes, and thus have the potential to reduce costs (Davenport et al., 2004). Integrated information systems provided by ERP-enabled organisations to react quickly to competitive pressures and market opportunities, achieve lower inventory, and maintain tightened supply chain links. ERP technology is even more appealing to organisations due to its increasing capability to integrate with the most advanced electronic and mobile commerce technologies (Al-Mashari, 2002). It is not surprising that the promise of an ERP solution to the problem of business integration is enticing (Davenport, 1998).

ERP systems have successfully enhanced the efficiency of a wide range of businesses by providing them with seamless access to the information they need. Many companies that have implemented an ERP system successfully have enjoyed operational and strategic benefits from the system. But implementing an ERP system is not an easy job. ERP implementation is a complex task that requires substantial time, money, and internal resources. It follows that ERP system implementations fail more often than not (Legare, 2002). One horror story of a failed ERP implementation occurred at Foxmeyer Drug, a $5 billion pharmaceutical company. The company filed for bankruptcy in 1996 and argued that the primary cause of its difficulties was a failed ERP implementation that crippled the business. (Legare, 2002)

ERP systems are business software packages that support daily business operations and decision making. These packages are capable of seamlessly integrating all the information flowing throughout a company, from financial and accounting information, human resource information, manufacturing information, supply chain information, to customer information (Davenport, 2000). For a long time, business organisations have struggled and have invested huge amounts of money in a search for a seamlessly integrated system within and across organisations. Most of these efforts ended up with disappointing results. That is why the promise of an off-the-shelf solution to the problem of business integration is very enticing.

ERP originated from material requirements planning (MRP) and manufacturing resource planning (MRP II) (Chen, 2001; Davenport, 2000). In a typical manufacturing environment, the master production schedule (MPS) determines the quantity of each finished product required in each planning period. Based on the MPS, the organisation then calculates requirements for the parts and raw materials that make up those finished products. MRP is a production planning and control technique in which the MPS is used to schedule production and create purchase orders for the part and raw material.

Following its useful application in manufacturing functions, MRP was expanded to include more business functions. In the early 1980s, MRP expanded to a company-wide system, which was capable of planning and controlling almost all the organisation's resources. This development was so fundamentally different from the original concepts of MRP, a new term, manufacturing resource planning, was coined. A major purpose of MRP II is to integrate various primary functions (e.g., production, marketing, and finance, human resources) into the planning process.

In the 1990s, MRP II was further evolved into enterprise resource planning, a term coined by the Gartner Group of Stamford, Connecticut, USA. ERP is capable of planning resources not only within an organisation but also across organisations in a supply chain. These capabilities distinguished ERP from MRP II, which only focused on the planning and scheduling of internal resources.

One major feature of ERP is that core organisation activities, such as manufacturing, human resources, finance, and supply chain management, are automated, and improved significantly by incorporating best practices in the industry, thus facilitating better managerial control, quicker decision-making, and lower operational cost (Al-Mashari, Al-Mudimigh, & Zairi 2003).

ERP systems started to gain in popularity in 1994 when SAP, a German based company, released its latest ERP systems package known as SAP R/3. Since then, companies have begun to spend billions dollars for ERP systems offered by SAP and other ERP systems vendors. According to Lea, Gupta, and Yu (2005), most Fortune 500 companies have already adopted ERP systems, and many midsize companies (less than 1000 employees) are planning ERP implementation. Many organisations have successfully adopted ERP systems, yet many more organisations have spent fortunes only to find that business performance has not improved to satisfactory levels within the expected time frame (Robinson & Wilson, 2001). Problems associated with ERP implementation are often classified into technical and organisational aspects. Technical aspects include the technology readiness of an organisation, the complexity of commercial ERP software, data loss due to the compatibility of data architectures between the old legacy systems and the new ERP software, and inadequacies of newly redesigned business processes. Common organisational factors may include employees' resistance to change, inadequate training, underestimated implementation time and cost, unwillingness to adopt new business processes, and strategic view of technology adoption (Mabert, Soni, & Venkataramanan, 2001).

As a relatively new system, ERP is recognised in the world by several different names. The synonyms for ERP, among others, are integrated standard software packages, enterprise systems, enterprise wide-systems, enterprise business-systems, integrated vendor software, and enterprise application systems (Al-Mashari et al., 2003; Davenport, 2000). Despite the difference in naming, the definitions of ERP proposed by various authors are relatively the same.

Rosemann (1999) defines an ERP system as a customisable, standard application software which includes integrated business solutions for the core processes (such as production planning and control, and warehouse management) and the main administrative functions (such as accounting and human resource management) of an enterprise. Slightly differently, Gable (1998), defines ERP as a comprehensive package software solution that seeks to integrate the complete range of business processes and functions in order to present a holistic view of the business from a single information and IT architecture.

The key points in this definition are that ERP systems cover multiple business functions, and they are packaged systems, not systems that are developed from scratch by user organisations. Shang et al. (2002) pointed out several characteristics of ERP systems, as follows:

- A set of packaged application software modules with an integrated architecture;
- Can be used by organisations as their primary engine for integrating data, processes and information technology, in real time, across internal and external value chains;
- Contains deep knowledge of business practices accumulated from vendor implementations in a wide range of client organisations; and
- A generic product with tables and parameters that user organisations and their implementation partners must configure and customise to meet their business needs.

In short, ERP is a computer system that keeps managers informed about what is happening in real time throughout a corporation and its global connection (Jacobs & Whybark, 2000). In the mid-1990s, the Gartner Group coined the term "ERP" to refer to next generation systems which differ from earlier ones in the areas of relational database management, graphical user interface, fourth generation languages, client-server architecture, and open system capabilities. The integration implies the use of a common database when all the subsystems "talk" directly to each other, and the data are made available in real time (Jacobs & Whybark, 2000). The information is updated as changes occur, and the new status is available for everyone to use for decision making, or for managing their part of the business. The decisions made in different functional areas are based on the same current data to prevent nonoptimal decisions from obsolete or outdated data. Expected benefits from ERP implementation include lower inventory, fewer personnel, lower operating costs, improved order management, on-time delivery, better product quality, higher productivity, and faster customer responsiveness (Robinson & Wilson, 2001).

A study by Deloitte & Touche Consulting, a consulting company, classified an organisation's motivations for ERP implementation into two groups, technological and operational (Al-Mashari et al., 2003). Technological motives relate mainly to:

- Replacement of an unintegrated system,
- Improvement of quality and accessibility of information,
- Integration of business processes and the supporting systems,
- Simplification of integration of business acquisitions into the existing technology infrastructure,
- Replacement of older and obsolete systems,
- Compliance to Y2K requirement, and
- Acquirement of system that can support business growth.

Operational motives, on the other hand, are related to:

- Improving inadequate business performance,
- Reducing high-cost structures,
- Improving responsiveness to customers,
- Simplifying ineffective, complex business processes,
- Supporting new business strategies,
- Expanding business globally, and
- Standardising business process throughout the enterprise.

There are many good reasons why organisations should adopt ERP system. Some of them are listed next.

- **Responsiveness.** In today's business, the speed of an organisation to respond to business requirements can be very vital. With its single database systems and integrated module, ERP systems enable an organisation to make faster and better decisions based on accurate and up-to-date information.

- **Maintenance cost.** The only alternative to the ERP systems is to keep a large number of unintegrated systems, which support various business functions or business process. Maintaining these systems is, of course, very costly, because each system requires a different maintenance programme and different skills.

- **Operational cost.** In an unintegrated systems environment, the data must be entered for each system. Each system may require a different format, which in turn requires data transformation. This "multiple entry" not only costs organisations much more, but also becomes a potential danger for data integrity.

- **Business process improvement.** Since the rise of ERP, many organisations have undertaken business reengineering (BPR) initiatives accompanied by ERP systems implementation, which have led to the invention of the term "ERP-enabled BPR." One of the best ways to improve a business process is to benchmark from the best practice that which has proven to be superior in the industry. Every ERP vendor advertises that their system is designed based on best business practice.

Swanson and Wang (2005) offered a model that explains a firm's success in terms of its adoption know-why and know-when and its implementation know-how. They examined this model in an exploratory survey of some 118 firms' adoption and implementation of packaged business software in the 1990s. Using multivariate methods, they identified business coordination as know-why, and management understanding and vendor support as know-how factors important to success, explaining nearly 60% of the variance.

Firms typically use consultants to aid in the implementation process. Client firms expect consultants to transfer their implementation knowledge to their employees so that they can contribute to successful implementations, and learn to maintain the systems independent of the consultants. Ko, Kirsch, and King (2005), drawing from the knowledge transfer, information systems, and communication literatures, developed an integrated theoretical model that posits that knowledge transfer is influenced by knowledge-related, motivational, and communication-related factors. Data were collected from consultant-and-client, matched-pair samples from 96 ERP implementation projects. A behavioural measure of knowledge transfer that incorporates the application of knowledge was used.

An ERP implementation cycle starts when an organisation realises the need for ERP systems. This need leads to the vendor selection process, whereby a solution is sought to meet this need. Then the organisation will have to decide on the implementation approach. Davenport (2000) identified four alternative implementation approaches based on two key dimensions. The two dimensions are speed, which refers to the time it takes to implement ERP, and focus, which refers to the amount of business change and value to an organisation. From the four alternatives, the slow, technical (poor implementation) is the only alternative that must be avoided because technical focus brings little business value. Therefore, it does not make sense to spend a long time on it. The other alternatives are up to the organisation to choose, depending on its business strategy.

An enterprise system is a generic solution which is designed based on a series of assumptions about the way companies operate in general (Davenport et al., 2004). Vendors, as mentioned before, try to structure the systems to reflect best practices, but it is the vendor, not the customer, that is defining what "best" means. In many cases, the system will enable a company to operate more efficiently than it did before (Davenport et al., 2004). In some cases, though, the system's assumptions will run counter to a company's best interests. When an organisation chooses strategic focus as an implementation approach, it must decide whether to change their business processes or to customise the ERP package to suit their business processes.

ERP implementation is a huge project that requires a substantial amount of money, time, and other internal resources. A huge project always represents a big risk, which is difficult to manage. For this reason, most organisations prefer to implement ERP systems gradually. It usually starts from accounting and financial modules, followed by manufacturing, supply chain, and other modules. Academics have different opinions about the validity of this approach (Davenport, 2000). Davenport advocates that an organisation should strive for business value in their ERP implementation.

After deciding which approach to be used in ERP implementation, the organisation should create and maintain conditions for project implementation such as

- Establish a project team,
- Define scope of the project,
- Establish procedure for monitoring and managing performance, and
- Provide required training for participants.

And then the implementation begins. At this stage, the organisation should define and develop processes, modify software if necessary, test (pilot) processes, establish and assign responsibilities for processes, design and create documentation, train users, and set up data. After all these steps are completed, the organisation "goes live" with its ERP. During the early stage of go-live phase, the implementation team will need to provide help desk for users before they get used to the new, process execution environment.

Even though ERP has been implemented and executed successfully, the real business value may not be realised quickly. ERP systems implementation is an ongoing process. To fully benefit from the ERP system, once it is installed and used in an organisation's operations, it needs to be reviewed and improved for better performance. The adoption of a continuous improvement programme after the go-live period enables the benefits of the system to be fully exploited (Davenport et al., 2004).

This book details the most important steps of the design and implementation process, while, simultaneously, providing knowledge about its basic steps. Chapter I defines the business process as the most fundamental concept of contemporary business organisation, and discusses the sequence of steps in business process redesign. We discuss at length the mechanisms for identifying key processes.

Chapter II discusses the step that follows the process identification step, namely, modelling the processes, as they exist in the organisation. Then comes process analysis — this part of the overall life cycle is about gathering more information about the processes that we have identified in the very first step. The next key step is process improvement/transformation, after which comes process implementation, which can have two distinct views: organisation point of view and information technology point of view. The next key step in the process is the monitoring and controlling of the processes that go on within an organisation. This monitoring could trigger another cycle of process change, where we move into the process identification, modelling, improvement, implementation and execution.

Chapter III is about the modelling of business processes, which is vital not only for business process management, but also for implementation of enterprise systems. Many frameworks and architectures have been proposed for modelling business processes. One of them is the Architecture of Integrated Information Systems (ARIS) that is tightly integrated with SAP R/3, and described in detail, including Event-Driven Process Chains (EPC). We focus on the ARIS House Of Business Engineering in this chapter because the ARIS models have a one-to-one correspondence to the way SAP R/3 models its business processes.

Implementation of enterprise systems is analysed in Chapters IV and V. Chapter IV focuses on implementation issues, while Chapter V focuses on implementation phases. Unfortunately, none of the traditional software development life cycles seem to capture the complexity of what was going on in the context of enterprise systems implementation. In this chapter, we focus not on the vendor's life cycle, but on the enterprise system adopter's life cycle. And we elaborate on what goes on in each of the phases of this life cycle. Three distinct phases in an enterprise system's implementation are recognised. The first phase is the project phase, in which the software is configured to suit the requirements of the organisation. The second phase is the shakedown phase, during which the organisation moves from the go-live status to the normal operation status. We look at the question, what is the time period that it takes an organisation to get back to normalcy? The third phase is the onward and upward phase. It is in this phase that the organisation attempts to realise all the benefits, or the majority of the benefits, that they believe they could obtain by implementing the enterprise system. After we have looked at all the steps to the implementation of the enterprise system, we consider what would be termed as a successful enterprise system implementation, and enterprise system implementation risks.

There is a variety of systems that go towards supporting processes in an organisation. Chapter VI describes one of them — the SAP Suite. SAP is one of the leading vendors of such integrated information systems. It provides integrated information from accounting to manufacturing and from sales to service. Whenever data is entered in one functional area for one particular transaction, this data is automatically reflected in all the related functional areas. The SAP system supports and integrates thousands of business processes. The core system uses a single database. The SAP system has strengths in certain industries, but it has offerings or reference models that have been specialised to most of the major industries in the world.

All subsequent chapters give an extensive case study. Chapter VII sets the case of SAP Production Planning module implementation at EA Cakes Ltd.

The market forced the company to change its sales and production strategy from "make-to-order" to "make-to-stock." The decision to change the strategy involved not only the company's decision to invest much more money in accumulating and keeping stocks of finished goods, it required also a complete redesign of its production planning system, which was an integral part of an ERP system that used SAP software.

In the EA Cakes case study, the management decided to change the production planning system. While there is evidence that the existing system had faults, it had nevertheless been developed to suit the existing situation and the people who managed it. This fact raises the question of where to start when attempting to improve a planning system. It is very rare to be involved in designing the planning system right at the firm's beginnings, and more often, the planning system has evolved over a period of time, and is designed to suit some form of management goals or objectives, or to suit the existing technology and processes. We can assume in most cases that the existing system has been designed with the best knowledge and understanding of the existing situation. To improve the situation, therefore, needs new knowledge, or the ability to see something that was missed in the original design phase. This is the material placed in Chapters VIII and IX. Chapter VIII concentrates on structural issues, while Chapter IX tackles the design of the capacity management business processes. Chapter X contains case solutions. Chapter XI presents some special topics in production planning redesign. After analysing the competitive advantage from production planning, we concentrate on advanced problems like balancing capacity vectors, and factors of the production environment, most influential in production planning. Chapter XII gives a tutorial case study using a pasta producing company. The case solution is given up to the end of the business process redesign stage. The SAP implementation (quite similar to the one described for EA Cakes Ltd, Chapter VII) is left to the readers of the book, or to the students, if the book is used in education. The main lesson of this case is the following: though the company does not look like EA Cakes Ltd, and the goals of the production planning systems are different, nevertheless, analogous SAP solutions can be used to give computer support to the production planning staff. The concluding Chapter, Chapter XIII, discusses some of the problems with ERP implementation with specific reference to the case, and it also looks at some of the lessons learned.

Chapter I

Business Processes:
Definition, Life Cycle, and Identification

Organisations as Systems

Organisations are fundamentally systems that convert inputs to certain outputs and hopefully, in the process, add value. Inputs could be anything from people, to materials, to money to information, while the outputs could be products, services, waste, or even intellectual property (Figure 1.1). To support this conversion, most organisations would carry out hundreds to thousands of processes that span functions such as production, research, development, and marketing. These processes, in turn, would be overseen by planning, organising and control mechanisms. While the flow of products and services occurs in the forward direction, there is an equally important flow of information backward that enables feedback and control. But for these mechanisms and flows to function effectively, business, information and decision processes need to be interwoven together synergistically. We club all these processes together under the umbrella term "business processes."

Figure 1.1. Organisations as conversion systems

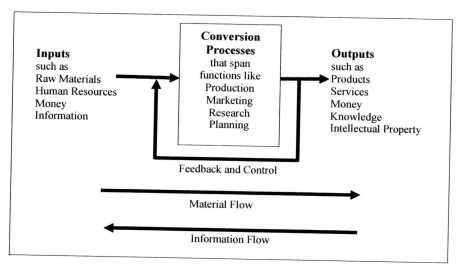

Business Process Definition

Many definitions for business processes have been put forward over the years. Davenport (1993, p.5), for example, defines a process as "a structured, measured set of activities designed to produce a specified output for a particular customer or market" and as "a specific order of work activities across time and place, with a beginning, an end, and clearly identified inputs and outputs: a structure for action." Rosemann (2001, p.18) defines business processes in a much more formal fashion as "the self-contained, temporal and logical order (parallel and/or serial) of those activities, that are executed for the transformation of a business object with the goal of accomplishing a given task." A business object may be an inquiry from a customer, an order from a customer, a quotation prepared for a customer, delivery note from a supplier, and so forth. Along similar lines to Rosemann, Sharp, and McDermott (2001, p.58) define a business process as,

a collection of interrelated work tasks, initiated in response to an event that achieves a specific result for the customer of the process.

It is worth exploring each of the phrases within this definition.

"achieves a particular result"
- The result might be Goods and/or Services.
- It should be possible to identify and count the result, for example, Fulfillment of Orders, Resolution of Complaints, Raising of Purchase Orders, and so forth.

"for the customer of the process"
- Every process has a customer. The customer may be internal (employee) or external (organisation). While the "Fulfillment of Order" process has an external customer, there are many other processes such as "Recruit Employee" whose customer is internal.
- A key requirement is that the customer should be able to give feedback on the process

"initiated in response to a specific event"
- Every process is initiated by an event.
- The event is a request for the result produced by the process.

"work tasks"
- The business process is a collection of clearly identifiable tasks executed by one or more actors (person, or organisation, or machine, or department).
- It is not a random collection of tasks.
- A task could potentially be divided up into more and finer steps.

"a collection of interrelated"
- Such steps and tasks are not necessarily sequential, but could have parallel flows connected with complex logic.
- The steps are interconnected through their dealing with or processing one (or more) common work item(s) or business object(s).

The business process enables us to understand the dynamism involved in the delivery of value by an organisation. Business processes may be generic, or particular to a given industry or organisation.

Distinguishing Business Processes from Business Functions

One of the most common mistakes made by anyone trying to understand and/or model processes is to mistake a business function for a business process. Business processes are by nature inter-functional, that is, they span multiple business functions. Functions are usually specific to departments which concentrate/specialise certain skills and/or knowledge. Common examples of such functions are Manufacturing, Marketing, Sales, Human Resources, and Finance. Even the simplest of processes involves the application of specialist skills found in different departments/functions.

A process such as "Sales Order Processing" would involve first, taking the order (Sales function), then, obtaining the raw materials to fulfill the order (Logistics function), making the product (Manufacturing function), shipping the finished product (Shipping function), invoicing the customer (Billing function), and obtaining payment from the customer (Collections function). Quite often, modelers define their processes so narrowly that they end up defining just what goes on within a single function. This again leads to the reinforcement of functional silos/stovepipes where functional efficiencies might be high, but overall enterprise-wide level-process efficiencies are low.

The Process Life Cycle

There are three key trends that characterise business processes: digitisation (automation), integration (intra- and interorganisational), and life cycle management (Kalakota & Robinson, 2003). Digitisation involves the attempts by many organisations to completely automate as many of their processes as possible. Another equally important initiative is the seamless integration and coordination of processes within and without the organisation: backward to the

Figure 1.2. Business Process Management Life Cycle (Adapted from Rosemann, 2001, p.2)

1. Process identification
2. Process modeling (as-is)
3. Process analysis
4. Process improvement (to-be)
5. Process implementation
6. Process execution (ES enabled)
7. Process monitoring and controlling

supplier; forward to the customers; and vertically of operational, tactical, and strategic business processes. The management of both these initiatives/trends depends to a large extent on the proper management of processes throughout their life cycle (Figure 1.2), from process identification, process modelling, process analysis, process improvement, process implementation, and process execution, to process monitoring and controlling (Rosemann, 2001). Implementing such a life cycle orientation enables organisations to move in benign cycles of improvement; and sense, respond, and adapt to the changing environment (internal and external).

The overall process life cycle that we have just seen as proposed by Rosemann can, in a sense, be thought of as being made up of just three main steps as

Figure 1.3. Three key steps of the Business Process Management Life Cycle

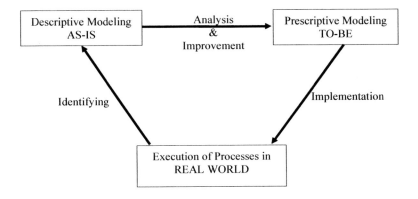

illustrated in Figure 1.3. First you look at the real world organisation and come up with a descriptive model of that real world organisation, which can be termed as the as-is model. And this descriptive model can then be analysed and improved upon to result in a prescriptive model of the world. That is, a model of the world that we think is better than the current model of the processes, and this prescriptive model is termed as the to-be model. The third and crucial step is to implement and execute this prescriptive model back into the organisation. Thus, we have the three steps of descriptive modelling of the real world, followed by prescriptive modelling that addresses some of the problems followed by the implementation of the prescriptive model. We look at the key step of "process identification" in the following section, and the rest of the steps are discussed in detail in the next chapter.

Process Identification

Process identification is the step where we identify the crucial processes that need to be reengineered and/or that need to be supported by systems that need to be implemented in a better fashion within the organisation. There are many ways in which we could identify these crucial processes; we discuss some representative ones in the sections below.

Process Evaluation

Peter Keen (1997), in the book *The Process Edge*, suggests a mechanism by which we can evaluate the process portfolio. The first question he asks is "Does the process define the Firm to customers, employees and investors?" If the answer is "yes," then it is a matter of identity and we do need to look at the process, it is an important process. But if the answer is "no," the next question that we ask is, "Is excelling at the process critically important to the performance of the business?" Again, if the answer is "yes," then we consider it as a priority process that does need to be considered. But if the answer is "no," the next question we ask is "Does the process provide a necessary support to other processes?" Then the process again needs to be considered, but it is a background process. But if the answer is "no," the final question that we need to ask is, "Is this process conducted due to legal requirements?" If the answer is "yes,'" then it is a mandated process, and again we need to consider it, but if it is absolutely mandatory, maybe there is no way in which we could change the process, but at least we can see whether we can improve it in some fashion. But if the answer is "no," to the final question, then the process is just being conducted because of historical reasons, and it is folklore, and hence, abandon the process.

Value vs. Need to Reorganise

Rosemann (2001) proposes another mechanism for identification of processes, and he suggests that whenever we look at processes, we look at them from two dimensions or perspectives. The first dimension is the need to reorganise, and the second dimension is the value of the process (Figure 1.4). If the value of the processes is high, and the need to reorganise it is high, then that is the very first process that we need to consider when we are reengineering or thinking of supporting, using enterprise systems. If the process value is low, but the need to reorganise is still very high, then that is the second set of processes that we need to consider. The third set of processes that we need to consider is the

Figure 1.4. Value of process vs. need to reorganise (Adapted from Rosemann, 2001, p.4)

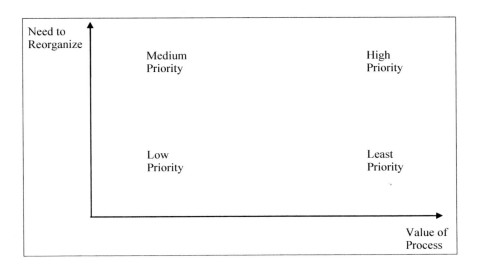

processes that have low value, and the need to reorganise is small. And only in the last case do we consider the processes that have a high value and a low need for reorganisation. In fact, it is very dangerous to reorganise this last set of processes because they do carry high value, and if, due to reorganisation we mess it up in some fashion, it is going to have a serious impact on the organisation. So when we do a reengineering exercise, we need to be cognizant of the fact that we consider the processes that carry a high value and a high need to reorganise first, and processes that have a high value but a low need to reorganise last.

Dysfunction, Importance, and Feasibility

Hammer and Champy (Rosemann, 2001) have their own set of criteria by which they identify processes that need to be reengineered. Three important criteria that they suggest are: Dysfunction, Importance, and Feasibility. Dysfunction is where we consider the processes that are in dire straits or deep trouble. Importance is where we consider the processes which have the greatest impact on the customer. Feasibility is where we consider the processes that are most amenable to successful redesign.

Davenport's Steps

Davenport (1993) not only comes up with similar criteria, but also a set of steps to identify processes that need to be reengineered. The first step is to list all the major processes that occur within the organisation. Step 2 is to determine very clearly the process boundaries. Step 3 is to assess the strategic relevance of each of these major processes. Step 4 is to analyse these processes, and make a decision on the health of each one these processes. Then finally, we qualify what is the background, the cultural, and the political implications of each of these processes, and we select only those processes that are filtered out as unhealthy for reengineering.

Value Chain

Another mechanism that can be used hand in hand with some of the proposals that we have seen above is the value chain proposed by Porter (1985). Porter, in his seminal work, suggests that we can divide activities that go on in an organisation into Primary Activities and Supporting Activities. Included in primary activities are inbound logistics, operations, outbound logistics, sales and marketing, and service. Inbound logistics include activities such as receiving, storing, disseminating, and inputs to the product. Operations are all the activities that transform the inputs into the final product. Outbound logistics is about collecting, storing, and physically distributing products to the buyers. Sales and marketing provide a mechanism by which the buyers, the customers, can purchase the product. But it also includes mechanisms by which we induce the customer to buy our product. Service is providing a quality of service so that we enhance the value that the product is offering to the customer. Supporting activities, which can also be termed as secondary activities, include aspects such as procurement, technology development, human resource management, and infrastructure. When we consider processes for reengineering, it is those activities that are on the value chain that provide value, that add value to the product as it goes through the organisation, as it gets transformed through the organisation, that are of absolute, vital importance. Hence, it makes sense to consider these primary activities for reengineering before we consider the secondary activities.

Competitive Advantage

Another mechanism to identify processes that are of vital importance is to look at the activities that an organisation conducts in order to be competitive. What used to be competitive advantages in the past have become competitive necessities these days. Thus, what used to be thought of as activities that an organisation had to undertake to be competitive are now activities that are necessities. For example, in the past, organisations could differentiate on aspects such as functionality of the product and cost of the product, and this would have provided competitive advantage. But nowadays, functionality and cost are taken for granted. There used to be a time when aspects such as time to market, flexibility, and service used to provide competitive advantage. But nowadays, these are taken for granted, and they have become necessities. So an organisation needs to be aware of the objectives that should guide it to remain competitive in the future. They could be as varied as market differentiation, mass customisation, the value for price, co-productivity, co-option, and so on. Depending on what we are using as a mechanism to be competitive, the supporting processes, which will support and provide that competitive advantage, are going to be different. Hence, identifying aspects that are going to make us competitive and identifying the processes that are going to support them will enable us to identify, in turn, the key processes that we need to look at from the reengineering perspective. Walters (2002) gives an excellent example of the issues that are involved in terms of competitive advantage. While we consider this, we need to keep in mind that though we have made a point saying that what used to be an activity that provided us competitive advantage in the past is a competitive necessity now, this is not the same for all organisations. Some organisations might still be competing on quality and innovation, whereas some other organisation might now be competing on time to market or flexibility or market differentiation. So it depends on where the industry that you are in is in terms of its life cycle. Is it still in its infancy where functionality, quality, and innovation are very important? Or has it matured over a period of time, whereby it has come so far that it is only on aspects such as mass customisation or market differentiation or prosumerism that it competes?

Goals

Another mechanism of identifying key processes is to look at this whole problem from the viewpoint of what are the strategic goals of the organisation. What is it that we, as an organisation, want to achieve? And how do we go about achieving those strategic goals? What are the processes that are going to help us achieve those strategic goals? This is slightly different from the competitive advantage that we talked about in the previous section because here, what we are saying is that the strategic goals can include aspects that relate to competitive advantage, but strategic goals, by its very statement, is much broader in its scope. Hence, another mechanism is to look at the goals of the organisation, then identify the processes that will help us to achieve those goals, and then look at these processes from the reengineering point of view, so that we can more efficiently and more effectively achieve these goals. This process can be made more explicit by specifying what are the strategic goals or objectives, and based on that, identifying the critical success factors (CSF) that will help us in achieving those strategic objectives. Once we have identified the CSFs, then we can identify what are the key performance indicators (KPI) that will help us in identifying whether we are meeting those critical success factors satisfactorily. Once we have identified the KPIs, then we can identify what are all the processes that are going on in the organisation that will enable us to improve the identified KPIs. For example, the strategic objective could be customer satisfaction, but then we ask the question "What are the critical success factors that will help us to achieve this objective?" It could be *error free order processing* or the *speed with which we fulfil a particular order.* Each of these critical success factors, in turn, has got performance indicators.

For example, when we consider *error free order processing,* how do we measure that this critical success factor has been met? We could measure it in terms of how often the delivery is on time. That is "What is the percentage of the time that the deliveries are on time?" Another measure could be "How often is the order correct in terms of the items that were delivered?" also known as volume accuracy. That is, "What percentage of the time do we get the volumes correct?" A third indicator could be the return rate. That is, "What is the percentage of all the products that are returned due to whatever reason — it could be a fault, it could be an unsatisfied customer?" Thus, we can verify whether we are meeting the critical success factor, *error free order processing* by monitoring the performance indicators such as *on time delivery, volume accuracy,* and the *return rate.* This, in turn, will help us to identify

Figure 1.5. Vision- and strategy-driven Process Change Management

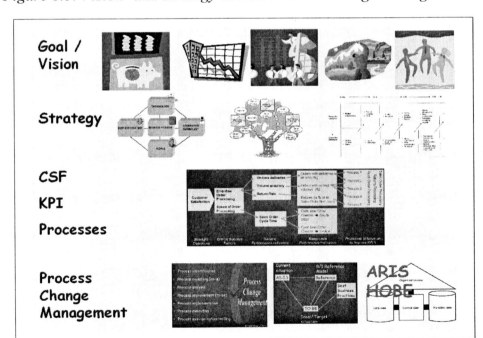

whether we are meeting the strategic objective of satisfying the customer. Now if we take something like orders with delivery on time, we know that this performance indicator has got many processes that will impinge on it, that will have an impact on how well we are doing against this indicator. Thus, we can trace from the strategic objective to the critical success factor to the performance indicator and to the business processes that will help us in improving those performance indicators, which will in turn help us in meeting those critical success factors which in turn will help us to meet the strategic objectives.

An overall picture of what we have been discussing so far is that goals or visions of organisations need to drive this strategy. The strategy will be achieved by looking closely at critical success factors. Critical success factors, in turn, can be monitored by key performance indicators. And key performance indicators can be improved by improving the processes that have an impact on the KPIs and CSFs. How do we go about this? This is through a benign process change management life cycle that constantly monitors, senses, identifies processes that need to be changed and that can be improved, models them, improves them, implements them, executes them, and monitors them to see to it that they are going fine, and if they are not going fine, again improves them, and so on, in cycles of better and better/improved processes (Figure 1.5).

Goal or Vision link to Strategy

The goal or vision of an organisation can be as simple as making money, or improving some aspect of their performance, or reducing some cost or waste. Or it could be to see to it that production is maintained, but not at the expense of harming the environment, or service is provided while seeing to it that the environment is not damaged. The goal could also be to keep the people employed happy, or it could be to balance the triple bottom lines of economy, environment, and society. But to achieve these goals or visions, the organisation needs to have a strategy. The strategy cannot be achieved on its own: there needs to be a sound organisational structure, there needs to be people, and there needs to be technology to support the strategy. But one core component that pulls all these things together, and is vital for achieving the business strategy, are the business processes that occur in an organisation (Figure 1.6).

Thus, we can see that to achieve this strategy, we need to have a sound organisation, sound business processes, good people, and good information systems in place. Thus, the overall organisation strategy can be achieved

Figure 1.6. The MIT90s framework (Adapted from Scott-Morton, 1991, p.28)

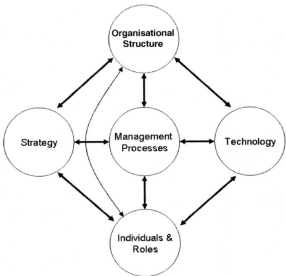

through a sound organisational strategy, a sound information strategy, and a sound business strategy. We also saw earlier that some of the strategies could be oriented towards gaining competitive advantage, and there were many mechanisms that we could adopt, depending on the life cycle of the organisation and the industry, to achieve competitive advantage, which in turn will help us to achieve the goal or vision of the organisation. And these strategies can be operationalised and achieved by focusing on the critical success factors, the key performance indicators that will tell us whether we are meeting those success factors, and, in turn, the processes that have an impact on improving the KPIs and CSFs.

One of the key strategies of organisations in the twenty-first century has been the "sense and respond" strategy. Sensing the changes in the environment, both internal and external, and responding at strategic, tactical, operational, and technological levels that will enable an organisation to adapt and survive. Some of the key elements that will enable the success of this strategy are:

- Adaptability
- Flexibility
- Versatility

- Ability to handle complexity
- Digitisation
- Moving from uni-channel to multi-channel
- Automation
- Reach
- Range

While adaptability, flexibility, and versatility might seem to be very similar concepts, there are subtle differences. Adaptability is the ability of an organisation to change, depending on positive or negative feedback, either in a gradual fashion, or in punctuated equilibria. In contrast, we look on flexibility as a quality of an organisation that allows it to dynamically and flexibly reorganise its strategies, people, processes, and systems. Versatility is a measure by which we can judge the ability of an organisation to move away from the beaten path. Can an organisation that was selling books now sell music: can an organisation that was brick and mortar now adapt to a clicks and mortar environment? The world in which organisations operate is very complex, and to survive in this complex web of interdependencies, an organisation needs to be adaptable, flexible, and versatile. Kalakota and Robinson (2003) identify three dimensions on which processes could be transformed, so as to enable an organisation to be adaptable, flexible, and versatile (Chapter II).

Two mechanisms to judge an organisation's ability to sense, respond, and interact through the value chain are *reach* and *range* (Broadbent, Weill, & St.Clair, 1999). *Reach* enables an organisation to evaluate how easily it can reach its stakeholders, customers, and suppliers, anywhere and at anytime. At one end of the spectrum, we find organisations that are able to connect easily within their business unit(s). And some have the ability to connect easily with all their units spread across geographic and/or national boundaries. Some can even connect easily with their customers and suppliers, whether they have the same IT infrastructure or not. The ultimate is for an organisation to be able to connect to anyone, wherever they are, at any time. And complementarily, we can ask the question, "How automatic and seamless are the *range* of avenues by which we interact with our stakeholders anywhere and anytime?" At one end, we have the ability to just send messages to other units or customers or suppliers. An improvement on this is to have all the key stakeholders have access to information. A more complex ability to support is to enable the stakeholders to be able to perform simple transactions on systems that are not their own. The ultimate is to enable the stakeholders to perform complex transactions on multiple application platforms that are spread across their partner landscapes.

Supporting these key elements necessitates a process-oriented approach. The *business process factory* and *ARIS house of business process excellence* (Scheer & Kirchmer, 2004) are attempts at coming up with a process that enables organisations to sense changes, and respond using best business practices.

SMART Objectives

An important part of coming up with strategies is not only to have a high-level strategic statement, but also to have strategic objectives that fulfil the requirements of SMART, that is, the objectives need to be *specific*, *measurable*, *acceptable*, *realistic* and *time related*. What do we mean by specific? It should be specific enough that we know what it is that we need to do, not something as broad as in "we need to provide better service." It needs to be measurable, that is, we need to say we would like to increase the profit by 5% or whatever, not just say we want to maximise profit. Maximised profit, again, is such a broad kind of an objective that we will never know when we have achieved that objective. Thirdly, the objectives need to be acceptable. That is ethically and morally acceptable to society and to the various stakeholders of the organisation, which will include shareholders, employees, management, and even our competitors. We cannot have an objective that says, "eliminate the competitor at all cost using all possible means"—that is totally unacceptable. Fourthly, the objectives need to be realistic, that is, we should not shoot for something that cannot be achieved either through lack of time or skills or funds or whatever. The objectives need to be something that is achievable. Finally, and not least of all, is the objective needs to be time related, that is, you need to give a concrete time frame within which you are going to achieve the objectives. Do not leave the objectives open-ended in terms of time. You need to say, "we would like to increase our profit by 5% in the next 12 months or 6 months or whatever." Thus, our objectives need to be SMART, but so should the key performance indicators.

Business Process Classification

American Productivity & Quality Center (APQC) has come up with a frame work which follows in the footsteps of the Porter's value chain. This framework differentiates between operating processes, and management and support processes. The operating processes are reminiscent of the primary activities of Porter, and the management and the support processes are similar to the support activities of Porter. APQC considers under operating processes seven key processes: (1) understanding markets and customers, (2) developing a vision and a strategy, (3) designing products and services, (4) marketing and selling the products, (5) producing and delivering the product in the context of the manufacturing organisation or (6) producing and delivering a service in the context of a service organisation and (7) invoicing and servicing the customers. These processes are vital, and add direct value to the product(s) and/or service(s) that are offered by an organisation. Under the management and support processes, APQC includes development and management of human resources, management of information, management of financial and physical resources, execution of environmental management programmes which would help us in meeting triple bottom line objectives, management of external relationships, and finally, management of improvement and change.

In contrast to these processes, Genovese, Bond, Zrimsek, and Frey (2001) of Gartner identify six key process areas, the first being *prospect to cash and care*. This process encompasses *sales order to cash* process as the core area, but prior to this would be the prospecting aspect, and after that would be the post sales, service, and care of the customers. A second key process identified by Gartner is *requisition to payment*. This essentially is the procurement process from the time you request a particular product or service from another organisation, and the time you pay that organisation for the product or service that they have provided. A third important process is *planning and execution*. This process is made up of all the processes related to resource planning, which could include materials, cash, labour, transportation, personnel, and maintenance. It doesn't just stop with planning, but it also goes to executing the plans and controlling the resources right throughout the execution. Another set of processes that Gartner have identified is *plan to performance*. This includes not just payables and receivables, but includes processes that are involved in consolidation, budgeting, treasury and financial management, and reporting. Another key process identified by Gartner is the *design to retirement* process. This is not just about research and development of new product, but it encompasses the entire life cycle of the product or service that the organisation is offering. From its conception in the mind of the researchers in the R&D department, to the time that it is beta tested, to the time that it is rolled out, to the time that it grows and becomes a cash cow, and finally to the time that it is retired. The final process that Gartner identified is *human capital management*, and this includes all processes that are related to the work force. It could be human resource (HR) as well as non-HR business processes, as long as it has an impact on the work force.

The *prospect to cash* process, like all the other processes, is quite involved, and it spans a huge spectrum of sub processes, multiple systems, and multiple organisations. For example, some of the key steps in this process that could be considered are logging of an activity, logging of an opportunity, checking for contract, checking the inventory, checking availability to promise or capability to promise, determining the price, giving a quote to the customer, creating a formal quote, generating of an order, checking the credit of the customer, confirming the order, planning and producing the product, sending advance shipping notice, shipping the product, invoicing the customer, and finally, applying for payment. Now this sequence of sixteen steps goes from the customer to the internal of the organisation to the supplier back to the internals of the organisation and then to the customer. And we can see that to support this process there are many sub-processes and many systems. Three of the key systems that could potentially support this involved, but very important process, are customer relationship management systems, enterprise resource planning systems and supply chain management systems.

Benchmarking

Benchmarking can be another important mechanism by which we can identify the processes that need to be reengineered or that need to be better supported through systems. There are four key mechanisms by which we can benchmark —historical, internal, external, and then theoretical. In historical benchmarking, we compare the KPI results that we are currently obtaining with historical results of those same KPIs from the past. For example, we might compare the KPIs of 2004 with the KPIs of 2003 or with 2002 and so on. Internal benchmarking is benchmarking within the organisation, where you might benchmark one strategic business unit (SBU) against another SBU, or you might benchmark one profit centre against another profit centre, or you might benchmark one department against another department. External benchmarking is one of the commonest types of benchmarking that is done, where we compare our company's results, our company's KPIs against the KPIs of other companies who are in the same business or industry. Finally, theoretical benchmarking is another very useful mechanism whereby we analyse the system and decide what is the theoretical goal against which we can compare ourselves. What is the theoretical but doable target that is possible, keeping in mind the current constraints that the organisation has? So, in theoretical benchmarking, the organisation sets for itself targets, and we compare the actual KPIs that we obtain with the theoretical KPIs that we believe can be achieved. These four types of benchmarking can very quickly tell us what are the KPIs in which we are lagging, either as a department, as an SBU, or as a whole organisation. Once we identify the key indicators in which we are lagging, we can then look at all the related business processes that can help us to improve that particular KPI. There are many organisations in the world which compare and publish KPIs of various organisations in various industries, for example PMG website (http://www.pmgbenchmarking.com) provides this kind of information, and will also conduct the benchmarking exercise on a consultancy basis.

Process Worth

Another mechanism that Peter Keen suggests for finding out whether a process is worth bothering about is to find out what is the worth of the process. The first question he asks is, "Does this process tie up substantial capital?" If the answer is "no," then you can consider its value as neutral and ignore it. But if the answer is "yes," the next question you ask is, "Does it generate more value than the cost of capital it uses?" If the answer is "no," then it is a liability, and we might need to look into the process to find out how we can convert this liability into an asset, even by eliminating the process as whole or by finding out how we can transform it. But if the answer to the last question is "yes," then it means the process is an asset. It is generating more value than the cost of capital that it uses. But that does not mean that we don't bother with trying to improve the process. There could still be more potential for improving the process making it more efficient and more effective, so that it produces more value or it produces the same value at less cost.

Conclusion

This chapter began with defining business processes, and we discussed the importance of distinguishing processes from functions. Following this, we introduced a process management life cycle. We spent quite a bit of time in looking at the first step of the process, namely that of identifying the business process. Though it is a simple step, it is one of the most important steps that one will undertake in this exercise. As the old proverb/adage suggests, "Finding what the problem is, is half the problem solved." And in the same fashion, finding out which process needs to be reengineered, needs to be improved, and needs to be supported by systems such as ERP, customer relationship management (CRM), or supply chain management (SCM) is half the problem solved. The other steps of the process management life cycle, such as modelling, analysis, and implementation, are discussed in the following chapter.

Chapter II

Business Processes:
Modelling, Analysis, and Implementation

Introduction

In the previous chapter, we introduced a useful process management life cycle, and we explored the first step of the same. In this chapter, we delve into detail of the other steps of the life cycle: modelling, analysis, and implementation, and we conclude the chapter by looking at a topic that has not had sufficient exposure in literature, namely mal-processes.

Process Modelling

Once we have identified the process, the next step is to model the process as it exists in the organisation. How do we go about modelling the process? A very useful heuristic proposed by stalwarts in the field is *staple yourself to an order*. Essentially what this means is attaching oneself to the business process, attaching oneself to the business object under consideration: it could be an order, it could be a customer, it could be a student, it could be an employee, it could be a manager, it could be a raw material, or it could be an enquiry from a customer. The heuristic suggests that you follow the business object or the person as they interact with the system, and you study the whole system by stapling yourself to the business object. You travel through the organisation, work in the different roles within the organisation, talk to the different people as they interact with the business object that you are considering. And as you do this, you model the process by which the business object is transformed: you model the process by which the value gets added to the product or service that the organisation is delivering. As you model, remember to keep in mind William of Occam's razor. Occam's razor states that as you model the real world, as you try to abstract the essentials of the real world that are of relevance, you need to be reasonably ruthless. Apply Occam's razor, and see to it that nothing inessential shall pass by it, but as you abide by this dictum, be careful that you do not omit the essentials.

Quite often when you are modelling the current way something is being done, people in organisations might suggest, "Why do we want to bother with the current way we do things, we know that it needs to be improved, so why don't we just model what we want to do and go ahead and implement that model?" Their argument for this is that the results of modelling the current way something is being done become obsolete the moment the to-be processes are designed and implemented. Another important point put forward is that it can be quite time consuming, as well as cost consuming. A third objection which has quite a bit of merit is that as you model the current processes, the analyst could become brainwashed into thinking that the current way something is being done is the best way. Or the analyst could become so narrowly focused, thinking only in the terms of current constraints, that he or she is not able to break out of the bounds of the current problems and constraints. This could result in to-be solutions that are very much like the as-is solutions, hence leading to very minimal improvements. While these objections all have certain merit, the advantages of modelling the current process far outweigh the disadvantages. One of the key advantages is that everybody gets to have a uniform understanding of the problem because it has been modeled, and this model can be shared with various people in the organisation, and you can understand, as an organisation how we are doing and what are the problems with what we are doing. It enables us to have the same terminology, and it also helps in convincing the user of the current process about the problems that exist in it. It is usually when we model the processes that the problems with the current processes become glaringly evident. Thus, it helps users of the current processes to unfreeze and move over to the new processes when they get implemented. The as-is model also acts as a basis against which the to-be processes can be compared. It acts as a benchmarking mechanism to help us understand how much we have improved from the past against various aspects of the process. It can also help us in moving from the as-is into the to-be in increments that help us successfully implement the process. Having the as-is also helps us in the design of the to-be. When we finish designing the to-be process, we can compare it against the as-is and see if all the essential elements of the as-is process are catered for and implemented in the to-be process. Thus, the completeness of the new process can be verified with respect to the old as-is process. Sometimes an analysis of the as-is process can result in a design that is not drastically different because the process may already be optimised. In that case, the as-is process itself becomes the basis for the implementation of an enterprise system or any other system.

There are many important steps that are undertaken, in the context of modelling the process. Chapter III goes in-depth into looking at the modelling of processes, and hence, we won't go in-depth into it at this stage. Once we have modeled the way we do things currently, the next important step is to analyse that process.

Process Analysis

The first step in process analysis is to gather more information about the processes that we have identified in the very first step and modeled in the second. Some of the mechanisms that we used to identify the processes (Chapter I) that need to be reengineered, or addressed in some fashion, come in very handy at this phase, and will provide us with the information that we need to collect. Some of the key questions that we ask in this phase are: What is the main purpose, or the goal or aim of this process that we are looking at? Why are we executing this process the way we are executing it at the moment? Are there any reasons: logical, historical, or legal? What are all the organisational units or departments or functions that are involved in this particular process, either as units that are actively transforming the product or service, or units that are the external or internal customers of this product or service? Another key question concerns the systems that currently exist that either support or have any impact on the process under consideration. What are the points at which the process and the systems interact? One of the questions that was asked in the process identification stage was with respect to problematic processes that needed to be reorganised or reengineered. And in this analysis phase, we go deeper into that, and find out all the different problems that beset this particular process under consideration. Here we might look at the flow of the process, the delays in the process, the problematic outcomes of the process, problems with the inputs to the process, problems with the transformational mechanisms in the process, problems with the personnel who support the process, problems with the systems, or lack of systems to support the process. Another important piece of information that we would have already collected earlier on which would become useful at this phase are the benchmarks. What are the internal, historical, external, or theoretical benchmarks with respect to the process under consideration? While we are doing this analysis, we also need to note down any changes that are going to happen in the environment. Any changes in the business environment, or the technology environment, or the personnel environment, could have an impact on this process in the future. Another exercise that is useful, to be conducted at this stage, is to identify all the problems with the process, but along with the identification of the problem, to also identify whether this problem is very serious, or of medium-level or of a low-level, and what are the potential solutions to solving each one of these problems. A useful mechanism to identify problems with the existing processes, and to list the potential solutions, is to look at generic reference models proposed by software vendors such as SAP, PeopleSoft, or Oracle. For example, the SAP R/3 reference model from SAP has literally thousands of business process models, both for traditional business, as well as for collaborative and e-commerce oriented business. These reference models are, in some senses, the best practices, as identified by the software vendors. And they do help an organisation to identify potential solutions, potential ways in which a particular problem has been solved by others in the field. It is useful to remember that these reference models are abstractions of many models from many organisations, and hence, they are a very lean, and succinct model of how a particular process could be implemented. They may not include all the possible variations: hence, these models are parsimonious by their very nature. These reference models encapsulate thousands of hours by consultants working with customers and getting a solution that is reflective of the best practice in the industry. Hence, using these models to identify problem areas in one's own organisation is a useful start. Sometimes when we are exposed to nothing else except our own way of doing things, we honestly believe that what we are doing is the best. But it is only when we are able to see what somebody else is doing, and we compare the way we do things with the way someone else does things, that it becomes easier for us to understand our own weaknesses, and also prepare us to change to a better way of doing things. Hence, using the reference model as the starting point in process analysis is advisable, once we have identified the problem processes and have collected all the information germane to this process.

Process Transformation

The next key step is process improvement/transformation. There are many dimensions against which a process can be improved or transformed.

Kalakota and Robinson's Process Improvement Dimensions and Categories

Kalakota and Robinson (2003) identify three dimensions on which processes could be transformed, as illustrated in Figure 2.1. The first dimension addresses the degree to which the process can be digitised. At one extreme, you have 0% automation, that is, it is completely manual; at the other extreme you have 100% automation, and there is no manual input as such. And you have a huge continuum in between with various degrees of manual and automation. An ideal to which you want to move is a process where everything is automated. The second dimension that Kalakota and Robinson identify is the scope of process integration. How well are the processes that go on within an organisation integrated together? Do the processes talk to each other seamlessly? At one extreme you have processes that are implemented in isolation, each supported by their own systems and personnel, and at the other extreme, you have processes that go on in multiple organisations (your suppliers, your own organisation, your customers), and these processes are integrated, and operate in a seamless fashion so that people are not aware of when they are working within their organisation, and when they have moved out of their organisation: the points of movement are unnoticeable to the participant of the process or the user of the process. In between these two extremes, we have situations where

Figure 2.1. Process improvement dimensions (Adapted from Kalakota and Robinson, 2003, p.10)

Digitisation	Integration	Interactions
Manual	Department	Single Channel
Semi-automated	Unit	
Completely automated	Multi-Enterprise	Multiple Channel

all the processes within a department are well integrated. And in an even better situation all the processes within a particular business unit or a particular organisation is well integrated. The third dimension refers to the type of process interactions that go on. Are these processes only single channel (brick and mortar) or are they multi-channel (Web site, brick and mortar, and call centre)? Here again, it depends on the industry, but one of things we want to aim towards is a situation where we have multi-channel process interactions.

While we have seen three dimensions of process transformations, Kalakota and Robinson also identify three categories of process execution. At one level, your effort in reengineering could be process improvement, such as what organisations such as Honeywell and Caterpillar have undertaken, where they have tried to reduce: hand off costs between processes; rework; variations of a process using six sigma; transaction costs; end to end process time primarily supported by technology, as well as supported by innovative process flows. And last but not least, improvements which result in enhanced customer satisfaction. At the next level, we have a strategic improvement of processes, such as the ones undertaken by Wal-Mart, Dell, Intel, and Cisco. They have gone beyond just improvement, and have replaced manual processes with digital processes, wherever and whenever possible. They have tried to improve the efficiencies in the whole chain, the logistic chain and the supply chain as a whole. They have not just tried to improve the end-to-end time of a process, but they have tried to also reduce the cycle time of much bigger complex processes. And here again, they have not just gone about improving customer satisfaction, but have gone about trying to improve the whole customer experience, and have shifted their entire operations, so that it now has the customer focus. The third level of process execution is business transformation, as undertaken by organisations such as IBM, AT&T, and Vivendi, where these organisations are changing the way the industry as a whole operates. This is only possible since they are big enough and have sufficient clout to be able to do this.

They are completely changing the way they do business, resulting in huge cultural change, not only amongst the employees of the organisation, but in the whole industry and amongst all the stakeholders in the industry. Here again, in terms of the customer, they have shifted their entire operations so that it is no more product-centric, but it is customer-centric.

Rosemann's Categories

Rosemann (2001) identifies three categories of improvements: (1) improvements related to the specific outcome or result of a process, (2) improvements related to the flow of activities and tasks of a process, and (3) improvements related to all the resources that go into supporting a process.

When we look at outcome related improvements some of the things that we can attempt are, first of all, see if we can eliminate the outcome. Elimination of the outcome eliminates the process as a whole. A key question to ask is, "Is this really required?" An equally important question to ask is, "Can this outcome be substituted by something else?" Another option could be digitisation of the outcome. Can we standardise similar processes, so that we have one common process? Or, looking at it from another perspective, can we focus on certain parts of the process and make it more efficient rather than clubbing it together with a whole lot of other processes?

When we consider activity-related improvements, one of the first things that we want to ask ourselves after we have looked at the model of the process is, "Can we eliminate any one of the steps of the process?" If we cannot eliminate, the next question is, "Can we automate it?" Other questions we ask ourselves are "Can these activities be conducted in parallel?" In that way, we reduce the overall lead time, or end-to-end process time. "Can we change the flow of activities so that it does not follow a push philosophy, but follows a pull philosophy?" An important consideration when we are looking at activities-related improvements is to focus on bottleneck activities, activities at which there are long delays due to whatever reason — insufficient capacity, and/or insufficient materials.

In the context of resource-related improvements, the kind of things that we look at are getting the correct resources in the right place at the right time, and integration of activities so that there are less handovers.

A Generic Approach to the Critical Examination of Processes

We examine the purpose for which the activities are undertaken, the place at which they are undertaken, the sequence in which they are conducted, the person by whom they are conducted, and the means by which they are conducted. All of this is done with the view to, first and foremost, eliminating them if possible, combining them if possible, rearranging them if possible and/or simplifying them if possible. Thus, the question that we ask ourselves when we look at purpose is, "What is the purpose and why is it being done?" With respect to place, we ask ourselves, "Where is it being done and why is it being done there?" With respect to sequence, we ask the question, "When is it being done and why is it done at that time and in this particular sequence?" With respect to person we ask, "Who is doing it and why should it be done by this person? Can it be done by somebody else?" With respect to the means, we ask ourselves, "How is it being done? Why is it being done in this particular fashion?" Here again, the reference models that we discussed earlier come in very handy. We look at our business processes, industry best practices as we know them, reference models that we are familiar with, or reference models that we think would be relevant in case we are going in for enterprise system implementation, so they could be software specific reference models. And using these three models, that is our current model as-is, best business practices as we understand them, and reference models from vendors, and based on the constraints that we have, we come up with a to-be model that is better than our current model and at the same time, closer to the ideal model.

This redesign exercise helps a company focus on their core businesses and focus on creating value for their customers. These activities help to integrate all the critical business processes together. It also helps an organisation realise that it is not just about optimising individual activities or tasks, but it is about management of processes that span the whole organisation, that span multiple stakeholders, including your customers and suppliers. And it is also about reducing, or even completely eliminating, the hand offs that occur between departments when we go across many steps. Many interesting quotes have been given about what is business engineering. I think it is useful to look at some of these quotes, since they help us to realise that this particular step in the business process management life cycle that we are considering is a vital step in the whole life cycle.

- "It is the search for an optimal flow in a company" (Messerli AF, Switzerland).

- "It is the streamlining of business processes to have maximum effect with minimum resources in supporting company goals" (Ernst & Young, South Africa).

- "Business engineering is the rethinking of business processes to improve and accelerate the output of processes, materials or services" (Philip Morris, Lausanne, Switzerland).

- "Business Engineering is the re-thinking of business processes to improve the speed, quality, & output of materials or services" (Philip Morris European Union Region, Switzerland).

- "Business Engineering revolves around information technology and continuous change. It is the constant refinement of an organisation's changing needs" (Esso, Austria).

- "Generally, it is a customer focus. It is also the designing of new processes using new information technology to create an efficient business network that involves creative staff in the process redesign" (Fahrzeugausriistung Berlin GmbH, Germany).

Childe, Maull, and Bennett's Levels of Process Improvement

Childe, Maull, and Bennett (2001) look at process improvement from a variety of perspectives. They say that process improvement can be as small as improvement of a personal process as undertaken by an individual, and at the other extreme, complete business reengineering, which impacts not just the organisation, but everyone else around the organisation. In between these two extremes, they identify group improvement, quality improvement teams, process simplification, process reengineering, and business integration (Figure 2.2). As you move from personal improvement to business reengineering, the scope changes from a very internal focus, to the external, involving external parties. And again, in terms of the nature of the change that occurs in personal improvements, it could be very incremental, but as you go towards business reengineering, it becomes quite radical. With respect to the potential benefit, at one end of the spectrum we have operational benefits, but at the other end, we could gain huge strategic benefits through business reengineering. While we can

Figure 2.2. Process improvement perspectives (Adapted from Childe et al., 2001, p.202)

Personal Improvement	Group Improvement	Quality Improvement Teams	Process Simplification	Process Reengineering	Business Integration	BPR
Internal			Scope		External	
Incremental			Nature		Radical	
Operational			Benefit		Strategic	
Low			Risks		High	
Low			Time to Implement		High	

get huge benefits through radical reengineering, we should also realise that the associated risks are very high with business reengineering, and quite low with respect to personal improvement. It is wise to remember that many firms have gone bankrupt when their reengineering exercises were conducted without proper precautions.

Function vs. Process-Oriented Organisational Structures

Holtham (2001) suggests that we need to be very careful when we consider process improvements, and apply BPR only when there is a need, and management is capable of undertaking the BPR exercise. We need to realise that business process reengineering is not just about changing processes. It could also result in a radical redesign of the organisation structures. Usually, the process improvement efforts would result in a change from functional organisational structures to process-oriented organisational structures. There are pros and cons for functional structures and process-oriented structures. But a via media that has worked very well is to retain functional structures, but supported by a process-oriented structure as well. Many organisations are interweaving their process-oriented structure with their functional structure, whereby they are not throwing away the benefits of functional specialisation, but retaining the functional specialisation benefits, at the same time leveraging the advantages obtained through the process-oriented structure. Thus, the move is towards flexible organisational structures that have a functional and a process orientation.

The processing-improvement exercise enables an organisation to think through their processes, and to come up with designs that are much more efficient and effective. And doing this exercise through proper self-reflection will enable organisations to not just automate obsolete processes. This critical, self-reflecting, self-evaluating step not only enables the weeding out of unnecessary steps, but it also enables organisations to move towards simpler processes that still get the job done. This is where the whole business process redesign, or improvement, is more an art than a science. This is where the ingenuity of the people involved in this exercise comes to the fore. It is quite easy to come up with simple solutions to simple problems. It is also easy to come up with complex solutions to complex problems. But the challenge in business process improvement is not only to come up with simple solutions to simple problems, but also simple solutions to complex problems.

When we looked at the business process management, we termed it as a life cycle. One of the key reasons for this is it is not an exercise that you undertake once in a blue moon, and forget about it for the rest of the period. The business process management life cycle needs to be something that is repeated every moment of the day. Different processes will be at different phases in their life cycle. You are constantly trying to improve the processes that you are undertaking, some in small ways and some in radical ways. Thus, business process improvement needs to become a philosophy that is a fundamental part of the organisational culture, and change becomes a constant. Process improvement is not an option anymore. The customers, the competition, and the change that is occurring in the world, demand that we constantly reengineer and improve the processes. Customers are becoming more and more sophisticated and demanding. They ask for a much greater range of products and services. Due to the Internet, they are aware of other choices, other options, and they are much more knowledgeable. This results in us having to constantly improve our processes to remain competitive. And our competition, again, is not the old fashioned gentlemanly kind of a competition, but it is a tough competitive environment that we live in, and it is no more just local organisations that we compete against, but we are competing against global organisations, because of the openness of the economies these days. In addition to these, the rapid change that seems to be constant these days motivates us to keep up with the change that is occurring around us by changing the organisation to survive.

While we consider process improvement, it is useful to keep in mind that many of the software tools that we might have used earlier in the process-modelling step also have features in them that support simulation of processes. When we are considering various alternative processes to the current as-is process, it is useful to model them, especially if they are very critical, and then run various simulations to find out the impacts of the changes, as well as the efficiencies or inefficiencies that could have crept in due to the change of the process. Tools such as ARIS for process modelling have in them a simulation module that enables one to simulate various things. Holosofx, another process-modelling software, also has a simulation component. Hence, using tools that also have simulation in them in the process-modelling phase comes in handy when we are in the process-improvement phase to evaluate various alternative paths. Once we have finalised on the process improvement, the next phase is implementing this process, and executing this process, and monitoring how well this process is being executed. These three steps are covered in extensive detail in Chapter IV, where we look at enterprise system implementation. Hence, we will cover these three steps briefly in the following sections.

Process Implementation

Process implementation can have two distinct views: organisational and information technology. From the organisation point of view, we look at the various people who would be involved in this new process: "How are we going to train them? What is the training that needs to be given to them in order that they function effectively within this new process?" This could involve educating them about the new objectives of the process, the new systems that would be in place. It could also imply that they become aware that they are not just a part of the traditional, functional, hierarchical, organisational structure, but they are also a part of the newly embedded cross-functional process structure. Thus, bringing the organisational human resources up to speed to cope with the changes that are going to occur is part of the organisational point of view. The information technology point of view looks at the new systems that need to be put in place in order for the process to work. This could involve the development of new software *ex nihilo*, or it could be the customisation of standard software packages like SAP, or PeopleSoft, or JD Edward's *One World*.

Thus, looking at the process implementation from these two points of view enables us to undertake the implementation of the software package; the training of the personnel; and putting in place the policies, the procedures, and the new documents that would arise as a result of the changes. Once these foundational requirements of the process have been implemented and put in place, then we look at the execution of this new process. And we need to remember that there will be a transitioning from the old process to the new process. Some organisations go for a complete cutover, some go for a smoother transition, where they run the old process and the new process for a little while, and once the new process is stabilised, then they stop the old process and just rely on the new process. We will be discussing these in much more detail in the process implementation chapter later on. But one of the things we need to keep in mind is that during this phase, there will be some amount of changes to the new process that we have implemented and are executing, because as we execute the process, we might realise some problems that were not apparent when we modeled it or when we conjured it up. These problems would need to be addressed, but the hope is that such problems won't be of very great magnitude. And secondly, as the process stabilises, such problems will reduce, and the number of such problems will reduce, and they will altogether cease. And once we reach a phase where most of the problems have been addressed, we freeze the new process. That means we do not allow any more changes to occur until another case has been made for undertaking changes. But for this to take place, for the new case to be made, we need to be able to document the usage of the processes and monitor the processes over a period of time. This is the main point of discussion in the next section. But before we move on to that, it is important to emphasise that it is here that we start realising the benefits of putting in the new processes. It is at this juncture that we start enjoying the results of improvement, of efficient and effective processes. But we need to keep in mind that immediately after the implementation of the new process, and in the early stages of execution, there will usually be a dip in the various KPIs. This is primarily due to the fact that people are still getting used to the new process: hence, their understanding of the new process may not be as high, and they may commit more errors in the early phases. But, hopefully, this dip is not too pronounced, and the dip slowly turns into an upward trend, which increases enough so that it goes above the previous level. That is, after the process has stabilised, the KPIs of the new process should be higher/better than the KPIs of the older process.

Process Monitoring and Control

The next, key step in the process is the monitoring and controlling of the processes that go on within an organisation. And here we are not just talking about the new processes that have been put in, but all the processes that go on within an organisation. We could monitor the processes from various perspectives such as resource, function, or the business object. And we need to constantly benchmark what we monitor and see to it that they are (1) within control and (2) as good if not better than the benchmark.

When we consider the process from a functional perspective, there are many other aspects that we can look at. Some of the common and most important aspects of the process that we monitor are, "What is the end to end processing time? What is the average of this for a particular period — compare this with the benchmark and see how well we are doing?" An important KPI in this context is work time vs. idle time. Similar to that, we could monitor how well the organisation is doing as far as learning the new process is concerned. This is more the internal benchmarking where we compare historical values of a particular process over a period of time. So in the beginning, we may compare our processing time with the as-is processing time: then we might compare the current processing time with the processing time of the new process 6 months back or 3 months back, to see if the processing time is decreasing. Usually, there will be a time when the processing time decreases rapidly but there will be a stage when it starts to plateau out, where the decrease in the processing time is not that noticeable. But hopefully, this plateau is as good as or better than the benchmarks obtained from other organisations. If not, then we need to question why we are not up to the mark. Other aspects that we might monitor are frequencies of the processes; deviation of the cycle times; the frequencies of the processes depending on customers, sales organisations, or distribution channels; or we could monitor processes against specific employees.

From an object perspective, we might conduct activity-based costing (ABC), or we might do time-related reports on the objects against various quality indicators. From a resource perspective, we might monitor the number/amount of resources involved in a particular process using the various benchmarking techniques that we have discussed earlier. And against all three perspectives, whether they be resource or object or process, we would not just monitor, but also raise exceptions to highlight when the process is going out of control.

Mal-Processes:
Negative Business Process Scenarios

Preventing Behaviour to be Avoided

An organisation may engineer a new process or reengineer an existing process for a variety of reasons. It could be done as part of implementing new strategies at the operational level, or as part of the implementation of an Enterprise Resource Planning/Enterprise System such as mySAP or PeopleSoft. Whatever the case, we would normally use requirements elicitation techniques to define the "as-is" business process and engineer "to-be" processes using, as much as possible, fragments of the reference model of a corresponding ERP system or the best business practices (BBP) of the industry.

As a result of the design, a set of business processes would be created, defining a certain workflow for the various roles that employees of the organisation take on as they interact with the system. These processes would consist of functions that should be executed in a certain order, defined by events. Particular employees/users would be responsible for execution of a business process, or a part of it. Every business process starts from a predefined set of events, and performs a predefined set of functions, which involve either data input or data modification (when a definite, data structure is taken from the database, modified, and put back, or transferred to another destination). When executing a process, a user may intentionally put wrong data into the database, or modify the data in the wrong way. The user may execute an incomplete business process, or execute a wrong branch of the business process, or even create an undesirable branch of a business process. We argue that most of these situations could be avoided at the design stage, rather than having to deal with them as they occur.

We focus on the actions, which may be done intentionally or through neglect. We do not consider similar effects produced accidentally, as they are a subject of interest for data safety. The focus of this paper will be on preventing the possibility of creating or executing such undesirable processes during the design stages of the business process. We term such processes as *mal-processes*.

- **Mal:** bad(ly), wrong(ly), improper(ly) (*New Shorter Oxford English Dictionary*, 1997)

- **Processes:** A business process is a collection of interrelated tasks, initiated in response to an *event* that achieves a specific *result* for the *customer* of the *process* (Sharp & McDermott, 2001). Hereafter we refer to such processes as *regular processes* to distinguish them from *mal-processes*.

- **Mal-process** can therefore be defined as a collection of interrelated tasks (executed in the place and time assigned for a *regular process*) that can result in harm for the customer or stakeholder of the process.

From this point of view, a mal-process can be considered as an undesirable branch of the complete business process, triggered by the same set of events, but achieving an undesirable result for the *customer* of the *process*. Hence, mal-processes are behaviours to be *avoided* by the system. It is a sequence of actions that a system can perform, interacting with a legal user of the system, resulting in *harm* for the organisation or stakeholder if the sequence is allowed to complete.

The consideration of mal-processes is extremely important from the security point of view. But apart from that, it has significant consequences for efficiency. Current reference models and implementations of enterprise systems do not consider mal-processes explicitly. Addressing of mal-processes involves business-oriented decisions that need to be considered by business analysts up front, rather than by technical configuration experts later on during the implementation.

Mal-processes are similar to *misuse cases, abuse cases, and failure cases* (Alexander, 2002; McDermott & Fox, 1999; Sindre & Opdahl, 2000), however, there is an important difference between them. *Misuse cases and abuse cases* assume hostile intent of an internal or external actor, so they are mostly concerned with the security of the system. Mal-processes do not suggest an external, hostile influence. Thus, mal-processes are not in the domain of systems and data security. Rather, they are subjects of study for the design methodologies and systems efficiencies.

However, the result of the mal-process is similar to the results of misuse or abuse cases: the system may function in a quite unexpected and undesirable fashion. It incurs losses to the major stakeholders, or to the organisation as a whole. So, from the point of view of the organisation, the mal-process is simply a poorly designed business process: the intent is correct, but the result may be different from the expected.

Hence, the field of mal-processes is a separate field of study, close to the fields of data safety and data security, but not intersecting with them.

What Causes a Mal-Process?

Some of the major causes for mal-processes in a business context are:

- Conflict of interests between an organisational unit (here we assume a representative of the unit who is a direct user of the system) and the whole organisation
- Excessive workloads of the organisational units; as a result a part (or even the whole) of the business process being neglected
- Deliberate violation because of a material and/or immoral incentive/reason
- Organisation and/or individuals may adopt mal-processes without realising they are mal-processes (mal-processes by ignorance)

We discuss each of these in more detail with examples and means of addressing them in the following paragraphs.

Mal-Process as a Result of a Conflict of Interests

All users have a position in an organisational structure. The structure is a hierarchy of positions, connected by the relation "superior-subordinate." We shall call the users *independent*, if there is no "superior-subordinate" chain between them in the organisational hierarchy. One of the reasons why mal-processes occur is a conflict of interests, when users have to put information in the system that can harm their own position in a hierarchy, or their superior's position.

Conflict of interests may affect the normal course of a business process when, for example, a part of the business process is an employee reporting on his or her own performance.

In this case the employee might be inclined to:

- Exaggerate achievements;
- Diminish faults; and
- Cover excessive waste in materials, labour or equipment use due to poor quality of production or services.

In this situation, the mal-process can be avoided by:

- Changing the user of the process, so the reporting is done by another independent employee, preferably of a higher level of hierarchy; and
- Duplicating the reporting process in another business process.

Examples

Customer Relationship Management

A company runs a Customer Relationship Management (CRM) system. The customer relations manager is a subordinate of the executive director. One of the functions of the system is to collect feedback from customers, process it, and to report the company's operational performance to the board of directors, and to the shareholders. Because the executive director -through the customer relations (CR) manager- has an interest to hide faults and to reveal only "good news," it is better to transfer the reporting of the CR manager directly to the board, or even better, to transfer this function to an independent body. The CR manager can distort the process of collecting the feedback from customers so that only the favourable response will surface.

Production

A line manager, after completing the daily assignment, puts data about the actual performance (feedback) into the database. The basic business process is realised through SAP shop floor control modules, *completion of order*, in particular. Very frequently, this data is incomplete or inaccurate or controversial, because it represents the results of the line manager's work. Sometimes, the results are poor because of errors in work organisation that are direct faults of the line manager. In this situation, this business process cannot be transferred to any other person (higher in the hierarchy), like the shop manager, because it will involve too much additional work for the shop manager, who is not involved in the operations management of the line. By duplicating the reporting process in another business process, say in the "Receipt of Finished Goods," designed for the manager of the finished-goods store, the validity of the information not only can be verified, but also significantly improved. When the line manager knows that the data will be soon double-checked, he or she will make fewer mistakes. On the other hand, the process cannot be completely transferred to the manager of the store of finished goods, because the line manager puts the data into the database immediately after the order completion, while the goods reach the store of finished goods much later. The time lag sometimes might be unacceptable.

Mal-Process as a Result of Excessive Workloads of the Organisational Units

Excessive workloads of the organisational units may affect the normal course of a business process, where the user simply does not have enough time to execute the whole process.

In this case, the user may:

- Execute only the part of the process that is considered the most important;
- Execute the process only in situations that are considered important; or
- Completely neglect all the procedures: "If I had time, I would find something more useful to do."

Example

As a typical example of such procedures, we can suggest "physical count," that is, a regular business process in inventory management of any ERP system, SAP included. The process is triggered by the calendar — this is a periodic procedure (monthly, quarterly). The goal of the procedure is to keep the inventory records in the database adequate to the physical levels. The record of the database for every item is compared with physically available stock. A standard for natural losses is set. If the difference is less than the standard, the situation is normal. If the difference exceeds the standard, the situation is recorded for the reconciliation committee, which will analyse the cause of shortage. In both situations, the record is updated according to the physical count.

This procedure is a very important pillar of the database. Effectiveness of many business processes is pinned to the accuracy of inventory records: production planning, sales, accounting, and so forth. Inaccurate inventory records will cause the malfunctioning of practically all ERP systems.

The main problem with this process is that it requires too much physical effort from staff already loaded with other duties. Instead of climbing the ladders and counting nuts and bolts, the store managers are inclined just to "tick the box." Sometimes they count only the most important inventory of A and B class, and sometimes do not count at all.

This problem was identified long before the development of ERP systems; however, traditional management depends not so dramatically on the accuracy of information. And when in doubt, the manager always could call and ask for a physical count of a particular item. Quite to the contrary, the super-efficiency of ERP requires super-accuracy in data, and the "speed-to-market" quality of ERP cannot be compromised by double-checking delays.

So, the remedy is to identify the possibility of malfunctioning of a business process, to stop its use, and to design a correct and effective process. For example, the complete physical count by the staff of the store can be supplemented by a sample count carried out by an independent person.

Mal-Processes Deliberately Caused by a User that has a Material and/or Immoral Incentive/Reason to Do This

This category includes, among other mal-processes, attempts to cover up petty theft of raw materials or finished products. Petty theft of raw materials or finished products frequently occurs in the food industry, and in consumer goods production. If the thief is the user, or a close associate, then he or she is inclined to cover up the theft by putting false information in the system. Apart from direct financial loss, it negatively affects the whole management system because of unreliable information about the actual amount of raw materials and finished goods.

It seems that this negative action can be eliminated through physical counting. However, the physical count is conducted rather rarely, say once per month. Suppose that the theft occurred early in the month, and the physical count was carried out at the end of the month. The difference between the record and actual exceeds the standard; the situation is recorded for the reconciliation committee, which will analyse the cause of the shortage. By the time of analysis, there will be no real possibility of discovering the guilty party, and most probably, the difference will be assigned to some input error, or to the inaccuracy of the bill of material.

The most useful best practice to cope with petty theft is a double check by another process, assigned to an independent user.

Example

The store of raw materials provides a raw materials batch for the daily production, using the daily line schedule and the bill of material (BOM). The line has a small storage in which raw materials not used during the day are kept for the following day. At the end of the day, the line manager sends the goods produced to the store of finished goods, and puts the amount of produced goods into the database. The process assumes that some of the raw materials might not be used, and remain in the line storage.

The excess of raw materials may occur for several reasons:

- The packed quantity of raw materials is not a perfect divisor of the required quantity. For example, butter is packed in boxes by 25 kg each. Suppose the required amount for the day is 30 kg, then two boxes will be sent to the line; the remaining 20 kg is supposed to be used in the next day's production.

- Due to the unplanned downtime, the amount of finished goods produced might be less than planned, then not all of the raw materials were used.

- Sudden change of the daily schedule was authorised by top management. The new products require other materials, which were urgently requested and delivered to the line (in addition to the already delivered daily package, which will stay in the store of the line).

According to the design of the process, the line manager should report any unused (for any reason) quantities of materials to the store of raw materials. These unused quantities are supposed to be deducted from the next day's package. At the end of the month, both stores make a physical count. This results in the creation of a list of materials sent to production. This list is compared with a similar list from the store of raw materials for reconciliation.

This business process is flawed, and gives a lot of space for petty theft of raw materials and finished goods in the factory. These lists may be significantly different, and there is no information that helps to find out the real reasons why. The obvious reason may be petty theft of the raw materials from the line storage, or theft of finished goods before they reach the store of finished goods. There may be other reasons, like an attempt of the line manager to conceal excessive waste. However, if something happened at the beginning of the month and has been discovered at the end of the month, it is practically impossible to find out the real reason, given the practical absence of necessary information.

The correct organisation of this business process would entail a few significant changes. There must be an independent user that verifies the actual use of raw materials. Such an independent user might be the manager of the store of finished goods. The normative amount of raw materials used might be verified through the BOM. As soon as the store of finished goods receives the daily production, the store manager puts the amounts in the database. These amounts overwrite the amounts put by the line manager (not physically overwrite, but in any dispute this amount is accepted as correct). Before computing the daily pack of raw materials, the manager of the raw materials store runs MRP on the actual amount produced the previous day. Thus, the actual amount of raw materials consumed the previous day, and the actual amounts of raw material left in the line store are determined. Any dispute involves the reconciliation committee, which has:

- All the information about passing of the raw materials down the track; and
- A time lag between the occurrence of the loss and its discovery, of no more than one day.

Mal-Processes by Ignorance or Lack of Knowledge

Organisations and/or individuals may be adopting mal-processes without realising they are mal-processes. A typical example here might be the following. The enterprise system design and implementation group, as usual, consist both of the employees of the company, and implementation consultants. The employees of the company, as a rule, promote and defend existing business processes. The reasons they give are:

- Their processes reflect the specific feature of the company's functioning;
- If the employees saw the way to improve their processes, they would have certainly reengineered them long before; and
- The company uses these processes and no harm has been detected; this is an evidence of maybe not the best, but reasonably good business practices.

The real reason for opposing change is the employees of the company are used to their processes, and therefore, frequently are not able to critically assess them. At the same time, these processes might produce a far from efficient management, and what is worse, might become unsuitable or even harmful in the ERP environment. However, the consultants of the implementation team may agree with the employees for political reasons (those who pay are always right), or simply because of lack of knowledge.

Unfortunately, there are no good recommendations how to avoid such mal-processes, apart from the obvious: stick to the reference model as close as possible, with the hope that the ERP developing company really puts in the reference model the best business practices.

Interplay Between Best Business Practices and Mal-Processes

Just as we have *best business practices*, mal-processes illustrate the *wrong business practices*. So, it would be natural, by analogy with the reference model (that represents a repository of best business practices), to create a repository of wrong business practices. Thus, a designer could avoid wrong design solutions.

There is, though, a very important difference between best and wrong business practices: while the best practice is unique, the wrong practices might be many. Significant deviations from the best practice are wrong, causing harm to the efficiency of the management system. Thus, it seems enough to put a warning sign on the reference model: *Do not deviate from the prescribed process!*

However, it is general knowledge that the reference model represents only a typical management system, and in this capacity, it does not reflect the specific features of any particular enterprise. At the same time, the specific features are mostly responsible for the efficiency of the particular management system. The role of the designer is to create an enterprise system that keeps the integrity and efficiency of the reference model, reflecting, at the same time, all necessary specifics of the enterprise. Thus, the designers deviate from the reference model as a rule, not as an exception. Do they create mal-processes? No, not all deviations from the best processes are mal-processes.

We argue that there are some *stable changes* in the business processes that we call mal-processes. The reasons they exist in the management system are explained in the section *What Causes a Mal-Process?* They are typical in the sense that they do not depend on the industry or the size of the enterprise. So, a mal-process is an intentional, stable deviation from the best process, and its stability is explained by the intent of the user.

A detective hunting a thief has only one path to follow, the path taken by the thief. But the thief can take any path he or she wishes, to escape the detective. In a similar fashion, while the best practice in a particular situation may be *one*, the mal-processes that could occur in that situation may be *many*! Practitioners and researchers in the area of *use cases* face very similar problems. The ideal use case path, usually known as the *basic flow* or *happy path*, is *one*, while the *alternative flows*, *worst-case scenarios*, *variants*, *exceptions*, and so forth, are *many*.

A repository of such mal-processes would enable organisations to avoid typical mistakes in enterprise system design. Such a repository can be a valuable asset in the education of ERP designers, and it can be useful in general management education as well. Another application of this repository might be troubleshooting. For example, sources of some nasty errors in the sales and distribution system might be found in the mal-processes of data entry in finished goods.

Conclusion

To conclude, we need to remember that last step of the business process life cycle, namely *monitoring*, that would trigger another cycle of process change, another cycle where we move into the process identification, modelling, improvement, implementation, and execution. Thus, this business process management life cycle is one of continuously identifying and evaluating not just the internals of the organisation, the process of the organisation, but also what is going on external to the organisation such as competitors, customers, the business climate, and the social climate, which in turn may lead us to change the way we do business. To be able to make this work, we need to reemphasise the point that we need to instil in the organisation a process-oriented culture which would consider that change is a constant. We briefly introduced the concept of mal-processes. Benefits of explicit incorporation of mal-processes into analysis, design, and implementation are many. We list just a few:

- Early identification and resolution of mal-processes by incorporating it as part of the Enterprise Systems Analysis and Design life cycle;
- Potential savings to the organisation and other stakeholders; and
- Identification of best business practices to remedy or prevent mal-processes would also be one of the benefits.

Chapter III

Modelling
Business Processes

Need for Modelling

The modelling of business processes is vital not only for business process management, but also for implementation of enterprise systems. For example, when we look at the process life cycle introduced earlier, three of the seven phases involve business process modelling, to a large extent. But apart from that, the models that are generated in these three phases are used in all the seven phases of the business process management life cycle. The phases where these models are developed are in the second phase of process modelling; and it is used in the third phase, where we do the analysis; and is used in the fourth phase, where we improve upon the as-is models, come up with the to-be models, and model them, using whatever tools that are available. But then, the to-be models that are developed in the fourth phase are used in the process implementation phase, in the execution phase, in the monitoring phase, and even in the process identification phase, when you think of it as a life cycle.

Even when we think of implementing the enterprise system, we have to deal with models. We have the current situation models, we have the reference model, as provided by the vendor, we have the best business practice models, and using these, we come up with the to-be model. Thus, we have to deal with models even in the context of enterprise system implementation, which might be thought of as a life cycle that fits in within the life cycle of business process management.

Process modelling has especially come into vogue in the recent past, when we have focused all our energies on cross-functional, integrated information systems that span the entire organisation. In the past, when we had monolithic applications, which catered just to activities that went on within one single department or unit, the need for modelling processes wasn't as high. It was only the industrial engineer who went about modelling these processes to do reengineering and other activities. It wasn't looked on as a necessity till recently.

Need for a Modelling
Framework/Architecture

Many frameworks and architectures have been proposed for modelling business processes and managing business processes: for example, CIMOSA, PERA, IEM, IRDS, OOIE and ARIS. These architectures and frameworks are essential if we want to have a guide for managing business processes and implementing enterprise systems. We need an architecture, or a framework, to guide us in the creation, analysis, and evaluation of business processes. And we need the architecture or the framework to support the development, optimisation, and implementation of an integrated information system to support the business processes.

Professor Scheer (1998) came up with the architecture of integrated information systems to overcome the problems associated with traditional business process modelling, as well as information modelling approaches. If we try to model all the complexity of a business process at the same time, the model can, quite quickly, become very large and incomprehensible. Hence, Professor Scheer suggested dividing up the business process model into different views: the data view, the function view, the organisation view, and the resource view.

The approach was a "divide and conquer" one, whereby Professor Scheer attempted to reduce the complexity of the business process model through providing different views.

In this chapter we will focus on Professor Scheer's architecture. There are two key reasons for this. One of the reasons is that ARIS is tightly integrated with SAP R/3. And the second reason is that ARIS not only has a robust conceptual foundation, but it also has software that supports that foundation. The Gartner (2001) group, in their magic quadrants, have regularly been identifying ARIS as the software which leads the whole pack of modelling software. It leads other similar software as far as vision is concerned, and is much ahead of the pack as far as their ability to execute is concerned.

House of Business Engineering

More formally, Professor Scheer titled his approach the *House of Business Engineering* (HOBE) (Figure 3.1). HOBE is made up of (1) the organisation view, which tells us who may execute a particular function or activity, (2) the function view, which tells us what are the functions that are there to support this

Figure 3.1. ARIS views/House of Business Engineering (Scheer, 1998, p.13)

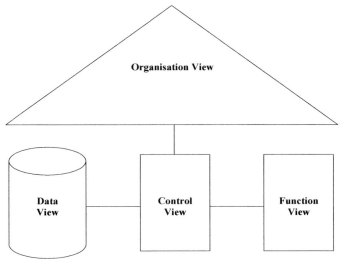

particular process, (3) the data view, which tells us which data is required to execute the functions, and (4) the control view, which tells us the logic according to which this particular process would be executed. The control view pulls together the organisation, function, and the data views, and provides, in a crisp form, the overall flow of the business process. In this chapter, we will focus on the control view, predominantly, but deal briefly with the organisation, function and data views as well. The control view, as mentioned, integrates and links functions, organisations, and data together.

The Control View and Event-Driven Process Chains

A diagramming methodology proposed to model the control view is the event-driven process chain (EPC). The event-driven process chain is made up of, minimally, four distinct elements: the event, the function, the organisational unit, and the data. The event tells us when something should be done. It describes the occurrence, or the raising of a status, which acts as a trigger to one or more functions. The function or the task essentially tells us what should be done, and it describes the transformations that need to be undertaken to move a particular

Figure 3.2. Basic components of the EPC

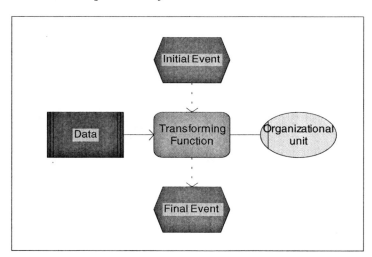

status from one value to another value. The organisation element essentially tells us who should be doing this particular task or function. And this could be at different levels of abstraction: it could be a department, a particular unit, an individual, or a whole organisation. The information or data element essentially informs us regarding the information or data that are required to execute this particular task or function.

Thus, the four key components of the EPC are events (statuses), functions (transformations), organisation, and information (data). Events (initial) trigger functions that then result in events (final). The functions are carried out by one or more organisational units, using appropriate data. A simplified depiction of the interconnection between the four basic components of the EPC is illustrated in Figure 3.2. This was modeled using the ARIS software (ARIS, 2001).

These fundamental elements of the EPC can be linked up together using logical operators such as *OR, AND,* and *Exclusive OR (XOR)*. These operators link the functions to the events and the events to the functions. They help us then model almost every possible situation under the sun. Multilevel operators help us in defining very complex relationships between the events and the functions, and functions and events. The following examples describe the various ways in which functions and events could be linked up together to represent a business process.

Example Illustrating Key Elements of the EPC

The example in Figure 3.3 illustrates some of the key elements of the EPC. The EPC can be rendered verbally as the following:

- In order for **M. Bernardy** to **open a customer inquiry**, one of two events must happen: *either* an **inquiry is received,** *or* there is a need to **create an inquiry from contact,** *but not both.* **Customer inquiry details** are received through fax.

- Once the **customer inquiry is opened,** M. Bernardy is responsible for **configuring the product** (car). In order to configure the product, M. Bernardy requires the customer inquiry details as well as the product (car) data.

- Once the **car is configured,** M. Bernardy is then responsible for not only **determining a price** for the product, *but at the same time*, **determining the taxes**.

Figure 3.3. A typical Event-Driven Process Chain (ARIS, 2001)

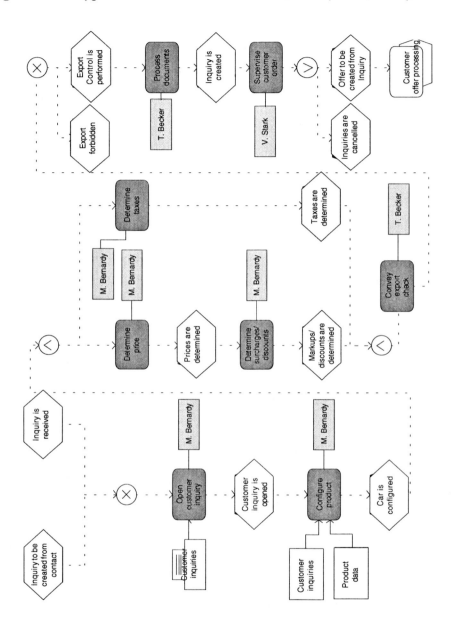

- Once the **price is determined**, M. Bernardy is also responsible for **determining any relevant surcharges and/or discounts**.

- Once the **mark-ups (surcharges) and/or discounts are determined** *and* the **taxes for the product (car) are determined**, it is then the responsibility of T. Becker to **convey an export check**.

- This process (convey export check) may result in *either* the **export of the product (car) being forbidden,** *or* the **export control being performed,** *but not both*.

- If the export control is performed, T. Becker is then required to **process the documents,** which results in an **inquiry being created**

- Once the inquiry has been created, V. Stark **supervises the customer order.** This could result in either the **inquiry being cancelled,** *or* an **offer to be created from the inquiry.** There may be circumstances where an **inquiry may be cancelled** and an **offer may need to be created from the inquiry,** at the same time.

- If the offer is to be created from the inquiry, the process of **customer offering** is triggered.

Examples Illustrating the Three Logical Operators Used in an EPC

We need to be aware that there are certain combinations of functions and events that are not legal. This is primarily due to the fact events cannot make decisions, only functions can make decisions. Hence, a triggering event should not be linked to two or more functions using an OR or an XOR logical operator. Figure 3.5 shows two situations, which are illegal. We need to overcome the problem produced by such illegal situations. An event does not have the ability to choose which function to trigger. When we find a model in this form, we need to resolve this problem by introducing a function which then enables us to come up with two or more different results, depending on the number of possible states, and these resulting events, in turn, trigger the two or more functions discussed earlier. Figure 3.6 illustrates such an illegal situation, and Figure 3.7 illustrates a solution to overcome the problem.

As mentioned earlier, events and functions can be linked using very complex operators. An example of such a situation is illustrated in Figure 3.8.

In the previous examples, we have only looked at one event triggering two functions, or one function resulting in two events. But two or more events could trigger two or more functions, and two or more functions, in turn, could result

Figure 3.4. Use of the logical operators in various event-function configurations (ARIS, 2001)

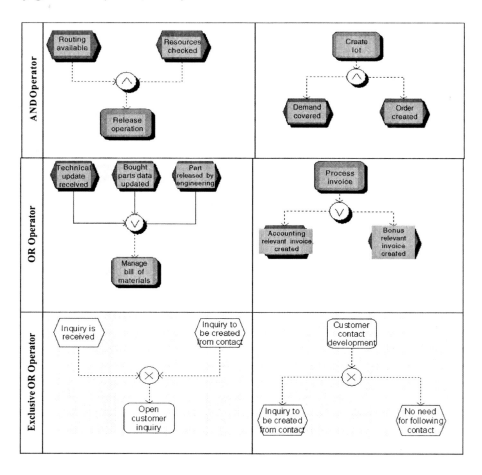

in two or more events. There are many ways in which this could be modeled; one of them is illustrated in Figure 3.9.

The control view of the EPC could also be organised against various elements in what is termed as swim lanes, either horizontally or vertically (Figure 3.10). In this view, all events for a particular process will be in one column after the other in chronological sequence: then, you could have all the functions of the process; and then, all the data of the process; and then, all the organisational units that are involved in the process. This type of view enables us to isolate and

Figure 3.5. Use of the logical operators in various event-function configurations (cont.) (Adapted from ARIS, 2001)

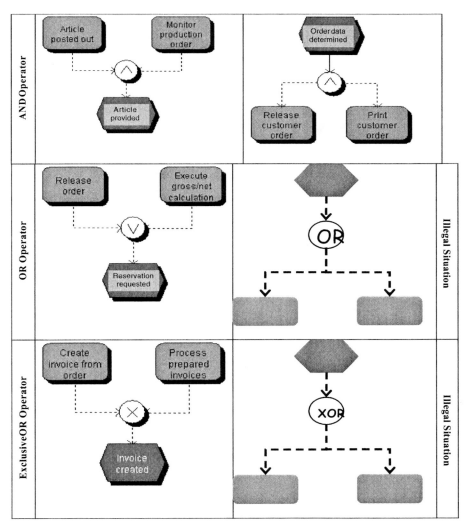

look at each one of these perspectives without being distracted by the other perspectives.

One of the things that we have not talked about, nor seen in examples so far, are the feedback mechanisms. Quite often, when the results of a particular process are inadequate either in terms of an error or in terms of incompleteness,

Figure 3.6. An example of an illegal situation of events making choices

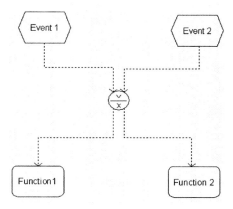

Figure 3.7. Illustration of modeling mechanisms to overcome the illegal situation of Figure 3.6

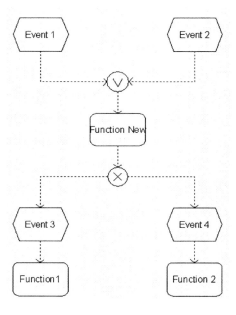

Figure 3.8. An example of the usage of nested operators

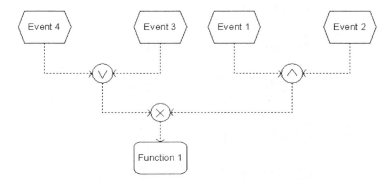

Figure 3.9. Modeling situations when two or more events are connected to two or more functions

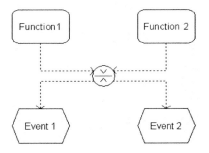

Figure 3.10. Depicting Swim Lanes (ARIS, 2001)

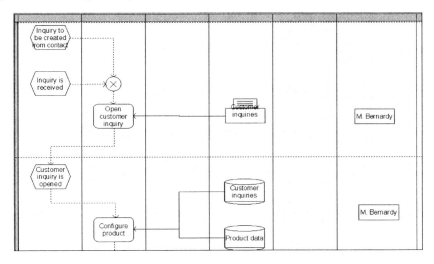

the process goes back to an earlier phase, and this is very simply done by drawing a line from the inadequate event back to the function from which the whole process needs to be redone. But the line cannot be joined directly to the function; it needs to be connected back through an Exclusive OR.

We could also start introducing probabilities into the model, whereby we could assign probabilities of a particular event occurring. The probability values could be based either on experience, or it could actually be based on data that we have in the system. In addition to that, we could enrich the model by specifying the data elements that flow into the function and out of the function.

Modelling Mal-Processes

Mal-processes can appear in an organisation in many ways. First, they may appear as a result of poor design. In the reporting example that we saw in the previous chapter, the designer may not see a reason for duplicating the feedback. As a result, the feedback process might be compromised. Second, even with the process correctly designed, one of the users may take a "shortcut." In the same feedback example, either the line manager or the manager of the finished goods store knows about the duplication of the feedback. Either one or another (or even both of them) may decide not to put in the feedback data. Third, the process may be assigned to a wrong person, who will deliberately mutilate it, as in the example of CRM reporting.

All this requires that the mal-processes be recorded in the same place and in the same format as best practices business process. Since mal-processes are equivalent in their characteristics to other processes except for their outcomes we can use standardised process modelling syntax and constructs to represent mal-processes. But the question arises regarding how we distinguish mal-processes from regular processes. One simple means of distinguishing is by colour but that may mislead if someone looks at a black and a white printout. Another option is to distinguish the events and functions of mal-processes from normal processes. Figure 3.11 illustrates some of the means (colour, weight of line, and/or shadow) by which we could distinguish mal-processes from normal processes in the context of constructs used to build event-driven process chains (Davis, 2001).

Figure 3.11. Modelling Mal-processes

Modelling Construct	Normal Process	Mal-Process
Event	Event	Mal-Event
Function	Function	Mal-Function
Organisation	Org Unit	Mal-Org

Figure 3.12. "No entry" sign

If we model a mal-process as a branch of business process, we need a special operator as illustrated in Figure 3.12 for:

- preventing the user to execute this branch of the business process, and
- preventing the designer to design a mal-process.

The application of these modelling constructs in the context of our first mal-process example is illustrated in Figure 3.13 and Figure 3.14.

Rules of EPC Modelling

Quite often, people eliminate events, and then just start putting one function after the other in their model. This needs to be avoided. Every function should result in one or more events. And it is only when events are explicitly modeled that we are able to capture the decision points that occur. The events enable us to understand the possible outcomes. Some simple rules that need to be kept in mind as we model EPCs are as follows:

- Every EPC should start with an event and end with an event.
- Within the EPC, events and functions should alternate; you cannot have one event triggering another event or one function triggering another function. Events trigger functions, functions result in other events, which in turn trigger other functions, and so on.
- When a particular rule is used to split a process path into two or more paths, then when these paths come back together, they should be linked back using the same decision rule, that is, if we split on an OR operator, then we need to join back on an OR operator; if we split on an AND operator, then we need to join back on an AND operator.

Figure 3.13. Application of mal-process and Best Practice or Regular Process modelling constructs

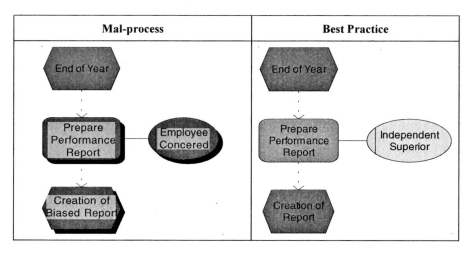

Figure 3.14. A model that integrates the mal-process and the regular process

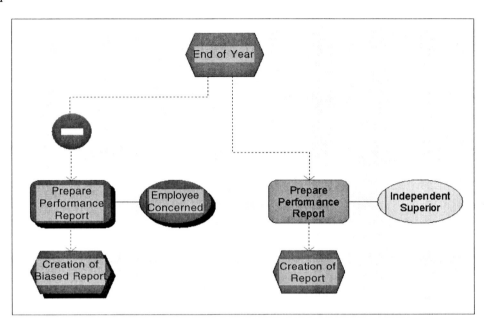

Enriching the EPC

What we have seen so far is the very basic EPC. This very basic EPC can be further enriched using other constructs, such as elements to indicate unstructured data (like an information carrier, a telephone call or a document), or it could be skills that are required to do the particular function or task, it could be instructions for doing a particular task, it could be the screen that will be seen when that particular task or function is executed, it could be a product or service that is delivered as a result of this particular function, or we could indicate objectives of the function. Thus, apart from showing the *who* (organisation), *what* (function), *where* (location), and *when* (event), we can also model the *how* in terms of skills and instructions, and the *why* in terms of the product or service or the objective of the function.

One of the fundamental principles in modelling is divide and conquer, and closely related with that is the use of different levels of abstraction to handle complexity. And EPCs lend themselves to this type of abstraction. Thus, we could have a very high-level EPC, and we could drill down on a particular function, and this could take us into the details of what goes on within that function. And there could be functions in this view, which could then be further drilled down upon, and so on (Figure 3.15). One of the things that needs to be kept in mind is, in this process of drilling down, if a function is triggered by an event and results in another event, those two events need to be present in the drilled down EPC as well. An alternative to drilling down is to split up a big EPC into smaller chunks, and use either process path connectors or use common events to link the split models. Thus, we could have hierarchical decomposition, with the ability to drill down to greater details, or we can have horizontal segmentation. The former uses levels of abstraction; the latter uses the divide-and-conquer principle.

Even EPCs, which by their very nature are very crisp and succinct in their representation of the process, can become complex. And to address this issue, we can model the EPC as a lean EPC, which has got only events and functions, but when we drill down on the function, then we will be able to see the organisational unit, the data, the screen, and any other information that we might want to attach to the particular function under consideration. The bare minimum EPC with just functions and events is called a lean EPC, while the function, with all its related elements like the organisational units, data, and so on is called a function allocation diagram (FAD).

Organisational View

Essentially, the organisational view informs us who does what and/or who is responsible for doing a particular function or task. The organisational view is quite important in understanding our current structures, allowing us to optimise them for the future. Thus, modelling the organisational view could help us to understand that our current organisational structures are rigid and hierarchical, and may enable us to see how we could move to a more organic, matrix and/or process-oriented organisational structure. But as mentioned earlier, while the process-oriented organisational structures provide simplified interfaces leading to optimised business processes, they also result in lack of specialisation. Specialisation is one of the key strengths of function-oriented traditional organisational structures. But the disadvantage of that is the interfaces are complex, and interactions are complex, and the flow is not as smooth as it is in

Figure 3.15. Hierarchical decomposition (Adapted from ARIS, 2001)

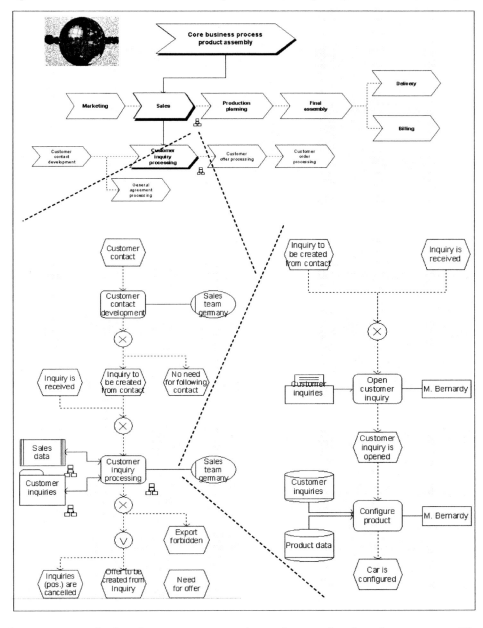

the context of a business process oriented organisational structure. The organisational view at the highest level would indicate the organisation as a whole. The next level could be the major divisions or departments, and then would come the position in the organisation, and then would come the persons who hold that particular position in that particular organisational unit (Figure

3.16). Since the organisational view does not exist in isolation, but exists along with an EPC, when we want to inquire about an organisational unit, we could very easily find out other business processes in which this particular organisational unit features. This type of inquiry could also tell us that some units seem to be doing a whole lot more work than other units.

Function View

The function view tells us what is actually done in the task. You could have multiple levels in the definition of functions (Figure 3.17). At the lowest level, you could describe the application as a whole; at the next level, you could only look at the functional areas that are relevant to a particular application. The next level could contain the tasks that are relevant to a functional area. And the final level could contain the subtasks under the main tasks. You could even go further

Figure 3.16. Organisational view (Adapted from ARIS, 2001)

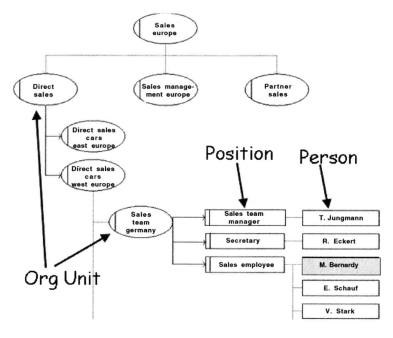

and drill down into the subtasks. Usually it is the tasks and the subtasks that would be linked with an EPC.

Data View

This view is the view of the data that is required to process or execute a particular function or task. Depending on the paradigm that the enterprise system is implemented in, the data view could be either an entity relationship (ER) view or an object oriented (OO) view. If it is an ER view, then we would need to model the entities (Figure 3.18), their attributes (Figure 3.19) and the relationship between the entities. If it is an object-oriented view then we would need to model the classes, the attributes, the methods of the classes, the

Figure 3.17. Function view (ARIS, 2001)

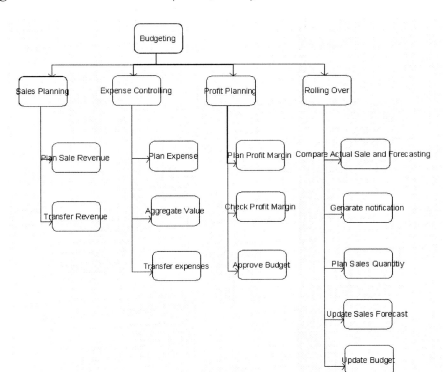

aggregation and generalisation relationships, and the association relationships, in the context of an object-oriented view.

Business Blueprints

As discussed in the earlier chapters, most of the vendors provide what is termed as a reference model. For example, SAP has its R/3 reference model. Essentially, these reference models are like an engineering blueprint, which shows the basic plan of what goes on in an organisation. And the purpose of the blueprint is manifold. One is to communicate to the users the complexity of the process in a simple fashion. Secondly, it enables business process managers to reengineer their business processes by looking at these blueprints. And thirdly, the blueprints become a basis for the implementation of the enterprise system itself. Very few organisations can model all the things that go on in the organisation starting from scratch. And the business blueprint, such as the SAP R/3 reference model, gives a huge impetus to the beginning of the modelling process. These blueprints encapsulate years and years of experience, and reflect deep knowledge of the domain, of the industry, and of specific processes. Blueprints thus serve as a good beginning point, as well as a lingua

Figure 3.18. SAP-structured Entity Relationship Model (ARIS, 2001)

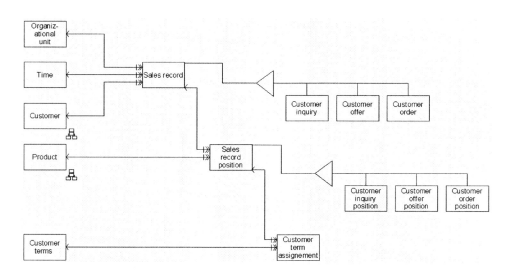

Figure 3.19. Extended Entity Relationship Model — Attribute Allocation Diagram (ARIS, 2001)

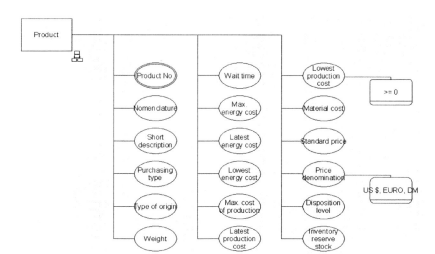

franca for the people involved either in a business process reengineering exercise, or in an enterprise system implementation exercise, and this enables the people to work in a manner that is accurate as well as quick. In many ways, blueprints act as an antidote for the paralysis through analysis syndrome that we discussed earlier.

While we find that the blueprints are quite extensive, they are also parsimonious. This may sound like a contradiction; they are extensive in that they cover most of the processes that go on in an organisation. There are literally thousands of processes in a blueprint, but the processes themselves are modeled in a parsimonious fashion. The models are quite lean in the sense they model the bare essentials of the process to be able to execute the process. These models are usually garnered by looking at multiple organisations, and taking the best from these organisations, as well as incorporating best business practices and consultant experience into the design.

In the context of these models, most of the vendors also come up with standards and variants. Standards imply this is the way most of the organisations implement the process. But sometimes, there are a significant number of exceptional cases where the organisations may implement it in a different fashion. And to recognise these significant exceptions, the vendors also come up with models that are termed as variants, that is, these are variations of the standard. Thus, when you are doing a business process reengineering exercise, you may look at the standard, and if it does not suit or it does not reflect what is going on in your organisation, then you may look at the variant.

SAP R/3 Reference Model and ARIS HOBE

One of the reasons we focused on the ARIS *House Of Business Engineering* in this chapter is because the ARIS models have a one to one correspondence to the way SAP R/3 models its business processes (Figure 3.20). For example, the organisational view of the ARIS HOBE is equivalent to the organisational models of the SAP R/3 reference; the function view/tree view of ARIS is equivalent to the component model of the SAP R/3. The data view of ARIS is equivalent to the data model of SAP R/3 reference; the control view of ARIS is equivalent to the process model of SAP R/3 reference.

And this equivalence goes even further: the ARIS software that supports the ARIS *House Of Business Engineering* is integrated tightly with the implementation management guide of SAP. Thus, once the model has been finalised in ARIS, it could be forward engineered into the SAP R/3 environment.

Capturing the EPC Model

The EPC is the core model in ARIS, and it is the model that represents the process as a whole. Hence, it is useful to be very clear about how to capture this model from the organisation. Here one can use all the techniques that we discussed in the chapter on business processes, especially the technique of stapling oneself to the business object whose flow we are following in the process. Davis (2001) suggests 13 steps to capture an EPC from the organisation.

Step 1. Work on the process one function at a time.

Step 2. For each of the functions, identify all the events that could trigger it, and all the events that could be a result of it. Here we need to be careful that the

Figure 3.20. ARIS-SAP R/3 reference model equivalence

ARIS	SAP R/3 Reference Model
Organisation View	Organisation Model
Function View/Tree View	Component Model
Data View	Data Model
Control View	Process Model

triggering events are absolutely necessary and that they are sufficient. When there are multiple triggers, we need to be sure about the logic with which these triggers are interrelated when they trigger this function. Is there only one logical operator connecting the multiple events, or is it multiple logical operators linking the events in a complex fashion? We need to again make sure that all the outcomes are clearly identified. Be sure to include not just the successful outcomes, but also the unsuccessful outcomes, as well as the odd variations in outcome. In the outcome events as well, be sure that the logical operators are modeled correctly when there is more than one possible outcome.

Step 3. Identify all the decision points in the flow. Some of this work would have already been done in step 2, but it is worthwhile to just go through the whole process flow and make sure that all key decision points have been identified; and in this context, one needs to keep in mind the illegal scenarios discussed earlier: the scenarios where the function can only make a decision; scenarios where an event making a decision needs to be remodeled in such a way that it is the function that makes the decision.

Step 4. We identify the branchings of the process into other processes. Here two issues that are quite important are: (1) Is the branch going to come back into the process? If it is going to come back into the process then you need to keep in mind that the operator on which you split should be the same operator on which you are going to join back. If it is not going to come back then it is not an issue; (2) A model is an abstraction and we should always be wary of the paralysis by analysis syndrome and ruthlessly put as out of scope processes that are not germane to our reengineering or system implementation efforts.

Step 5. For each of the functions and the process, identify all the key attributes such as processing times, waiting times, and set up time. Identify all the relevant costs, and any other information that would help someone else understand the process, and reengineer it if required.

Step 6. Identify the data input and the data output for every function. If possible, attach copies of these documents/data inputs and outputs to the function as a rich object.

Step 7. For each function, identify the organisational unit that is responsible for its execution, the systems that will be there or already exist to support it, and any other resource that is required to support it. Sometimes some functions have been aggregated to such a high level we might find that the function is implemented or executed by multiple organisational units. In that case, in that higher level of abstraction, put in an organisational unit that expresses the multiple units put together. But then, drill down on that function to another detailed EPC where it is very clear that each of the functions or sub functions are executed by one unique organisational unit.

Step 8. Model the special knowledge skills and steps that are required to implement or execute the function. Attach these documents to the function.

Step 9. Create a function allocation diagram, once the process has been modeled, with all the necessary elements in place.

Step 10. Review the EPC and verify that the now lean EPC truly reflects the process.

Step 11. Iterate over the first 10 steps until all the processes have been modeled.

Step 12. Review data elements of the model. See to it that all the data inputs to the EPC have a creation point within the EPC. If it is not created within the EPC, then identify the external source or process that is the source of this data.

Step 13. Review the organisational elements and any other system or resource object that is of importance. If it becomes difficult to understand the relationships between the organisational units, then it is worthwhile to create an organisational chart using the organisational view. Follow a similar exercise for the systems and other resource objects.

Modelling Guidelines

When we model, we need to be concerned about the correctness of the modelling. Correctness has got two elements, semantic correctness and syntactic correctness. In the previous sections, we looked at a few syntactical issues, such as an EPC should begin with an event and end with an event, and also the need to alternate between events and functions. We also discussed issues related to splitting on an operator and joining back on the same operator. These are all syntactical issues of correctness, which are important, but of even greater importance are the semantic issues. Does the model correctly represent the semantics of the real world? We all know that the process model is an abstraction, but in that abstraction, has it abstracted the real world correctly as far as the current problem that is facing us is concerned? Not correctly in all the dimensions of the real world (which is impossible), but correctly in terms of the problem that is under consideration. Closely related with semantic correctness is the relevance of the model. Here we need to use Occam's razor, which we discussed in the previous chapter. Ruthlessly model only the essentials, but as you model only the essentials, ruthlessly keep out the inessential items. Models need to be very clear and understandable, and they need to be useful, useable, and used. Follow the *keep it simple, stupid* (KISS) principle.

Break down the process model into chunks that are of reasonable size. Do not model more than what can be assimilated by either an analyst or a user. Use multiple levels of abstraction and hierarchical decomposition. Use divide and conquer, and horizontal segmentation, so that the models are of reasonable sizes. While you are modelling, remember Pareto's 20:80 principle. Model the 20% of the most important processes: don't model everything. And even within a process, there can be so many variations in the process that you may not be able to model all the variations, unless it is an extremely important and vital process that you are modelling. Only if it is an important process is it worthwhile to look at all the worst-possible case scenarios, as well as the most commonly occurring scenarios. If the process is reasonably important, but it is not of a very high importance, then model 20% of the variations that occur 80% of the time, rather than modelling 100% of the variations.

See to it that the models follow similar language and approaches ,because models are there to be shared. Even though you might be using the same symbols, you might be using very different languages for expressing the same ideas. Hence, it is useful, especially in the early stages of a modelling exercise, to get all the people who are involved in the modelling exercise to meet at reasonable intervals, so that everybody is using not just the same symbols, but also using similar language, and have the same understanding of the issues. And see to it that the models that are created are integratable. Integratable not only in terms of the different views, but also integratable in terms of horizontal segments being integrated together and decomposed models being integrated with higher level models.

Some key questions that we need to ask ourselves as we progress with the modelling is, "Why are you modelling?" And depending on the answer to this, the type of model that we would use would be very different. Are we modelling from the point of view of business process reengineering? Or is it from the point of view of developing an enterprise system? Or is it for the purpose of configuring an enterprise system? Or is it for both? So the answers to these questions would enable us to decide which modelling view is the most important. Is it the EPC view (which is the most commonly used one) or is it the organisational view, or is it the data view. A second question that is of relevance is, "What is it that we are modelling?" Is it the process, or is it the function, or is it the business as a whole, or the subunit within it, or are we modelling only the flow of a business object through the organisation? Another question is, "Who is it that we are modelling?" Is it a unit, is it a line management team, or is it some roles that individuals play in some of the key processes? Another key question is, "What is the time dimension as far as the model is concerned? Are we modelling the current process, or are we modelling what the process ought to be in the future? Or are we modelling just for the sake of simulation? And even so, is it the current situation or a potential future situation?" While we do this, we also need to be aware of the time scale that we are using in our models. We cannot put a blanket order and say, "We model only processes that take more than 10 minutes." Some processes might be conducted by a computer system, for example, an automated process which might take only a few seconds. But we would definitely want to model all the detailed steps in that process. Some processes might take days and months from the beginning till the end. And we might need to model even this process, which takes such a long time. Another key question that we need to consider in terms of the time dimension is the modelling of delays. Sometimes in the function attribute itself, the delay could have been incorporated. We can specify time to set up, processing time, as well as the delays that occur within the function. But especially in the as-is process model, we might want to highlight to management the problems that exist currently. And to do that, we might explicitly model the delays so that management is aware of the problems that exist in the current situation.

Chapter IV

Enterprise Systems Implementation Issues

Many software development life cycles have been proposed in the past. Boehm's Waterfall Model (Figure 4.1), incorporates, project definition, analysis, design, coding, testing, implementation, and maintaining, with feedback at every stage to the previous stage.

The prototyping model (Figure 4.2) involves listening to the customer, building a prototype that reflects the customer's requirements, followed by testing of the prototype by the customer, and then listening to the customer again regarding the prototype, and then revising and rebuilding prototype. Then we again get the customer to test drive the prototype, and this goes on in benign cycles where the customer requirements are honed in as time progresses.

One of the most popular approaches for major software development projects nowadays is the rational unified process (RUP), with its iterative approach involving four major phases: inception, elaboration, construction, and transition (Figure 4.3). Each of the phases involve major workflows such as business

Figure 4.1. The Waterfall Model of software development (Boehm, 1981, p.36)

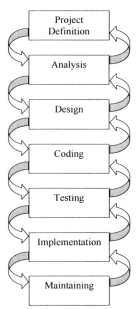

modelling, requirements, analysis and design, implementation, testing, and deployment, as well as supporting workflows such as project management, configuration, and change management. As we go through the rational unified process, we do multiple iterations of business modelling, requirements, analysis and design, implementation, testing, and deployment. But the effort that we spend on business modelling peters out as time progresses, whereas, there is more testing and deployment as we come towards the end of the phases. That is, in the earlier phases such as inception and elaboration, we do more of business modelling requirements, analysis, and design. And then during the construction phase, obviously, we do a lot more of design, implementation, and testing, and in the transition phase, we do a lot more of testing and deployment. And throughout all these phases, we have configuration and change management and project management to support each and every one of those phases. The spiral model of systems development is similar to the prototyping approach in terms of cycling/iterations, but closer to the waterfall method in terms of phases. Essentially, the spiral model has four major steps: *analysis*, *design*,

Figure 4.2. The prototyping approach to software development (Pressman, 1992, p.27)

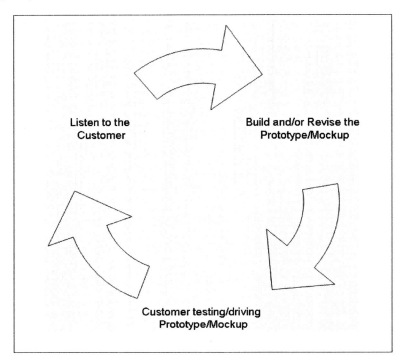

coding and testing, and *releasing and implementation* (Figure 4.4). You do this in a cyclical fashion, starting with the core and important phase, important parts of the project or rather important parts of the system, in the beginning, and then implementing that core, and then building around it as time progresses. Or you do this by building a core module in the beginning, and then building the other modules as time progresses.

Unfortunately, none of these traditional software development life cycles seem to capture the complexity of what goes on in the context of enterprise systems implementation. To address this problem, Brehm and Markus (2000) propose a divided software life cycle that captures the unique aspects of developing and implementing enterprise systems. Essentially, what the divided life cycle does is to split up the process into two distinct processes (Figure 4.5).

The first process goes on at the site of the vendor, the other process goes on at the site of the organisation, or the enterprise system's adopter. What

Figure 4.3. The Rational Unified Process: Workflows and phases

		Phases			
		Inception	Elaboration	Construction	Transition
Process Workflows	Business Modelling				
	Requirements				
	Analysis & Design				
	Implementation				
	Testing				
	Deployment				
	Multiple Iterations in each Phase				

Figure 4.4. Spiral Model (Pressman, 1992, p.29)

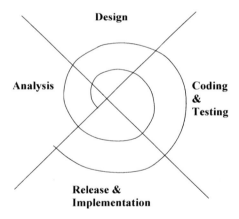

happens at the vendor's site could be any one of the above life cycles that we have looked at; it could be the rational unified process or it could be the spiral model or it could be the waterfall model, but most organisations nowadays would adopt something more formal like rational unified process or the spiral model. Once the vendor has come up with a product, this product is then released to the organisation which is adopting/implementing the enterprise

Figure 4.5. Enterprise system divided software life cycle (Adapted from Brehm & Markus, 2000, p.4)

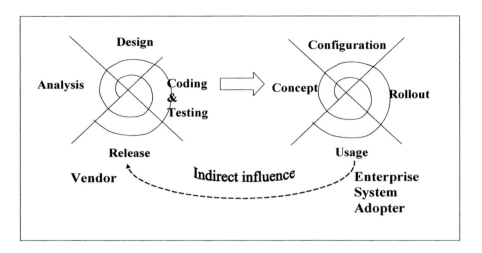

system. And when the product is released into the organisation, the organisation initially has a conceptual idea of what they want to do Based on that, they go and configure the enterprise system that is being released to them, roll out the implementation, and use the system. They cycle through these steps again and again until they have implemented the entire enterprise system with all its modules. Thus, on the ES adopter's side, we have concept, configuration, rollout, and usage. Especially in the context of the enterprise systems, there is an indirect influence from the enterprise system adopter to the vendor, whereby some of the best practices that the enterprise system adopter adopts get included in the vendor's next release, while the problems and issues that the adopter faces are taken on board by the vendor. This is true of most software development life cycles where the software user influences, to some extent, the vendor's plans for the next release. But it is worthwhile to note that this indirect influence is stronger in the context of enterprise systems than traditional software systems.

In this book we will not focus upon the vendor's life cycle, but we will focus upon the enterprise system adopter's life cycle (Chapter V). Before we go into the details of the life cycle, it is useful to understand the foundational forces that need to be resolved in the context of enterprise system implementation (Figure 4.6). First and foremost, every organisation has their current way of doing something, also termed as as-is process and then there is the best business practice, as understood by the industry in which the organisation is situated. Apart from this, we have the reference model that would be implemented when the software gets implemented. Thus, we have three distinct models available to us: (1) the as-is model of the current situation, (2) the reference model of the software, and (3) the best business practices of the industry.

Keeping these three things in mind, the fundamental purpose of the enterprise system implementation is to come up with a target model or configuration of the system, also termed as the to-be model, which will help an organisation to implement: (1) the very best business practices, (2) using the best reference model that reflects the business practice that is there in the industry, and (3) ideally not having to change their current situation too much. This is asking for a bit too much, but in an ideal world, you do not want to change your current practices too much because too much disturbance could lead to failure, and disturbing or changing over drastically, or radical change, can cost a lot. On the other hand, changing the reference model too much implies changing the software too much, and that too can be very risky and expensive. And finally, if we go too far away from the best business practice, then the purpose of implementing new business processes or implementing an enterprise system may not result in the benefits that we are looking for. Thus, in an ideal world, the as-is, reference, and BBP are clustered close together, and it is an easy matter for us to come up with the to-be, which is again found within that cluster.

Figure 4.6. Forces that need to be resolved to move from AS-IS to TO-BE

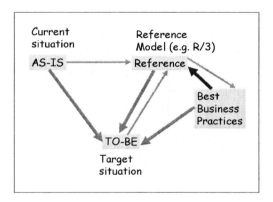

Figure 4.7. Process follows software or software follows process (Adapted from Martin, 1999, pp. 95-97)

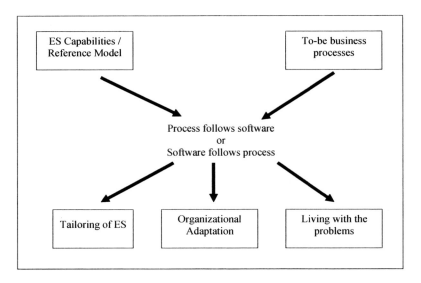

But unfortunately, in many situations, there is a big gap between each one of these four situations. This chapter and the next look at how to resolve this in a manner that results in a successful implementation of an enterprise system in an organisation.

Martin (1999) suggests that we need to consider the capabilities of the enterprise systems' package and the to-be business processes that we want to implement, and furthermore, he suggests that there could be two key ways in which we could address this (Figure 4.7). The process could follow the software, that is, the to-be business processes that we are designing can be exactly the same as the processes as proposed in the reference model of the enterprise system package. The second option is where the software follows the ideal to-be business process that you have designed, that is the software follows the process. Thus, in the case of the former, what we need to do is change or adapt the organisation to suit the software. In the latter, what we need to do is to modify or tailor the enterprise system package to suit the process. But there is the third option, which is we do not do anything, we do not implement the package, we do not change the process, we just live with the current problems that we have. Between the three extremes of *process follows software* and *software follows process*, there is a huge continuum of options, and most organisations' implementation of enterprise systems would be found somewhere in that continuum, sometimes closer to *process follows software*, and sometimes closer to *software follows process*.

Enterprise Systems Project Management

Like traditional projects, the three pillars of functional requirements, costs, and deadlines still play a key role in ES projects. The organisation still wants the products to be made/configured better that is, with more functional requirements, faster, and cheaper (Figure 4.8). But in addition to these three elements, one other element that is of great concern, especially in ES projects, is how does the organisation move from the as-is to the to-be? How is flexibility built into the system? How is flexibility built into the processes to enable the organisation to manage the evolution from the current state to the future desired state?

Unlike traditional projects, the enterprise system project is so massive in scope and impact that Davenport (2000) suggests that we need to think of enterprise system projects as akin to a new business venture, or a business change programme, and not just an ordinary project.

Figure 4.8. The Project Management Triangle

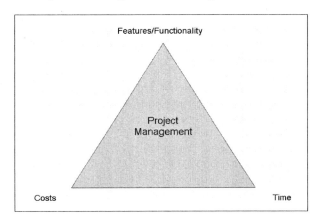

People, Process, and Technology Issues

Three key issues that need to be kept in mind in ES implementation are issues that affect people, issues that affect processes, and issues that affect technology. People related issues predominantly revolve around the change management activities. How do we move people from one process to another process? This would involve assessment of their current capabilities, assessment of the future requirements as far as their capabilities are concerned, and putting in place appropriate training mechanisms to move the people from one level of expertise to another level of expertise. Apart from this, formation of the project team, composition of the project team, issues related with working with consultants, issues related with commitment to the project not only from the member of the project, but also from the other stakeholders who are involved, especially the users of the new system or the new process. Process-related issues generally revolve around managing the enterprise system implementation project as a whole: issues that are related to implementing the new and reengineered process, issues with moving from one stage of the project to the next stage of the project, issues with moving from one phase of the implementation to another phase of the implementation, and finally issues with completing the project and starting to realise the benefits of the implementation. The final set of issues that are of relevance to any enterprise system project is the software functionality. What is the core functionality that we need to have, that we need to use? This is of vital importance since most enterprise systems have thousands of processes with many different ways in which those processes can be configured. So what is the functionality that we need, and how do we configure that functionality? Other aspects that also pose challenges as far as technology is concerned are the setting up of the various reports, preparation of the data, interfacing with legacy systems, and managing all the applications. On a long-term basis, how do you evolve the system as far as new releases and upgrades that come from the vendor? If one goes for a multiple vendor solution, how do you keep the multiple modules or applications from the multiple vendors synchronised together over a period of time? So upgrading, evolving, and managing the enterprise system applications over a period of time is an ongoing challenge.

Critical Success Factors for Enterprise System Implementation

Throughout this chapter and the next we will discuss critical success factors and the aspects that will lead to a successful implementation of enterprise systems. But here we will briefly outline some of the key CSFs that have been identified by implementers over many projects. First and foremost, the project needs to have very clear aims. It needs to have a good organisational structure, as far as the project is concerned. And the members of the project team need to be highly competent. There needs to be good communication processes set up between the members of the project team, as well as between the project team and the key stake holders such as the employees who will be using the system, the power users of the system — the customers, the suppliers, and key decision makers — who will all be using the system, or be impacted by the system in some fashion. Another key aspect, which we will discuss in detail later on, is the ability of the project team to come to quick decisions regarding what needs to be done. In the first chapter, we looked at mechanisms to identify the key business processes that need to be reengineered or that need to be supported by systems. Deciding on those processes needs to be done pretty quickly, but quickness should not lead to suboptimal results. It is just a warning so that projects teams should not get into the paralysis through analysis mode. Another aspect that comes through repeatedly in the literature, both academic and practitioner, is the inclusion of key power users and end users very early on in the project life cycle, not just at the end to test out the system, but right in the beginning itself. And this, in the end, will garner for the organisation, and for especially the project team, much higher acceptance of the decisions that they had taken as far as the users are concerned. And like most activities, here again Pareto's principle comes in handy. We need to focus on the 20% of the key questions that is going to resolve 80% of the problems; 20% of the key processes that is going to give us 80% of the benefit.

Implementation Strategies

There are many strategies that we need to consider when we think of enterprise system implementation. And none of these strategies are mutually exclusive.

Figure 4.9. Horizontal module by module implementation strategy

Human Resources

Production Planning

Materials Management

Sales and Distribution

Financials/Control

Hence, in the following sections, be aware that though the strategies are being discussed individually, very rarely would one strategy alone be used in the implementation. Most of the time it is the combination of strategies that usually brings about the best results.

One strategy that has been adopted quite often is to implement the core components of the enterprise systems first, and then add the other components in a phased kind of a manner (Figure 4.9). For example, quite often the financial (FI), and control (CO), and other core modules of the enterprise system are implemented first, followed by modules like sales and distribution, materials management, production planning, project management, human resources, and so on, in that order. One of the main reasons why FI and CO are usually selected for implementation right in the beginning is that they are vital for the rest of the modules to hang on. The other modules would not be implementable without these core modules being in place. The reason why the HR module comes much later, as compared to sales and distribution and materials management is purely because sales and distribution is a core value adding activity that lies on the value chain that we discussed in Chapter I. In contrast, HR is a module that supports a department that is only a supporting function that does not lie on the value chain. Hence, even in implementation, we see to it that the modules that are going to support the core value chain are implemented first, so that we can start enjoying the benefits of these core modules and enjoying the efficiencies that are brought into our value adding process much earlier than the efficiencies that are brought through the supporting processes.

While this horizontal strategy has worked, another strategy is to implement these modules, strategic business unit by strategic business unit (Figure 4.10).

That is, we do not implement all the modules at all the units at the same time; this could lead to a huge failure. Rather, we implement the system in one unit first, which is representative of many of the other units, and then we progress to the next unit and so on. In this context, it is also wise to first implement it in a small business unit, a business unit where the cost of failure is not too much, in a business unit that is representative of quite a few of the business units that are there in your organisation. All these help in reducing the risks of failure.

So far we have seen two strategies: one is implementing it module by module, the other is implementing it strategic business unit by strategic business unit. We can also go for a combination of these two strategies (Figure 4.11). We could implement all the FI and CO, and aspects such as procurement right, across all the business units right in the beginning. And then, once we have implemented these core modules across all the units, we can go and implement, say, the sales and distribution, or any other modules that are of interest, business unit by business unit. Thus, this strategy brings in the benefits of both those earlier strategies that we looked at. Apart from that, one other key reason for this strategy, whereby we combine the previous two strategies, is because the financial, procurement, and control processes are quite similar even across business units. So it may not make sense for us to split up this aspect for each and every business unit that we have. The financial, procurement, and control in many organisations would follow a centralised kind of an approach, as opposed to a decentralised approach. In this case, it makes even more sense to implement these modules right across the board, across all the units, since it is the same system that is going to work across the units. And only after that implementation has been done, do we go and implement the other modules business unit by business unit.

Figure 4.10. Vertical SBU by SBU implementation strategy

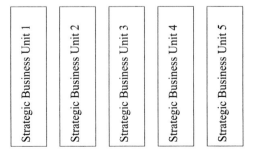

Phased vs. Big-Bang
Implementation Approaches

As we have already hinted, the strategies that we have looked at so far follow what is termed as a phased approach. What we have seen is the phasing is done by business unit, or by module or application. Another way in which it could be phased is also by geographical location. That is, the ES may be implemented in all the U.S.-based units first, and then go to your European units, or implement it in one particular state where the rules and regulations are unique, so it makes sense to make the implementations state specific. Quite often, geographical location is not just because of geographical distance, but it is more because of the changes that could occur in some of the modules that relate to the legal and tax aspects of doing business. And hence, if your organisation has spread across multiple countries or multiple states which follow different rules and regulations, even with respect to tax or legal issues, it is advisable to go for the geographically distributed/phased approach to the implementation.

As opposed to these phased approaches, another approach that has been implemented in the past is what is popularly known as "the big bang approach."

Figure 4.11. Mixed strategy of implementation that integrates Figure 4.9 and Figure 4.10

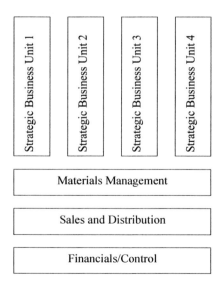

In this approach, essentially what is done is an enterprise wide implementation, all at the same time. That is, we implement the enterprise systems in all our units and implement all the modules that we want to implement at the same time in all the units. The complexity of this project is so high that most big firms adopt a phased approach. In the context of smaller firms, sometimes it makes sense to go for a big bang approach. But before venturing into the waters of either a phased approach or a big bang approach, it is worthwhile to consider the pros and cons of each of these approaches.

Pros and Cons of a Phased Approach

One of the key reasons why an organisation would go for a phased approach is that the phased approach breaks up a whole implementation into chunks of activities that are much more manageable. We are able to reduce the radical nature of the change when we make it in discreet chunks rather than one huge change. It also allows us to learn from experience, allows us to take the knowledge and learning that we have gathered as a result of the first phase of implementation, and take it over and use it in the second and subsequent phases of the implementation. This is especially true when we are implementing it, say, business unit by business unit. What we learn in the first business unit, which is hopefully representative, we are easily able to take that experience and understanding and transfer that knowledge across to the second business unit, and this will hopefully result in a much quicker and much cheaper implementation. The same applies when we do the implementation module by module or application by application. Though the business processes that we would be supporting are different, still the very fact that we have implemented a module of the enterprise system in one unit gives us a certain understanding into the complexities of the process, and helps us in making the second round of module/application implementations much more efficient and quicker.

There are many disadvantages to a phased approach, but here we will consider the two main disadvantages. The first disadvantage is that the overall scope and time frame of the project can be significantly increased by a phased approach. There are many reasons for this. Some of them are related to projects, some of them are related to having to build temporary interfaces to existing systems. Let us consider the temporary interfaces to existing systems. It is worthwhile to explore this problem in a little more detail. This problem occurs because we are not going in for a big bang approach. What this means is we are only implementing module by module. Assume we have implemented the financial (FI) and control (CO) module, but we still not have implemented the sales and distribution (SD) module. The newly implemented FI and CO modules have to talk to the legacy systems that implement the sales and distribution functionality, or all the other functionalities of the rest of the systems. We need to build temporary interfaces between the new modules that have been implemented and the old applications that exist. And these temporary interfaces have to be thrown off once the other modules have also come online. For example, now that you have implemented in the second phase the sales and distribution module, the interfaces that you have built between the FI and CO and the legacy sales and distribution systems need to be thrown out because it is not of relevance any more. Thus, splitting the project into many finer modules could sometimes result in having to build these bridges to legacy systems that then have to be thrown out. The cost of this aspect could be significantly high, and needs to be kept in mind. And the final thing that we need to realise is that though a phased approach carries less risk, the time before we can start enjoying the benefits of the enterprise system also gets elongated. The complete benefits of having reengineered business processes across all units well supported by an enterprise system would not be felt until all the modules in all the units have been implemented.

Pros and Cons of the Big Bang Approach

The big bang approach helps an organisation to transition to the to-be model of business processes much more quickly than the phased approach. And it is the quickest path to implementing the entire enterprise system. This also overcomes the problems that we mentioned in the previous section regarding temporary interfaces that need to be built between the new modules of the enterprise system and the old legacy systems. Since we are implementing all the modules at the same time, there is no need in a big bang approach to build any temporary throw away interfaces. But as we mentioned earlier, the big bang approach does have its problems. One of the key problems is there is no going back, there is no learning from the past. You have just one opportunity to implement the system and if you get it wrong, there is potential that the whole organisation might go down the gurgler. But if you get it right, you have a lot to gain. There is no leveraging and using the knowledge gained from one phase to another in a big bang approach. While the phased approach might take a long time for the entire implementation, it allows one to see the benefits of implementing an enterprise system quite early, as soon as, in some cases, the first modules are in place. But in the context of the big bang approach, since the whole project comes to an end only when all the modules are implemented, it can be quite a long time before the benefits of implementing an enterprise system are felt. Apart from that, the most complex module that gets implemented, and/or the most complex business unit where they are implementing the enterprise system, becomes a part of the critical path for the rest of the implementation as a whole. This increases the risks of such an implementation tremendously. Overall, the advice is, go for a phased but quick implementation, and definitely avoid the big bang approach. As mentioned earlier, phase your implementation, implementing base modules such as financial, control, and procurement, across all units, and then implement sales, manufacturing, distribution, and HR, in business unit after business unit. And as you implement, start with a business unit that is representative rather than being unique. Also start with business units which are not as critical for the functioning of the whole organisation, just so that in case the implementation is a failure, the whole company does not come down, but it is just one part of the company that is affected. To support the phased and quick approach, many methodologies have been suggested by various vendors, as well as by various consulting partners, and it is wise to go for one of these methodologies to enable you to get through this difficult implementation process reasonably quickly. Some of the key drivers in this whole decision making process are the number of existing systems, the age of the existing systems, and the complexity of existing systems. And this, in itself, will tell us how to go about the phased approach.

Another aspect that we need to consider is how long a company can put up with constant change. It is very difficult for an organisation to survive a long and tortuous implementation. Before an organisation decides to go for the phased approach that can extend many years, they need to question carefully whether they have the organisational will to sustain that kind of a situation. Another aspect that will play a role in the implementation of an enterprise system is the desire for integration. How great is this desire: Is it great enough that they are able to put up with long drawn out implementations? How focused are they on making changes to the business processes to deliver value? These kinds of questions will help an organisation to decide which strategy they are going to go in for, whether it is going to be a phased approach or a big bang approach. And in most contexts, it is not as if it is one or the other: you could go for a phased approach at the global level, but in some units, go for a big bang approach as well. Thus, even in this context, one can have a mixed strategy

Figure 4.12. Scope vs. function (Adapted from Davenport, 2000, p.173)

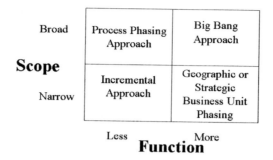

where phasing predominates, but if the unit is small enough, then you might go in for a big bang approach within the context of the phased approach.

Davenport (2000) recognises that there are two major dimensions to enterprise system implementation (Figure 4.12), the first dimension being the scope of the implementation. Is it broad, that is, across all units? Or is it very narrow? The second dimension relates to functionality. What is the functionality, what are the modules that will be implemented?

If we have a situation where we are happy with minimal functionality and a narrow scope, then we can go in for an incremental implementation. But if we desire minimal functionality but a broad scope, we go for a phased implementation. If we desire a high functionality with a narrow scope, we go for a geographic- or business-unit-phased implementation. If we want high functionality with a broad scope, we might consider a big bang approach. And here again, there are no hard and fast rules. Hybrid approaches are the norm rather than the exception, hybrid approaches that make the best of many strategic options.

Chapter V

Enterprise Systems Implementation Phases

Introduction

Markus and Tannis (2000) recognise four distinct phases in an enterprise systems implementation as viewed from the adopter's perspective. The very first phase is called "chartering." They suggest that even before the project starts, a business case is usually made whether to go ahead with the enterprise system implementation or not, and it is only after the business case has been made, and the constraints of the solution have been understood, that the project actually starts. The project never starts if the constraints are too much, or the business case is not strong enough. The second phase is the project phase in which the software is configured to suit the requirements of the organisation and implemented in the organisation. The third phase is the shakedown phase, during which the organisation moves from the go live status to the normal operation status. This is the time that it takes an organisation to get back to normalcy. The fourth phase, according to Markus and Tannis, is the onward-and-upward phase. It is in this phase that the organisation attempts to realise all the benefits, or the majority of the benefits, that they believe that they could obtain by implementing the enterprise system. But apart from realising the benefits, this is also the phase when the organisation plans ahead for future enhancements to the system, as well as to the processes and the organisation. In a cycle of continuous improvement, this phase merges into the next project phase where the software is reconfigured, or new software is configured, which will enhance the current operations. Thus, Markus and Tannis identify that each of the four phases have specific activities: Phase 1, project chartering where ideas are turned to dollars; Phase 2, the project phase where dollars are turned to assets; Phase 3, the shake down phase where assets are turned to impacts; and Phase 4, the onward-and-upward phase where the impacts are turned to performance.

Parr and Shanks (2000) identify three phases that have similarities with Markus and Tannis' phases. Phase 1 is planning, which is equivalent to the chartering that we looked at earlier. Phase 2 is the project phase, which is in turn divided up into setup, reengineer, design, configure, test, and installation. And this cycle of steps in the project could be repeated either for the different modules that we are implementing, or for the different business units where we are implementing. Phase 3, according to Parr and Shanks, is enhancement, which maps with the onward and upward phase of Markus and Tannis. The only difference between this model and the previous model is that Parr and Shanks have not explicitly considered the shakedown phase that Markus and Tannis identify in their model or life cycle.

Callaway (1999) proposes a more elaborate set of steps. Callaway suggests that any enterprise system project would be comprised of the project preparation phase, planning of the business processes, configuring the system according to the planned business processes, testing and validating of the configured system, final preparation of the system, and finally, going live with the system. These six phases encompass most of the activities that go on in an enterprise system project. In addition to this, we would like to suggest that project preparation should be preceded by the chartering phase, as identified by Markus and Tannis, because it is in the chartering phase that you decide whether to go ahead or not with the project. And if you decide to not go with the project, then you never even start on the project.

Chartering

This is the very first phase of any enterprise system implementation. This is the phase where an organisation considers, first and foremost, the question whether they should implement an enterprise system. And they make a business case which helps them to evaluate the cost and benefits of an enterprise system. If the benefits outweigh the cost, then they proceed further with vendor selection and partner selection, and then actually prepare for the implementation project.

Prerequisites

Before we start on the enterprise system implementation, we need to consider whether the organisation fulfils some of the key prerequisites that are required for a successful enterprise system implementation. First and foremost, the organisation needs to have a clear strategy about how they are going to implement an enterprise system, and how that enterprise system would support the goals of the organisation. Secondly, does the organisation have data in the format of specified quality and of specified characteristics, and is it in a position to implement or start using the enterprise system. From a people perspective, we need to consider whether the organisation has the skill, knowledge, experience and expertise to either implement the enterprise system on their own, or implement it in partnership with a consulting firm. From a technology perspective, we need to ask the question whether the organisation has the infrastructure to support and execute an enterprise system. Some of the technology requirements are quite high when it comes to enterprise systems, especially in terms of the servers, the networks, and even the client. From a financial perspective, one of the things we need to ask is, can we really afford it? Here the costs are not just the cost of software, there are many other costs that are involved, and we will be looking at them in detail in a few more paragraphs. Again from a people perspective, we need to ask ourselves whether the management understands and supports the implementation of the enterprise system. Here it is not just a question of supporting the enterprise system, but also the changes to the processes; and the organisational structures, policies, and procedures, that will result, due to such an implementation.

If, and only if, these prerequisites are satisfactorily met, do we progress further. In the chartering phase, as well as through the project, the team needs to have a good mix of people with not just technical skills, but also business skills. Some would even suggest that, especially in an enterprise system implementation, business skills are of paramount importance, and only then the technical skills. It is the business skills that help us to identify the correct problem, and once we have identified the correct problem, the technical skills enable us to implement a system effectively and efficiently to address the problem.

We need to obtain involvement from the grass roots of the organisation, from the power users of the organisation, from the key people in the organisation who understand business and understand systems. In the chartering phase, we need to have the chief executive officer on board, key members of the senior executive team, as well as the board of directors involved in deciding whether to go with the enterprise system or not. Many organisations have not taken seriously the implementation of an enterprise system, and have made a shipwreck of the implementation. And some have even gone bankrupt as a result. The decision makers need to not only think of the present requirements, but also of the reasonable future requirements. Balanced with this, they also need to manage the scope of the enterprise system implementation project. While they need to consider the future, they should not think so far ahead that they come up with a project that will take forever to implement. So here again, there needs to be a decision where future requirements are balanced against current constraints.

Business Case

Once a team of decision makers have been formed, the next phase is to come up with a business case. The purpose of the business case is not to just sell to the management the need for an enterprise system, but it is to take a balanced, unbiased view of whether the organisation should really go in for an enterprise system, and if so, which one should they go in for, and who should be the implementation partners? In the business case, we consider the cost versus the benefits of putting an enterprise system in place. It is an iterative process where we cycle through many different options. We start by being generic in our requirements, identify the key requirements, and then hone in on the specific requirements. While we do the cost-benefit analysis, we need to keep in mind that it is not purely a financial exercise. That is, financial considerations, on their own, should not dictate whether we go in for an enterprise system or not. Sometimes it may be a case of catching up with the competition and/or catching up with an industry. Here we do not have a choice but to adopt an enterprise system, otherwise we will be left far behind, as far as the technological battle is concerned. For example, in the classic case of Brittanica, their inability to adapt led to their demise. Many organisations do not spend enough on technology and start lagging behind, and some see putting an enterprise system into place as a means of, at one-shot, putting into place all the systems that they need to have.

Costs

There are many costs that are incurred during the enterprise system project: hardware, software, change management, consultants, data conversion, training, integration, and disruption costs. Hardware costs involve setting up the servers, the clients, the network infrastructure, and other tools and technologies to support this hardware infrastructure. And when we consider servers, it is not just servers to support the software: we also need to have backup and testing servers, in addition to the production servers. In the contest of software, we have costs related to licences, which are usually based on the number of users, but sometimes could be a company-wide licence for the software. And we also need to keep in mind that most of these costs are not just one-off costs, but there are annual maintenance costs, as well as licensing costs involved. In the context of hardware and software, we need to keep in mind the concept of the total cost of ownership of the whole system throughout the life cycle of the enterprise system.

Apart from the hardware and software cost, one of the major costs (actually this cost can be much more than the cost of hardware and software) is the cost of change management. In some organisations, change management costs have been as much as 70% of the total cost of the project. Hence, it is a pretty substantial part of the cost, and we need to be aware of this. Quite often organisations think, "Ah, we have got the hardware and the software, and we have got some consultants to just configure the system." But these costs are not the main cost; they are just the tip of the whole iceberg. Seventy percent of the costs are hidden costs which cannot be clearly quantified. Thus, we need to bear in mind that change management is a vital part of the implementation process, and the better we do it, the lower our total implementation costs are going to be. Sometimes associated with change management are the costs of consultants and contractors who have been involved in implementing the project. Apart from the costs of the software provided by the enterprise system vendor, other software costs are also involved in an enterprise system. Two key costs are the costs of the database and of the supporting tools, such as modelling software, testing software and monitoring software. Quite often, the data that we have from the legacy system is very dirty, that is, it has a lot of errors and inconsistencies that need to be addressed before it can be loaded up into the new enterprise system. This cleaning-up cost can be quite substantial. Apart from cleaning up, the new system might require new data to be captured over a period of time so that it can be loaded into the enterprise system. And this in itself could bring about a whole new set of costs which are associated with converting the old and existing data into a format that is acceptable with the new enterprise system.

Associated with change management is another cost, which is the cost of training the users of the system in different capacities; users within the organisation and administrators of the system. Since an enterprise system almost covers the entire organisation, it will touch almost every employee in the organisation in some fashion. So we need to bear in mind that the cost of training could potentially be quite high, since every employee would need to be trained, to a greater or smaller degree.

The integration of the system with existing systems using bridges, whether temporary or permanent, is again a costly exercise. And integration, more and more, is not a one-off exercise, since organisations keep upgrading their systems almost every year, and that implies new systems are coming up, or new versions of the systems are coming up, and it is not always that the newer versions are going to coexist with our existing system easily. Quite often the protocols of the new systems are different, and not always backward compatible with the protocols of the older systems. Thus, integration can be quite expensive.

Testing costs, again, are something that needs to be borne in mind. Testing is an activity that occurs almost from the early phases of the project right to the end. Testing occurs at different levels of abstraction where we do low-level programme tests, medium-level module tests, intermediate-level application tests, and finally, integration tests of the complete system that involve all the modules and all the applications. And these tests are conducted each time a programme or module is changed or configured slightly differently. Not only should the programme or the module be tested, but also how this programme or module is functioning within the context of the entire system. Thus, integration tests are something that is repeated again and again and again through the life cycle of the project.

Related with change management, but not necessarily considered explicitly always there, is the cost of disruptions that occur due to putting the new system and new processes into place. This is a major cost that is incurred during the shakedown phase immediately after going live, and before the system reaches normalcy. The cost of disruption, due to implementing the new system, could include a drop in profit, a drop in customer satisfaction, an increase in lead times, cycle times, and an increase of waste. Thus, the period of disruption needs to be minimised as much as possible, so that the cost of disruption drops low. The final cost that might have to be borne, unless appropriately addressed, is the loss of good employees who have been involved in the project. Their value, due to their involvement in the enterprise system project, has gone up, and unless the organisation remunerates them according to their new level of expertise, the employees are going to search for greener pastures. Other costs that we need to keep in mind are costs related with building up the infrastructure while keeping in mind the existing infrastructure. The breadth of impact of the implementation on the organisation has an impact on the costs. The amount of redesign work undertaken in terms of the processes has a significant impact on the costs. The number of legacy systems that need to be integrated into the enterprise system, again, increases the cost. In case we do not change the processes, but change the enterprise system, then the costs of customisation goes up. How many reports do we need to create, how many new user interfaces do we need to customise, how many interfaces do we need to build — all these costs can add up very quickly.

Benefits

In terms of benefits, one of the key benefits identified by Davenport (2000) is the automation of work processes. A prime example is employee self-services. In the past, there would have been somebody in HR who would have taken care of a request from the employee. But with an enterprise system in place that supports self-services, the employee goes directly to the system and makes whatever changes that need to be made, as far as their employment is concerned. Or in the context of ordering a particular product, instead of going through procurement, some things could be ordered directly by the employee.

Rationalisation of the data is another key benefit that is obtained as a result of an enterprise system. The integration of the data, the cleaning of the data, and having one single entry of the data provides so many advantages that quite often, organisations put enterprise systems in place just for this.

Revenue enhancement is also a potential benefit of implementing enterprise systems. Improved customer services could result in the same customer purchasing more, as well as new customers coming on board, which would in turn increase the revenue. Since the enterprise system is in place, it might be easier for the organisation to expand and grow. And the availability of enterprise wide data, and clean data at that, provides more opportunities for better decision making than ever before.

Enterprise systems also bring down the total cost of ownership. Instead of having five different systems with overlapping features, integration problems, and synchronisation issues, we have one single system with one single database where changes in one part of the system flow on to the other part of the system seamlessly. The enterprise system itself comes with so many features that problems of programming new features, as is the case in the context of customised or domain specific applications software is concerned, do not arise that frequently in the context of enterprise systems.

Since an enterprise system usually replaces many legacy systems, many of the problems associated with maintaining legacy systems, upgrading them, and supporting them, are reduced substantially. Usually enterprise system vendors attempt to keep up and ahead of changes in the field. They are not always successful, but they do attempt to, and this usually prevents the need for an organisation to be building specialised functionality in-house.

Other benefits that result are improved visibility within the organisation as well as outside the organisation, tighter integration between processes and departments, and lower handover costs because of this tighter integration. The systems, to the most part, generally possess WYSIWYG (*what you see is what you get*) characteristics. This is a big improvement from the interfaces of the past, but at the same time, enterprise system vendors sometime lag a little behind specialised application vendors as far sophistication of their interfaces are concerned. But some vendors have taken onboard this problem, and have explicitly addressed user interface issues. And for the most part nowadays, the interface provided by an enterprise system vendor is as good and in some cases much more sophisticated and better than the interfaces offered by specialised application vendors.

Finally, but not least, is the fact that the enterprise system implementation is just the beginning of the journey. The enterprise system provides the basic infrastructure above which we could build other systems, such as supply chain management and customer relationship management. Many organisations nowadays implement an enterprise system with the primary motive of being able to implement, on top of the enterprise system, the sophisticated functionality that is being offered by SCM, CRM, and Business Intelligence systems.

Vendor Selection

The selection of the vendor of the enterprise system is a very important decision. Some even go as far as suggesting that it is the most crucial decision of the whole project. And we really may not be able to do a good business case and understand the costs and benefits until we have selected the vendor, because the costs are so closely linked with who the vendor is, what the software is, and what the reference model of the software is. Thus, there is an intrinsic and very tight link between the functionality provided by the vendor and the business case.

There are many factors that affect vendor selection. One key factor is whether the vendor supports the industry vertical in which the organisation lies. For example, PeopleSoft specialises in the tertiary education sector, Baan specialises in manufacturing, while SAP specialises in health care, petrochemicals, and a whole lot of other industries. Depending on the industry vertical that you are in, sometimes the vendor is a foregone conclusion, because there might be only one vendor who does that particular industry vertical very well. Some of the vendors have a stranglehold on certain industry verticals. Though this situation is changing, it is not changing rapidly enough.

The second key factor is how well the enterprise system fits the organisational strategy, as well as the organisational processes. What is the degree to which we need to customise the software? The less that we need to customise it, and the better it fits with the strategy of the organisation, the higher the reasons for selecting the vendor.

The third critical factor is the identification of the vendor who supports the core process of our organisation. And then we look at the secondary processes and their support. Certain vendors specialise in certain modules and sets of processes. For example, SAP does finance well, Baan does the manufacturing module well, while People Soft does the HR module well. Especially if an organisation is very large and would like to go for the best of the vendors for each of their modules or applications, then it is not just a matter of vendor selection, but it is *vendors* selection. Who are all the vendors who will be supporting the modules that are of interest to us?

The final key factor is the scale of the organisation. Certain vendors specialise in certain areas. For example, SAP dominates the larger firms, while there are a host of vendors who play in the medium and smaller firms. Thus, depending on the size of your organisation, certain vendors are either excluded or included in your deliberations. Another important aspect is the match of the technical and the business functionality with organisational setup and requirements. What is the degree of centralisation or decentralisation that is offered by the system? How much autonomy is provided to the user? Does the system allow us to drill down to the details or only provide us with the aggregate? Does the system support global organisations or only local organisations? Does the system support centralised or decentralised or federalist approaches as far as data and processes are concerned? With respect to software modification, does the vendor allow one to do simple configuration as well as radical programme-code modification? Depending on the answers to these questions, our choice of vendor could be short listed.

Ease of use of the software is another important criterion in vendor selection. Of special importance is matching the ease of use with the capabilities of our staff, and the implications for training. Does the system run on multiple platforms (hardware, software) in terms of operating systems, as well as in terms of databases? How flexible is the software in terms of working across multiple networks? How well does the software fit the culture of our organisation? Is it very rigid and expects the organisation to be very hierarchical? Or does it support a matrix or an organic kind of an organisational structure and culture? This process of vendor selection should not take more than a few months. As mentioned earlier, the selection of vendor is tightly enmeshed with the selection of the business case, and within the vendor selection itself is enmeshed other related selections such as the hardware, the implementation partner, and consultant. Sometimes selection of vendor automatically decides who our implementation partner will be, and it works the other way as well. That is, sometimes the selection of implementation partner necessitates us to go for one technical solution due to the expertise of the implementation partner. But it is advised that the vendor is selected first, based on the merits of the software and its match with the organisation, and only then the implementation partner is selected based on that.

Kuiper (Callaway, 1999) suggests a funnel approach whereby a whole series of questions are asked, and the answers to the earlier questions constrain and filter the vendors, resulting, in the end, with only a handful of vendors for deeper questioning. If you go for the funnel approach, the basic factors that we discussed earlier should be asked right in the beginning, and that in itself will constrain and limit very quickly a number of possible vendors. And then we can ask the more detailed and subsidiary questions of the few vendors who are left. Otherwise, we might end up in a situation where we are asking thousands of questions to 20 or 30 vendors, rather than asking hundreds of questions against a few vendors. Here again, we need to keep in mind that usually the core modules such as FI and CO can be very similar across most vendors in a particular industry and scale of organisation. It is only in the more advanced modules, or subsidiary or specialised modules, that we find differences between vendors. If the main purpose for us to go for a vendor is to take advantage of the advanced modules, then it is very important, at this stage, that we compare the functionality of the advanced modules rather than just the functionality of the core modules.

Once we have identified a vendor, or a couple of vendors, we could use scoring models that help us to focus on the crucial processes in the organisation and how well the short-listed enterprise systems fare as far as these crucial core processes are concerned. You will want to use case studies of vendor implementation, as far as these core processes are concerned, as a guide in this finalisation process. Visiting reference sites at this point is highly recommended. Vendor and user conferences, such as the Sapphire conference run by SAP and related vendors, are a useful venue to get to understand the problems faced by the customers of a particular vendor. Getting the vendor to demonstrate their product, and getting the vendor to allow the organisation to test drive the product before finalisation, is very important. You might even want to get the vendor to test drive their software with your own data.

The cost of the product, the payment structure and licensing structure, the one-off costs, and the repetitive costs that occur annually would all help us in comparing the final short-listed set of vendors. Verifying the integrity of the claims of the vendor from reasonably unbiased third parties such as the Gartner Group or the Forrester Group is a must. While implementation partners and consulting firms could provide some advice in this matter, they tend to be biased because of their close relationships with the vendors whose products they specialise in. Hence, third parties like Gartner are a useful source. The Gartner Group, for example, publishes the magic quadrants on a regular basis, where it compares various vendors in the different sectors, such as the large, medium and small, as well as in the different industry verticals. Gartner classifies them based on their ability to execute, as well as their visionary character. This again helps us to understand the capabilities of vendors from two important perspectives. Closely related with the visionary aspect is the viability and future plans of the vendor. In the cutthroat market of enterprise systems, will the vendor survive? If not, it is a dangerous move to go for an enterprise system vendor just from a cost perspective, though you might feel that they might not survive in the long term, for two key reasons: (1) an enterprise system selection could become a life long selection and you want the vendor to be a partner throughout, and (2) it is difficult to change over from one vendor to another vendor after implementation. Attending the user conferences also help us to understand the level of customer support provided by the vendor. Finally, we also need to consider the level of support that we can expect from consultants as far as implementing, maintaining and evolving the systems are concerned. We should not go in for solutions for which it is very difficult to find consultants.

Another ERP/ES software selection methodology that is quite useful is the Clarkson-Potomac method (Callaway, 1999) that starts off by assessing the IT environment and the plans of the organisation, followed by defining and prioritising of requirements. The assessment of the IT environment helps us to identify contenders, and the definition of requirements helps us to come up with test scenarios for the key requirements. The next step is to get the contenders to show off their product against the test scenarios that have been created. Get them to use your data for the test drive, and based on the results, select the winner of the test drive, negotiate with the winner, and plan for the implementation. While some might consider the Clarkson-Potomac approach and Kuiper's approach to be distinct, we can easily see how these approaches can be integrated together. For example, we could adopt Kuiper's approach to start with in order to short-list the list of contenders, and then move over to the Clarkson-Potomac methodology.

Implementation Partner Selection

Just as in the case of software selection, cost should not be an overriding factor in implementation partner selection. There are many other important considerations apart from cost. The size of the organisation, the reputation of the organisation, and its ability to implement the software of the vendor, all play an important role in the selection. Some of the key questions to ask are: What does the industry have to say about this implementation partner? What references do they bring to the table? Are they committed to the vision of the organisation? Have they been able to manage change in other organisations as part of their implementation? How well did they manage that change? Has this organisation extensive experience in your industry, and also extensive experience with the software product? Does the organisation possess enough skilled resources to be in a position to undertake your implementation? In a few cases, leading consulting partners have sent rookie consultants to undertake implementations, resulting in suboptimal implementations. How well do they know and understand the processes of your organisation and of your industry? While the selection of a vendor can be based on the above factors, we might find that if we go for a best-of-breed solution, then we might, in a similar fashion, have to go in for a best-of-breed implementation partner selection. Another issue that is vital is to take a decision on who is going to control the project? Is it going to be the implementation partner whom you hire at a fixed cost for the whole implementation, or do you take on yourself the project responsibility and hire the services of one or more vendors/partners for different aspects of the project? There are pros and cons in terms of costs and risks. Obviously, the cost of the former is higher, and the cost of the latter is lower. But at the same time, the risk of the former is lower, and the risk of the latter could be higher. If a firm has not had much experience in implementing enterprise systems, if this is the first time an organisation is implementing an enterprise system, it is advisable to go for a single systems integrator or implementer at fixed costs, rather than the organisation taking on the responsibility of managing the implementation project.

Preparing for
the Enterprise System Project

Once chartering has been completed, and the organisation has decided to implement an enterprise system, and has decided who will be the vendor, the next critical phase is preparing for this important project. First and foremost, the organisation needs to identify the resources required in terms of funds, in terms of people, and in terms of time. As usual, the three key components of a project, functionality, cost, and time are quite closely interrelated. In an enterprise system project, formation of the project team is absolutely vital. And the project team is not just the internal people in the organisation, but also the contractor and the consultants who will be your partners in the implementation process. The internal project team needs to be made up of hand picked people, people who are vital for the functioning of the organisation. Callaway (1999) suggests that if the organisation can function normally, as usual, without the personnel who have been dedicated to the enterprise system project that indicates, that they might not have selected the right people for the team. That is, the personnel whom you should put on the project team need to be personnel who are very knowledgeable, very experienced, and who will be missed when they spend most of the time working on the project. And, as alluded to earlier, the project team needs to be made up of not just technical people, but also business people. In fact, the leadership of this project team should be people who are more business oriented rather than technically oriented. A business-oriented leadership has more chances of succeeding in this type of project, where business skills are of paramount importance.

Knowledge Required

There are three core types of knowledge that are required to not only oversee an enterprise system project, but also to be a part of the enterprise system project. And depending on what role you play, the level of knowledge you need to have in each of these three areas could vary. The participants in the project need to have knowledge about business processes, about the enterprise system that they are putting in place, as well as enterprise systems in general. And they also need to have knowledge about the process of implementing the enterprise system, and realise the benefits from the enterprise system. It is in some ways the aim of this book to impart these three core sets of knowledge. Chapters I, II, and III focus on business processes; Chapters IV and V focus on the enterprise system implementation process, and Chapter VI focuses on enterprise systems. The latter chapters use a case study to reinforce all three types of knowledge.

Sponsorship

The project needs to have sponsorship from the very highest level: the chief executive officer. Apart from that, the sponsor should be from the part of the organisation where the enterprise system is being implemented, if it is a strategic business unit and not the entire organisation. Usually, the executive sponsors are the chief executive officer, chief information officer and/or chief operations officer. The sponsor plays a very important role in the enterprise system project. It is the sponsor's role to actually link the implementation of the enterprise system with the strategy of the firm, and communicate this linkage, and the value of implementing such a system to the organisation as a whole. Apart from communicating the value and the importance of the enterprise system, this sponsor needs to create a climate in the organisation that will enable the implementation to go through smoothly. The sponsor needs to put in place measures that will enable the organisation to change and evolve to accommodate the enterprise system. The sponsor also needs to advertise and inform, through various channels, to the employees, the goals and visions of the organisation that are driving the implementation of the enterprise system. But apart from that, the sponsor also needs to explicitly link the implementation of the enterprise system with key performance indicators that will be improved, hopefully, as a result of such an implementation. In organisations that are not very keen on taking on board enterprise systems, or may have the culture that is one of *islands of power*, it is difficult to implement enterprise systems. And it is especially, in such contexts, that the sponsor needs to enforce the inevitability of change and improvement to the existing business processes supported by the new enterprise system. Thus, the key role of the sponsor is to provide all the necessary conditions, such that the project proceeds on budget and on time.

Leadership

Next to the executive sponsor, the most important role in the project is the project leader or manager. Most projects will have just one leader, but some of the very big projects have multiple leaders for various facets and for various phases of the projects. Especially with the leadership role, it is important that there is an equal mix of skills as far as business and information technology. Davenport (2000) suggests that the project leader needs to be a jack-of-all-trades combining the skills of a technologist, with that of a business expert, with that of a drill sergeant, a motivational speaker, a politician and a psychologist in one. Taking over from the sponsor, the leader needs to be even more explicit in linking the business changes that will occur as a result of the system changes.

Process Owners

The implementation of the enterprise system will lead to changes to some of the core processes within the organisation. And as a part of the project team, we need to identify business process owners who will own each of these core business processes, who will take responsibility for the changes that will take place in those processes, and will see to it that those processes fit in with the system. This person has to be someone with very good experience in the business and in the process, with excellent design skills, who will be able to gather the information about the process, or who will know the information about the process. This person should be able to understand the alternatives for implementing the process in different ways, and will be able to evaluate these alternatives. Last but not least, this person should be able to link their process with the overall process that goes on within the organisation.

Super/Power Users

Apart from business process owners, we need to also identify super users within the system. Usually they will be drawn from the middle level of the organisation, either managers or employees or non-managers from the departments or functions that will be affected most by the enterprise system. Their primary purpose is to understand how the implementation of the enterprise system will affect the tasks, activities, and the processes that go on in their part of the organisation. Apart from that, they will also be used for recommending to the consultant or contractor who is doing the configuration, the actual system configuration that will work in their context. Due to their understanding of their work, they are also ideal candidates for testing and piloting the system once it has been configured. So they act as typical users of the system, testing it against normal, as well as worst-case scenarios. Since they are super users or power users, they are usually well respected in their part of the organisation, and hence, they are also ideal candidates for selling the system to the other employees in their department or function: selling and training the others in the use of the new enterprise system. The super users also have certain responsibilities after the implementation of the system: to see to it that the business processes and the systems work hand in hand during the transition from implementation to shakedown to normalcy. And they would also be actively involved in taking care of the teething problems that are a natural part of implementing any system: optimising the processes and the system so that the shakedown period is as short as possible. Usually, the super or power users are hand picked by the managers from among their employees based on their performance.

Teams

There are two distinct teams that will need to be formed. One is the vision and planning team, and the other is the implementation team. The vision and planning team is made up of a very small number of people, maybe 5 to 10, depending on the size of the project, who are highly skilled in business and technology. And it is this team that fits the enterprise system to the organisation. It is this team that decides whether process is going to follow software or software is going to follow process. Whatever the situation — by how much the software is going to follow process or by how much process is going to follow software — these decisions are taken by this particular team. And these decisions have a tremendous impact on the overall project. Thus, this team would be responsible for the time frame of the whole project. They will decide the benefit and cost that will be incurred. They will decide how the key processes will be structured, and how they will flow within the organisation. Any changes to the organisational structure, again, will be decided by this team. This team will identify processes that will be common across the whole organisation, and usually it is better to make the processes common, unless the case can be made against commonality and for uniqueness. This team would also be responsible for the phasing of the project over a period of time, phasing of implementation in terms of process or module or geographic unit or business unit. It is this team that will see to it that the goal and vision of the organisation is met by the implementation of the enterprise system.

In contrast to the vision and planning team, the implementation team would be made up of a much larger number of people. This team will have some members from the vision and planning team in it to ensure that the vision is actually being implemented, and not something else. But apart from these, the implementation team will have people drawn from the organisation, as well as people drawn from the implementation partner or contractor. The implementation team is made up of people who are full-time on the project. Depending on the size of the project, it could be anywhere from fifteen to hundreds of people. These are the people who actually do the implementation and are responsible for the as-is model, for the improvements with the as-is model, and to come up with the to-be model. And it is this team which is responsible for implementing the to-be model by configuring and/or modifying the enterprise system to support the to-be model. The implementation team is also responsible for training the employees in the configured system. It is also the implementation team who will be responsible for seeing to it that the organisation's transition to the new system occurs in a smooth and, as far as possible, seamless fashion. While we are making up all these teams, we need to be careful that we do not forget the local information technology or information systems department, and expertise that exist within the organisation. Some organisations have completely gone for implementation using external partners leading to absolutely no role for the local IT experts. And this results in a situation where the local IT employees are very dissatisfied. At the same time, you are letting yourself in for a lifetime of dependency on the external implementation partner. An ideal situation is to have a mix of your own IT people, your own business people working side by side with the IT and business people of the implementation partner. This will enable your people to pick up sufficient skills that will enable them to evolve the system, to some extent, as the years go by.

Profiles

Apart from these roles and teams that we have seen so far, there are very specific skills that are needed for the implementation of such a complex system. For example, SAP suggests that the application consultant should have advanced knowledge with respect to mySAP.com components, mySAP.com Core, the Accelerated SAP or Value SAP process of the implementation, and have an advanced level of industry experience in that particular module that is being configured. Apart from this, SAP also expects the application consultant to be proficient in project management and testing, and have a basic level understanding of ABAP programming, quality management, interface design, operating systems, programming languages, networks, and databases. Thus, we can see that any one who is involved in this project needs to have a wide level of experience in business as well as in technical areas, and very advanced level knowledge in certain areas. For various other roles, SAP has given very specific guidelines about the kind of profile that is expected. For example, the SAP consulting profile, in contrast to the application consulting profile, is heavily oriented towards technical know-how. They expect the SAP technical consultant to have advanced level knowledge of database networks, programming languages, operating systems, interfaces, testing, Internet technology, ABAP programming, and industry experience. But in addition to this advanced level, they also expect the technical consultant to be proficient as far as mySAP.com workplace, components, and core modules are concerned. Between these two extremes, one at the application level, the other at the technical level, we have a whole range of other roles with intermediate level or combination of skills, such as a cross application expert, corporate strategy expert and programmer or developer.

Planning of the Business Processes

Once the project team has been put in place, the next key step is planning of the business processes. This phase is absolutely crucial to the success of the enterprise system project as a whole. It is in this step that we follow some of the early phases of Rosemann's life cycle introduced in Chapters I and II. The identification of the business processes that need to be supported by the enterprise system, the modelling of the processes as they are occurring now, analysing those processes and suggesting improvements to those processes, and coming up with the to-be model, all these steps would be undertaken within the context of planning of business processes. Especially in the context of enterprise system implementation, the company not only needs to keep in mind their current as-is process, they also need to keep in mind the reference model of the vendor whom they have selected, and the industry best practices, and combine these three to design an improved business process model that has the chance of succeeding both in terms of working in the organisation, as well as succeeding in terms of providing benefits. Quite usually, organisations use the reference model as a starting point for their redesign efforts. But some organisations follow a clean sheet approach where business process improvement is paramount, and it is only then that they consider how well the business process is going to be supported by the vendor. This approach, made popular in the early 1990s by Hammer and Champy (1993), has not been very successful.

Davenport (2000) goes as far as suggesting that reengineering should not be done in isolation, but it should be done hand in hand with the requirements and constraints placed by the enterprise system that you have selected. Thus, Davenport's approach is closer to an IT led reengineering/improvement effort, while Hammer and Champy's (1993) approach could be considered as an improvement led IT approach. Davenport's approach is the one that is predominantly used in industry. And it acknowledges that business processes, and the systems that support these business processes are tightly linked, and you cannot consider one without considering the other since they are so intrinsically and completely linked together. Davenport's (2000) approach is somewhat like Owen Corning's good-enough reengineering approach: that is do not go all out on the reengineering but do enough reengineering so that you leverage the enterprise system. Thus, this approach does not suggest a radical reengineering, but a pragmatic reengineering that keeps in mind the requirements of the enterprise system, keeps in mind that change management can be expensive and can be very risky, and attempts to make only those changes that are vital for the organisation.

While we consider this phase of planning of the business processes, we need to be careful that we do not spend too much time in analysis. We could be caught up in the paralysis by analysis syndrome. Some organisations have looked at the as-is, the could-be, the to-be and best business practices, and the reference model, and based on all of this, they have come up with a solution that would work for the organisation. Unfortunately, though they did everything correctly, they went far over the budget and over time. While this idealistic approach is attractive, it can, at the same time, lead to failure if proper constraints are not put on the amount of analysis that is done.

Davenport (2000) suggests an ES-enabled reengineering process whereby the organisation first asks itself whether the desire to improve the process is there. If it is there the next question is, is the enterprise system a likely option? If "no," then conventional/traditional reengineering needs to be done to improve the processes. But if the answer is "yes," then the organisation needs to adopt an ES-enabled reengineering approach. If this is the case, then the organisation needs to conduct an analysis of the existing processes, and then develop enterprise-system-enabled design principles. And based on that, configure the enterprise system and the process to suit the enterprise system. The ES-enabled reengineering step is made up of decisions that relate to which enterprise system should we go in for, based on aspects such as the industry vertical and the business processes that we are implementing.

As we mentioned earlier, the modelling and analysis of the existing process is important, as it provides a baseline so that we can understand the improvements the new process is going to bring in. It also highlights the problems, issues, constraints and the requirements of the future processes. These also act as a good case for change that can be put to the management, to sell the enterprise system.

In the ES-enabled design, we see to it that the design is driven by strategy. The design needs to take into consideration critical success factors, the key performance indicators that will enable us to monitor the critical success factors, and the business processes that would enable us to improve the KPIs.

In the enterprise system and process configuration step, we decide on the enterprise system modules that we will be implementing, and the sequence in which we would implement them, based on the business processes that are of vital importance to us. We could go for either a single vendor approach or a best-of-reed approach, where we consider all the vendors who supply us with enterprise systems, and take the modules from these vendors which best suit our own operations. The best-of-breed approach is a very expensive approach, but could also lead to the greatest benefits, if implemented properly. Another approach is the portfolio approach where we have a core enterprise system, a backbone from one vendor, and then plug on to this backbone other vendors who are the leaders in particular areas, and we plug in the modules in which they excel. The portfolio approach also enables us to have the best of both worlds, in a sense. We have a core backbone from a single vendor, and then we have the advantages of a best-of-breed approach. Whatever the approach, most vendors of advanced modules of enterprise systems package their products in such a way that they can be bolted onto existing enterprise systems. In this whole mix, we should not forget that sometimes we might continue to go along with legacy systems in case the legacy system proves to be superior to the existing offerings made by vendors. While an enterprise system is a must for most organisations these days above a particular level of operations, not every module in an enterprise system would be the best as far as exactly meeting the requirements of the organisation is concerned. And it is in this situation where if an organisation feels that they will be able to obtain strategic advantage by retaining certain of their legacy systems two options present themselves to us. One is to go along with the legacy system and integrate it to the enterprise system. The second option is to take the code of the legacy system and programme it using the programming language that would be available within the context of the enterprise system. For example, SAP provides the ABAP programming language that allows one to design a simple programme or a whole module within SAP itself. The second option provides

Figure 5.1. Footprint of a modern enterprise system (Adapted from Genovese et al., 2001, p.11)

		Multiple Domain	Single Domain	Specific to Vertical
Domain Unique Modules	Catch Weight			
	Recipe Management			
Primary Bolt-on Modules	Supply Chain Management			
	Customer Relationship Management			
Traditional Modules of Enterprise Systems	Production Planning			
	Materials Management			
Core Modules of Enterprise Systems	Financials, Controls, Procurement, Sales			

a tighter integration, but obviously more effort is spent in coming up with a solution. In the first option, the integration is not as tight, but the effort spent is not as much since integration is a bit easier than creating a whole module *ex nihilo*. Thus, in this step we need to map out the functionality required by the system, some of which will be available from a core base enterprise system, some of which will be available from other vendors, some of which can be available from third party providers as bolt-ons, and some of which will be available as legacy systems. But there is the possibility that there is a certain amount of functionality that may not be available with any system, whether it is the enterprise system or a bolt-on or a legacy system. And it is here that we might need to programme, from scratch, either within the enterprise system environment itself or outside it, the functionality that is not offered by any of these systems. Genovese, Bond, Zrimsek, and Frey (2001) provide a good example of the footprint of a modern enterprise system.

Processes and Information: Common or Unique or Federal?

In this step of planning of the business processes, we need to take a decision on commonality of processes and information. For an organisation which has got many units spread across different geographical locations and different countries, it becomes even more important to decide whether all the units will have common processes, or will each unit have a unique way of doing something. Or will it be a federalist approach where some of the processes are common across the units, but then there are some processes that are unique.

Apart from the commonality of processes, another key decision to be made is the commonality of information. Is the information that will be available in every unit of organisation going to be common? Or would each unit have absolutely unique information? And here again, we can have the via-media federalist approach where we have certain information that is commonly available throughout the whole organisation, and then certain information that is unique in each unit.

Thus, in this step we need to decide very clearly which of our processes and which of the information is going to be common and which is going to be unique. And it is advisable that the project team makes a blanket requirement that processes will be common across units unless a case is made for it to be unique. So if someone wants to follow a very idiosyncratic process that cannot be supported by the enterprise system, they have to make a strong case for that. They have to make a case saying that it is going to provide benefits in terms of differentiating yourself from your competitor, or some kind of a case which shows that the financial benefits or other qualitative benefits far override the costs of the uniqueness of the process. Apart from commonality of process, we also need to differ from the reference model only when we truly believe that our process is better and adds more value than the process as advised by the reference model. Here again, there will be a point at which the cost of changing the process and the cost of changing the system would meet, and at this ideal point, total costs are minimised. Another approach that can work in some organisations is the approach of *common in time*. What this approach suggests is that we will try to make as many of the processes common in the beginning, but then we will leave out those processes where it is difficult for us to make changes and make them common now. But then, over a period of time, introduce changes in the units that are under consideration, and then bring about this commonality over an extended period of time.

Some of the decisions that are made in this phase have implications for the hardware, as well as the software configuration which comes later on. How many instances of the system would we be running, would there be an instance for every unit, would there be an instance for every region? The strategy of commonality that has been adopted has implications on these matters.

Business Process Modelling

Many conceptual tools have been used for business process modelling: ARIS (Architecture of Integrated Information System), KIM (Kolner Integration Model), CIMOSA (Computer Integrated Manufacturing Open Systems Architecture), and PERA (Purdue Enterprise Reference Architecture). These tools provide us with a set of concepts, as well as modelling methods that enables us to capture the complexity of the processes that go on in an organisation. They capture them in such a fashion that it is easier to implement these processes in the context of a particular enterprise system. ARIS, proposed by Professor Scheer, goes even further and provides a software tool set, that not only enables one to model the process, but also to simulate the process. Other software tools that support the business process modelling are Holosofx from IBM, Visio from Microsoft, and Live Model from Intellicorp.

Apart from providing an environment where we could create models as well as simulate these models, many of them also have reference models of various vendors; for example ARIS provides the SAP R/3 reference model. This allows implementers to directly start looking at the reference model of the enterprise system even before the implementation starts. And the modelling tool sets also provide an environment that enables us to modify the business blueprint and integrate processes from multiple sources. Once the models have been created, we can run various simulations with different parameters and different base settings. This will enable us to not only understand the process, but also understand the constraints within which the processes are operating.

Once we are comfortable with the improved process, then we can start the process of carrying out the changes to the enterprise system. And even here, some of the vendors like ARIS have direct linkages with vendor software such as SAP R/3 whereby the models that have been created in ARIS can be forward engineered or moved over into the bare SAP R/3 system.

BPR to Implementation Scenarios

While we are doing this planning of the business processes, it is useful to consider how this is going to link with the implementation. Are you going to do the business process modelling and the reengineering and the changes, isolated from the implementation? That is, do the business reengineering in the beginning, and once everything has been completed, do the implementation of the enterprise system that reflects the business process reengineering exercise. Is it going to be done in isolated modules or phases, or are you going to go in for a parallel approach where business process engineering is conducted side by side with enterprise systems implementation. And if you go for a parallel approach we could have two main ways of doing it. We could spend equal effort and time on BPR as well as software implementation, or we could spend more time on BPR in the beginning, and as time progresses, we reduce the time we spend on BPR and increase the time we spend on enterprise system implementation. This would be the preferred model, but even more preferred is to start the whole exercise keeping in mind the requirements of the enterprise system. Based on that, do the BPR exercise and start working on the enterprise system implementation, but as time progresses, steadily increase the enterprise system implementation effort while simultaneously decreasing the BPR effort. This scaling down of BPR effort and scaling up of enterprise system implementation effort results in a situation where enterprise system implementation can be carried out smoothly and successfully. One of the key reasons for this is you are not making too many changes to the process much later in the project phase. You are finalising most of the key processes early on, and only after those have been done are you really gearing up on the enterprise system implementation. This leads to a much more stable implementation environment. Another approach that some organisations have taken is what is termed as jump-start implementation, where they initially go in for an extremely narrow implementation of the enterprise system consisting of the core modules, and after they have finished that implementation, they go in for an approach where BPR and enterprise systems implementation go hand in hand in a cyclic fashion over the entire life cycle of the enterprise system.

As mentioned earlier, the implementation and consulting costs can be much higher than the costs of the software and the hardware. In some cases, it is three to eight times the cost of the software license. Enterprise systems are massive in their size as well as in their scope, and in their impact on an organisation. And that implies that the changes that will occur in an organisation as a result of implementing such a system are also going to be massive. The change management costs are quite often underestimated. In reality, this is one of the biggest costs of any enterprise system implementation. Some organisations have spent as much as 75% of the total cost on change management. The total cost of an enterprise system implementation project can very easily run into the tens and hundreds of millions of dollars for a medium- to large-sized firm involving thousands of months of labour.

Configuring the System

One of the first steps that is involved in configuration of the system is to build up the information technology infrastructure that is needed for the execution of the enterprise system. This usually entails bringing in heavy-duty servers with huge amounts of memory, and hard disk space with capability for mirroring, and multiple processors and fail-safe modes of operation. Apart from the servers, quite often the graphical requirements of the enterprise system can be so high that even the clients might need to be beefed up in terms of their memory, as well as their graphic processing capabilities. Since all enterprise systems have a client/server architecture, a reasonable amount of the processing is done on the server side, but some of the processing could be done at the client end. The third part of the technology puzzle is the communication networks. These might also need to be upgraded to accommodate the increased traffic necessitated by the enterprise system. Many enterprise systems are not very efficient at their implementation, and they might move the graphics that are involved in the screen presentation up and down the network. But SAP avoids this by having a very fat client that has loaded onto it all the graphics that will be required to create a form or screen. The only thing that passes up and down the network is just the data and not the graphics of the form. The graphics are generated at the client end, leading to efficient use of the network infrastructure.

One of the key decisions that we would have made earlier on would have been with respect to the number of system instances, and this has flow on effects in terms of the IT infrastructure. The higher the number of instances, the higher the technical complexity of the whole IT infrastructure in installation is, and the cost of the installation commensurately goes up. While the hardware costs are higher in the context of a multiple installation system, it might be more attractive from a business point of view since it allows individual businesses in the organisation, or when the business is spread out geographically, to have their own information system environment, while still allowing the exchange of information between the multiple instances.

Quite often, the unique as well as federalist approach towards process and/or information will lead to a higher number of instances, as opposed to a completely common approach to process and information. Along with the number of instances, a closely related decision that needs to be made is the number of systems that will be there in the implementation. Traditional software environments usually have just a two-system landscape, whereby there will be a development system that the developers use to develop the software, and then the production system where the software actually runs. In contrast, SAP advises that the organisation adopts a three-system landscape whereby there are three distinct systems: the production, the development, and the quality assurance systems. This three-system landscape allows for the testing of upgrades in a fashion that is isolated from the production system. Thus, the organisation might develop and modify programmes on the development system, and these are then transferred to the quality assurance system that has two instances, one for quality testing and another for training. And only after the system has been checked on the quality test instance will it then be transported or transferred into the production system. Obviously, the training instance and the quality assurance system is also for training of employees on the system. This prevents employees being trained on the production system and pulling it down or making errors. Thus, the training system would be a complete replica of the production system, enabling the employees to experience the system and use it without the fear of the implications of making errors. While the quality testing system instance in the quality assurance system is used for module testing, integration tests, complete system integration testing, and even within the development system, there could be a testing instance where individual programmes are tested, or individual processes are tested before they are transferred to the quality assurance system. The development system generally contains another instance, like a *sand box*, which allows anyone to play around with the system. This allows people to customise the system without having to worry too much about what will be the impacts. And the third instance that is of relevance in the development system is the customisation instance where the actual settings are made, and then it is tested in the test system and moved to the quality assurance, and once it is tested in the quality assurance, it is moved over to the production.

Once the hardware and software infrastructure has been put in place, configuration can begin. Configuration usually occurs at different levels of abstraction. Organisations usually will do what is termed as high-level scoping, which is then followed by a detailed scoping, and this in turn is followed by a detailed configuration. Usually the detailed configuration is realised by making changes to the configuration tables in the system. There are literally thousands of these configuration settings that need to be made, and the process is quite complex and needs expertise, and is not usually feasible for the IT personnel of the organisation to undertake. Hence, configuring is usually carried out by external consultants, and can take anywhere from a few months to a year. It is the configuration phase that decides the success of the implementation to a large degree. How well has the configuration team translated the business process requirements identified earlier into the pathways of the configured system?

Brehm, Heinzl, and Markus (2001) identify eight different types of mechanisms to configure a system: from simple configuration to very complex package code modification. *Configuration or customisation* entails the setting up of parameters in the tables that enables processes to be executed in particular ways. Apart from the execution of process it is also about the functionality that one is going to use from all that is available. This would usually involve the definition of organisational units, creation of standard reports, and a decision on the logic by which certain things get implemented. This type of configuration involves all layers of the system, that is, the communication layer, the application layer, as well as the database layer.

The second type of configuration that Brehm et al. (2001) identify is *screen masks*, where the predefined screens available in the system are modified to suit the requirements of the organisation. This modification may entail removal of certain attributes, changing certain language, or combining multiple screens into one screen. Usually the defaults in many of these systems would involve anywhere from a single screen to 10 tabbed screens for doing one particular activity. And usually this might be much more than what the organisation needs, and hence, one of the most commonly undertaken activities in screen mask configuration is the integration of multiple screens into fewer screens. This activity usually involves the communication layer.

The third level/type of tailoring in terms of complexity is workflow programming. In this type of tailoring, we do not just accept the workflow that is suggested as a default in the reference model. We may either take the standard as the starting point and then modify it to a lesser or a larger degree, or we look at that workflow and create an absolutely new workflow, since the old workflow does not seem to meet our requirements. Another activity that could be done is integrating multiple workflows: taking elements from multiple workflows and putting them together in a new fashion. Many reference models have what are called *standards* and *variants* in their workflow. If the standard does not meet our requirements, then we can look at the variants. And only when we find that the variants are also not meeting our requirements do we explore mechanisms by which we could either change the standards or the variants to come up with a modified version. When both of these are not satisfactory, then we come up with a totally new workflow. Workflow programming usually impacts on the application layer.

The fourth type of tailoring is to do with reporting. Most of the enterprise systems come packaged with thousands of predefined standard reports. And usually it is more a matter of selecting those reports we need from the predefined ones, rather than creating new reports. Here there are two types of tailoring that are usually done. One is where we change some of the criteria on which the reports are based: maybe the attributes on which the reports are created, maybe the way the reports themselves appear, or the look and feel of the reports. These are usually minor changes. Apart from that, we might find that we require a particular report which is not being catered to by any one of the reports that came with the system, in which case we have to come up with a new report. Since the reporting is closely linked with access to databases, this type of tailoring has impacts on not only the application layer, but also on the database layer.

The fifth type of tailoring is termed, in technical lingo, *user exits*. This is the provision of extra functionality that goes beyond what the current programme does. For example, the current system may calculate EOQ (economic order quantity) in one particular fashion and you might want to calculate it in a slightly different fashion. To accomplish, this we could write an user exit that calculates EOQ in the way we want it to, but the rest of the environment remains the same. Though programming is involved, the level at which we are making changes is not so drastic. This again involves the application layer and the database layer.

The next level of tailoring is what is termed as ERP programming, where additional modules or applications are developed without making any changes to the existing modules or the application code. For instance, SAP has its own language called ABAP, which enables one to write simple programmes, as well as entire applications. Obviously, this has an impact on all layers of the system from the communication layer to the application layer to the database layer.

Interface development is the next type of tailoring in terms of complexity. When we say *interface development*, we are not talking about development of user interfaces, but rather the development of interfaces to other systems. Interfaces to legacy systems, third-party systems, third-party bolt-ons, advanced modules provided by other vendors, or if we are adopting the best of breed approach, then interfacing between the different modules obtained from different vendors. All of this comes under the ambit of interface development. This is a very complex exercise and needs to be undertaken with great care, and it usually affects the application and the database layers of the systems or modules that are involved.

The final type of tailoring is package code modification, where the existing code of the enterprise system is changed at the programme level, or it could be major changes to the whole module. And this again affects all layers of the system.

Within each one of these eight types of tailoring, from configuration to package code modification, there could be different levels of tailoring. One could do minor configuration or moderate configuration or extreme configuration. And the same applies to the package code modification. It could be something very minor or something moderate or it could be extreme tailoring of the code. Usually you do not want to go in for package code modification if possible, but if you are forced to go for it, you do not want to do extreme package code modification, but only minor to moderate. The risks of implementation increase dramatically as we move from simple configuration to major package code modification. The risks of an organisation or an enterprise system failing increase as complexity of configuration increases. When we consider the different levels of tailoring, it is not only the success or failure of the system in the short term that we need to keep in mind, but also how difficult is it going to be in terms of maintaining the system in the medium to long term? If the tailoring type is configuration, then the effort required to maintain the system is very little. But as we go up in complexity, for example in workflow programming, the maintenance effort becomes moderate, and when we go to package code modification, the effort of maintenance could become very heavy. And some organisations have gone bankrupt because they have gone in for such heavy package code modification that they have not been able to execute the system properly nor maintain it. Some vendors actually wash their hands of the system if it has been configured heavily as far as the code is concerned. Vendors are not willing to support upgrades if the organisation has heavily changed the code that came with the system.

Once the system has been configured, the next important step before starting the testing is to prepare the data and load it up into the enterprise system. This would involve obtaining the data from all the legacy systems, cleaning the data up, converting the data into a format that is acceptable to the new system, loading it on to the new system, testing that the data that has been loaded is in the format that is required, and maintaining the data for a period of time before it can become useable by the enterprise system. Since the data usually comes from a variety of systems which have used a variety of formats, there always tends to be problems of mismatches and semantic issues. Integrating the data so that it is useable by the new enterprise system can be quite a difficult and long, drawn-out affair, and should not be taken lightly. Nor can the length of time required to get hygienic data that can be used by the enterprise system be underestimated.

Testing and Validation
of the Enterprise System

The next step, once we have configured the system and loaded the data, is the testing and validating of the system. In this phase, what we essentially do is to verify that the system works as it should from business, technical, practical, effectiveness, and efficiency perspectives. This is where we normally use the super users and the power users that we identified as part of the project to test, and validate that the system operates as it ought to. Though we have put testing and validation almost towards the end of the process, this is not really true. Various steps in testing are actually carried out from an early stage of the whole process. Some of the key phases in testing are planning of the testing, setting up of the test environment, construction of the unit tests, development of the interface programme and their testing, integration test planning and test execution, user acceptance testing, performance testing, data testing, and conference room pilots. It is worthwhile to just mention that the user acceptance testing is not just from the view point of whether the system works as it ought to, it is also from the perspective of how easy is it to use the system from the user interface point of view. Thus, we need to make sure that the system has been designed in such a way that people use the system, find the system useful, and the system is useable.

Conference room pilots are an effective way to test out various business process scenarios. Conference room pilots enable us to verify that the flow of the entire process under consideration is as it should be. In the context of conference room pilots we bring together the power users of the system and the process under consideration, set up the system and the clients in one room, and then we step through the process. We verify that not only is the process executing as it should, but the data flow is also accurate. Thus, we make each one of the users of the process mimic what they would do in the real world in the safe environment of testing. We make the users react to events, enter the data that is required, execute various actions and see if those in turn trigger the appropriate processes down the line. If issues arise, we try to find appropriate solutions, which could entail a small change to a major redesign, and the data flow is checked again. Sometimes we might need to reconfigure the system, in which case we come back to the conference room and go through the exercise of the users putting the data in when appropriate, and checking the execution of their various actions, whether they in turn are resulting in appropriate status changes in the system, resulting in triggering of other related processes. It is an iterative process that is conducted for all the key processes that have been identified.

Long before we test the process as a whole, as in conference room pilots we would have conducted extensive testing of programmes, testing of units equivalent to individual transactions, testing of modules, testing of all the modules integrated together, and testing of all the units that support a business process or a scenario. All these tests are carried out not only in the development system, but the total system integration tests are carried out in the testing system or quality assurance system before it is rolled on to production.

Thus, there are four key types of tests that are done: unit tests of individual transactions, module tests where application modules are tested, scenario testing where whole business process scenarios are tested, and then integration tests where the whole system is integrated together and tested as a whole. Whenever changes occur, either at the programme level or at the unit level, we need to retest the modules, the scenarios, and the total system.

Final Preparation

Once all the testing and data have been validated, the next step is to prepare for going live. In this phase, we attempt to resolve all the issues and problems that have arisen during the testing. We resolve the issues and then do retesting. All the user interfaces (UI), all the interfaces to the various systems are tested. The testing from the UI point of view involves ease of use, usability, and usefulness. Interfaces between systems are checked: we see to it that data is being transferred correctly and that there are no issues of accuracy of the transfer. We verify the semantic accuracy of the transfer and we also verify that all the data that has been brought into the system, either on a one-off basis or in a continuous basis from legacy systems that might still be running, are all in the appropriate format and are all ready to use. Once all these data and interface issues have been resolved, then we go on to training all the users of this system. Here again, we could use business process scenarios to do conference room pilots, but unlike the previous context, here we would be using it to train rather than just test.

Going Live

The final step in project implementation is the going live phase. There are two sub-steps in this: one is switching on the new system, and the second is transitioning from the old system into the new system. This going live is usually done on either holidays or weekends when there will be minimal disruption to the regular running of the business. And it also enables you to check how the system functions as a whole, without disturbing the business and having minimal impact on the customers and other stake holders who would interact with the system.

There are many ways in which you could transition from the old system into the new system. One way is what is termed as a clean cut over, where the old system is stopped and the new system is started. This generally carries with it very high risk. What if the new system crashes? We will end up with not having the old system, or new one. Hence, a parallel approach or a phased approach is used in the transition. We run both the new and the old system in parallel till all the kinks have been ironed out in the new system, and we are reasonably confident that the new enterprise system is working according to our specifications. Once we are happy with the new system, we start phasing out the old system and relying totally on the new system. Phasing over, or the transition over from the old to new, could be business unit by business unit, or it could be module by module, or business process by business process. This enables us to learn from our experiences, and to carry that experience and the learning over into the new modules or new business units where we are implementing.

Some people think once we have implemented an enterprise system that there won't be much work. But usually the implementation of an enterprise system enables the organisation to move into a business process orientation mode, which results in an organisational realisation that business process management is vital for the survival of an organisation. And this will entail revisiting the Rosemann's life cycle, that we saw in an earlier chapter, on a regular basis, either in the small scale or in the large scale, where we constantly monitor the systems and the processes that we have implemented, and see to it that we are equal or better than the benchmarks. We try to improve our business processes and the systems to higher and higher levels of effectiveness and efficiency.

As we have seen, the process of implementing an enterprise system can be quite drawn out. Some of the vendor-recommended implementation processes such as Value SAP have got in them more than 500 discrete steps in the implementation process. Thus. the implementation exercise is very long and difficult. To ease this implementation problem, most vendors and most consultants have come up with solutions for a rapid implementation of an enterprise system. Two approaches have been quite successful. One is to start with a preconfigured system: that is a system that has already been configured for the specific industry in which the organisation lies. This results in a much shorter configuration and roll out for the organisation. Another approach, which is not mutually exclusive to the first approach, is the rapid implementation approach suggested by vendors as well as by implementation partners. For example, SAP's Value SAP (formerly called Accelerated SAP) attempts to cut down on the total duration of the project and prevent projects from going over time and over budget, by using templates, accelerators, and a whole host of techniques. The rapid-implementation approach has become such a norm that almost all implementations now follow one form or the other of the rapid implementation approach. We need to bear in mind that rapid implementation does not imply elimination of certain steps of the implementation, rather it suggests ways and means by which those same steps are done, but they are done in a way such that they are done either quicker, or they are done in parallel, so that the overall project time is reduced. At the same time, some of the detailed steps that are relevant for the large organisation may not be relevant for a medium-sized or small organisation. And it is up to the project team to go through the recommended steps of the vendor, as well as the implementation partner, and come up with a project plan that best fits their needs. While rapid implementation has been reasonably successful and widely adopted, Davenport (2000) rings a warning note. He makes the point that usually in the rush to complete the project, we might not implement the whole system, nor may we make it truly cross functional. And sometimes we might overlook idiosyncratic processes that define a company and define its competitive edge, and put in place a common business process that is the same as the process used by our competitor. This could lead to the loss of our competitive edge. Thus, we find that while rapid enterprise system implementation can save time and money in the short term, it could potentially result in the loss of money and the loss of time in the long term, because we have not redesigned the process nor the system as it should be.

Enterprise Systems Success

Now that we have looked at all the steps and the implementation of the enterprise system, we need to consider what would be termed as a successful enterprise system implementation. Markus and Tannis (2000) correctly identify that success is a dynamic concept, and could be very different, depending on the phase of the implementation. During the project phase, success could be measured in terms of how well we did the project: in terms of the cost of the project, in terms of the time that it took to complete the project, in terms of the functionality that we delivered. In the shakedown phase, success could be defined by the impacts of the system on the key performance indicators, and how quickly we negotiate the difficult phase between go live and normalcy. The quicker we are able to negotiate the phase, the more successful we would term enterprise system implementation to be. In the onward and upward phases, success would be defined by how well the system achieves the business results that we wanted it to achieve. Does the system meet the vision and goal that was charted out in the business case?

Another key dimension that would indicate the successes of the enterprise system is how easy is it to evolve the system as the business, the environment, as well as the organisation changes over a period of time. How easy is it to adopt the new releases of the vendor? How easy is it to plug in new functionality offered by third-party providers of software? How easy is it to move on to a new hardware and software platform, but keep the same enterprise system? How easy is it to change the workflow as the business processes change in the outside world? Does the implementation of the system result in better decision making? Does the system enable the organisation to be on a continuously learning and evolving path? Answers to these questions ultimately enable us to decide whether the system has been a success or a failure.

Thus, success can be defined in terms of technical terms, it can be defined in terms of project, it can be defined in terms of economic or financial returns and impacts, and it can be defined in terms of how smoothly the organisation runs. Apart from this, we also need to know whether the key stakeholders involved in the enterprise system project are happy with the system. Do they consider it as a success? Some of the key stakeholders are the employees who use the system, as well as the external stakeholders, like the customers and the suppliers, who also interact with the system in one way or the other, directly or indirectly.

Enterprise System Implementation Risks

Enterprise system implementation is accompanied by enormous risks to the organisation. There is technical risk; there is financial risk, as well as organisational risk. We can define risk as a problem that has not yet happened, but could cause loss or failure of your project. This definition implies that risk itself will be different in different phases of the enterprise system life cycle that we have seen. Risks during the project phase are different to the risks during the shakedown phase and the risks during the onward and upward phase. Risks are very closely associated with success.

Scott and Vessey (2002) have come up with a model (Figure 5.2) that attempts to explain to some extant the various risks that are involved in enterprise system implementation. They divided up the risk into three major categories, the most important being risks associated with the external business context, the next important being the information systems context, and the third where the risk is associated with the enterprise system project.

The risks at the strategic level or the outermost level are much more important, and have a greater impact on the success or failure of the project/implementation than the risks in the inner circle related with the enterprise system project and the information system context. But that does not mean that lower-level issues are less important. Actually, the risks at the higher level are managed through responses at the lower, tactical levels. But if the strategic level is not done well then the tactical level is done even less well. But if the strategic level is done well, then even if we do not do the tactical level well, we would still be able to gain benefit. It is more a question of effectiveness and efficiency. The strategic level decisions are the issues that help us in being effective while the tactical level issues help us in being efficient in carrying out the strategic level directions.

In terms of the external business context, they identify key risks as being the competitive environment and its stability, the collaborative environment and its stability, and the co-operative environment and its stability. In the organisational context, they identify organisational culture, firm's strategy, organisational structure, business processes, knowledge, skills and the IT infrastructure. A poor understanding of the corporate culture, or a poor strategic vision or organisational structure, or badly reengineered processes, or lack of knowledge and skills leading to ineffective change management, or poor infrastructural planning could all lead to failure of the enterprise system project. In the context

Figure 5.2. Enterprise System Implementation Risks (Adapted from Scott & Vessey, 2002, p.75)

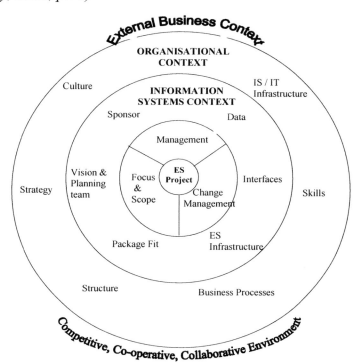

of the informational systems, they identify having a good champion or sponsor, having a steering committee, seeing to it that the package fits well with the organisation and its business needs, training the people so that they have knowledge in terms of processes, technology, and implementation, technology infrastructure for the enterprise system, interfaces to legacy systems and to third party products and between multiple ES where applicable, and data conversion as playing a crucial role in seeing to it that the project is a success.

Within the project context itself, Scott and Vessey (2000) perceived project management issues, project focus and scope, and organisational management, as key factors in the success or failure of the whole mission. With respect to project management, they identify bad leadership, ineffective resource management, lack of empowerment of key decision makers in the project, inappropriate composition of the project team, not using consultants in the very first project or enterprise system implementation, and ineffective customisation of the enterprise system, as key factors that have an impact on the success of the project. In terms of the project focus and scope, they identify the lack of alignment between the business and the package, or over-scoping of the project or scope not being defined well, or the time of the project being either too short or too long — all have a significant impact on the success. In terms of organisational change management, they identify insufficient commitment by the top management to the project, ineffective communication between the members of the project as well as between the project team and the organisation as a whole, and inadequate training of the people involved in the project as leading to failure.

Conclusion

Enterprise systems have been on the horizon for around 30 years now, and all large organisations and most of the medium-sized organisations possess enterprise systems. But that does not mean that the new market is only the small- to medium-sized firms that are starting to implement enterprise systems. Many of the larger and medium-sized firms that already have enterprise systems either are in the process of implementing new modules, or are adding bolt-ons or are implementing a best of breed approach, so that knowing about the implementation process, and being effective and efficient in the implementation process can be a very useful thing. As mentioned earlier, most organisations have a business process management orientation these days, and are moving into continuous improvement as a philosophy. Another key reason for understanding enterprise system implementations and the issues associated with it is the fact that most organisations are moving into what is termed as the ERP tool era, where more advanced modules are being plugged in into the existing enterprise systems, or enterprise systems themselves are changing drastically in terms of their functionality and features. Thus, the new implementations are almost as difficult and complex as the initial implementation of the enterprise system. Therefore, many of the lessons that we have learned in the past 30 years in enterprise system implementation are valid for the future. Some of the key lessons that have been learned are that most of the projects do not fail because of technological reasons, but fail due to the management issues that surround the implementation, as mentioned by Scott and Vessey. If the environment or the strategy changes, we need to respond to those changes at the tactical/ project levels. We need to ensure that we have a clear vision and a strategy. And this will overshadow the entire implementation and its effectiveness. We need to recognise that organisational culture and change management is of vital importance, and we need to encourage an open culture where there is free communication between the key stakeholders and the project team. We also need to be aware of the fact that technology is not everything. Quite often people involved in these projects get so razzle-dazzled by the technology that they forget that getting the business processes right is more important than getting the technology down precisely. A phased approach to implementation is advised. Phasing can be module by module, unit by unit, geographical location by location, or by using a strategy that mixes and matches the best, using the knowledge gained in the early phases, or implementations in the latter phases and implementation. The team that you form is very important, and it needs to possess a good strong sponsor, a good leader, a good vision and planning team, and a good implementation team that is made up of core users who are super users and power users, whose absence in the organisation will be felt. Data conversion and building interfaces to legacy and third-party systems can be quite time consuming and need to be factored into the project. Managing risks proactively is a must: we need to develop contingency plans to address risks that arise in the middle of a project. We need to be flexible and react to unforeseen circumstances. It is better to know the go live date or reduce the project scope than to do a half-complete job. It is better to put more people on the team, when appropriate, than try to go with a very lean team. But at the same time, we need to keep in mind economies of scale do not work well in these kinds of projects. If you add new team members right at the end. it is not really going to increase the functionality nor decrease the time of implementation. In reality, it might actually take longer to implement because we have to bring the new members up to speed on the project.

Finally, we need to remember that enterprise system implementation is not a bed of roses. Lozinsky (1998) identifies the typical phases that people experience in the course of working on one of these projects. The people in the projects start with great enthusiasm that soon turns to concern, and then might turn into panic. Then there is the search for the guilty, and then hopefully, they might start seeing the light at the end of the tunnel and experience the results of the success of the project. And finally end up by praising those who did not participate in the project.

Chapter VI

Enterprise Systems :
The SAP Suite

Systems in an Organisation

To support processes well, we need to have information systems and integrated information system support processes even better. There are a variety of systems that go towards supporting processes in an organisation (Scheer, 1998). Figure 6.1 illustrates some of these systems.

At the lowest level, we have quantity-oriented operating systems in areas such as production, engineering, purchasing, sales, marketing and personnel management. At the second level, we have value-oriented accounting systems to support inventory accounting, fixed assets accounting, accounts payable, accounts receivable and personnel accounting. At the third level of abstraction, we have reporting and controlling systems such as investment controlling, purchasing controlling, personnel controlling, production controlling, sales and marketing controlling. At the fourth level, we have the analysis and information

Figure 6.1. Systems in an organisation (Adapted from Scheer, 1998, p.5)

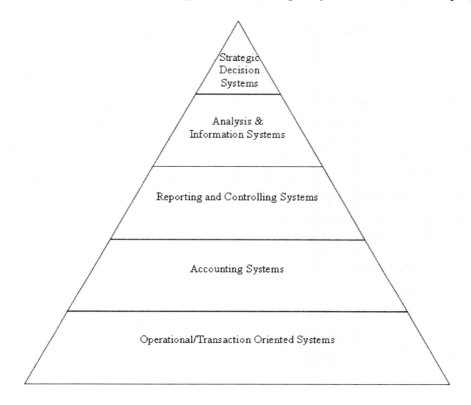

systems such as the production, investment, purchasing, personnel, and sales and marketing information systems. And at the very top of the pyramid, we have strategic long-term planning and decision support systems.

Integrated Information Systems

In the past in most organisations, these horizontal as well as vertical systems have been isolated in the design and deployment, leading to islands of information. Such islands of information pose many problems, and to overcome these problems, organisations started designing MRP systems in the 1960s that had the master production schedule, the materials requirement planning, the capacity requirement planning, and the ability to execute capacity plans and material plans all integrated together. In the 1970s MRP was expanded to MRP II, which in addition to the base MRP modules, included sales and operations planning, forecasting, and simulation. And in the 1990s, MRP II was expanded to include a whole host of functionality from controlling, materials management, sales and distribution, financial accounting, investment, quality, personnel, and plant maintenance management. In the more recent past, ERP itself has expanded, and it now includes advanced modules, called by the Gartner Group (Genovese et al., 2001) as ERP II. ERP II packages include, in addition to the core packages, E-procurement, integrated plant systems, supply chain planning, collaborative product commerce, customer relationship management, and supply chain execution. Thus, from transaction- and accounting-oriented roots, ERP systems have come a long way, and now they are viewed as a strategic business solution that integrates all functions, horizontally as well as vertically, in terms of Scheer's pyramid.

SAP

SAP stands for *Systems Applications and Products in data processing.* SAP is one of the leading vendors of such integrated information systems. It provides integrated information from accounting to manufacturing, and from sales to service. Whenever data is entered in one functional area for one particular transaction, this data is automatically reflected in all the related functional areas. The SAP system supports and integrates thousands of business processes. The core system uses a single database. Some of the key characteristics of SAP are discussed in the following sections.

First and foremost, SAP is a packaged software solution. That is, it comes ready to run and it is up to the organisation to customise it to suit their particular requirements. Secondly, SAP is modular, that is, it has got many modules, and it is up to the organisation to select the modules that they need to have. Some modules are dependant on other modules already being there. Hence, there is to some extent a prerequisite arrangement between the modules. To a large extent, the processes that are supported by SAP cover most of the transactions that go on in an organisation. SAP follows a client-server architecture (Figure 6.2) and supports traditional as well as Web-based modes.

The data that is obtained from SAP is real time, at least from the core system. The core system offers real time access to all the information. The data

Figure 6.2. SAP R/3 client-server architectures

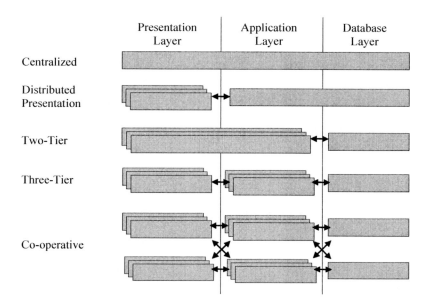

warehouses that sit on top of the core system might provide batched data. SAP is enterprise-wide, and can be deployed across geographical boundaries. SAP attempts to encapsulate the best business practices. We also need to keep in mind that big systems have high inertia, and generally, it takes a while before core functionalities change in a drastic fashion.

SAP can be deployed in most of the major languages that are used throughout the world in business, and one implementation itself can use multiple languages. Each time a user logs in, the user could use the system using a different language. SAP supports multiple currencies, not just in terms of the fact that you can change the currency that is being used by the system, but also it can support multiple currencies at the same time. There is a default currency that is used, but in addition to this default currency, you could use other currencies as well. SAP is a very secure system with different levels of security offering hundreds of roles with a variety of combinations. The SAP system has strengths in certain industries, but it has offerings or reference models that have been specialised to most of the major industries in the world. As mentioned before, it is a packaged software, but more importantly, SAP offers a huge level of customisability. From a very simple configuration we can go on to a very complex package code modification. This aspect was discussed earlier in Chapter V.

The integrated nature of SAP allows the business processes to be much simpler than in an unintegrated system where there are many islands of information. SAP provides a standard definition for the data, and has a common business language that enables communication within SAP, as well as interface in a consistent manner with third-party providers of bolt-on modules. These advantages enable an organisation to focus on their core activity rather than wasting time in integration activities.

Modules of SAP

Some of the major modules of the core SAP system are logistics, accounting, and human resources. But apart from these, SAP also has got a number of information systems to support higher-level analysis and decision making. The logistics module, in turn, is made up of materials management, sales and distribution, logistics execution, production, plant maintenance, customer service, quality management, logistics controlling, project system, environment, health and safety, and a host of central functions. The accounting module, in turn, has got sub-modules such as financial accounting, treasury, controlling, enterprise controlling, investment management, project system, real estate management. The human resource module has personnel management, time management, payroll, training, event management, organisation management, and travel management. The information systems are made up of executive information systems, logistics information systems, accounting information systems, human resource information systems, ad hoc reports, and a host of other functionality.

SAP as Process-Ware

SAP can be thought of as process-ware. It provides a structure for work that goes hand in hand with process-oriented thinking. A fundamental aspect of SAP is that it is process oriented. Though the modules that we have mentioned earlier seem to be independent under the hood, they are all integrated together.

Let us consider, for example, the purchase order process. To raise the purchase order, we need to have support of the materials management, the financial, the control, and the production planning sub-modules. Once the purchase order has been raised and we receive the goods, at the time of goods receipt, we need to have the support of the materials management, financial, control and quality management sub-modules. Once the goods have been received and we are starting the manufacturing process we need to have the support of the materials management, financial and control, and production planning sub-modules. And once we have manufactured the product and want to deliver the product, then we need to have the support of the materials management, sales and distribution, finance, and control sub-modules. Thus we can see, to support any process, we need to have multiple modules integrated in a seamless fashion. Another aspect that would have become evident as we looked at this process earlier is the fact that almost every step needs to have the support of finance and control. And as we saw in the implementation chapter, usually it is the finance and control modules that are implemented right at the beginning, for the very good reason that without them, none of the other modules can work.

One of the key components of the enterprise system, apart from the integrated database is the work flow management system that orchestrates the flow of activity and information that goes on in an organisation. As can be seen in the earlier discussion, SAP provides support for most of the functions of an organisation and most of the processes of an organisation. And the modules of SAP correspond to how organisations specialise their work, and how organisations divide their processes. Since the work flow management system is an integral part of the enterprise system, it also allows the performance of the various processes to be measured and monitored in terms of time as well as in terms of cost. While adopting SAP would predispose a company to a business process orientation, it does not mean that this process orientation is achieved automatically. To support such a process-oriented system, we also need to have process-oriented management and leadership, process-oriented compensation, process-oriented organisational structures, process measurement, process improvement, and cross functional communication.

Evolution of SAP

SAP has evolved in many ways over the years: from being a system that supported enterprise resource planning, it now supports collaborative supply chain and collaborative distribution. It has systems that support the supply chain management, and systems that support customer relationship management. From an enterprise resource planning orientation SAP moved to an inter-enterprise co-operation mode some years ago, and now it is oriented towards e-community collaboration.

Thus, from an orientation of integration, SAP has moved to an orientation of collaboration. This does not mean that integration does not exist any more. Integration exists, but in addition to that there is co-operation and collaboration. The three common themes in the SAP philosophy are integrate, empower, and collaborate. The SAP product suite integrates a number of applications, modules, and services. The SAP product suite, as a whole, tends to empower all the stakeholders of an organisation, from its customers to its partners to its employees. Thirdly, it provides very good support for collaboration, anywhere, anytime.

Figure 6.3. SAP R/3 modules and their support for the operational, tactical, and strategic levels of organisations

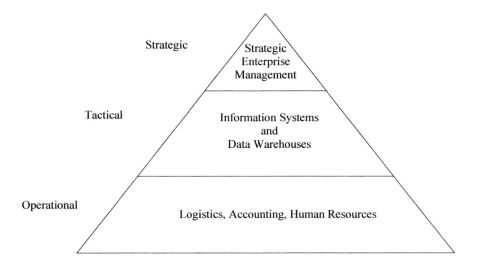

Figure 6.4. Enterprise Management, SCM, and CRM

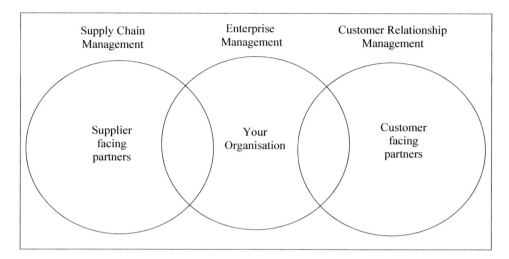

The various products of SAP support the various levels in an organisation (Figure 6.3). SAP has excellent support for the operational level with its logistics, accounting, HR, e-commerce, and work flow systems. SAP has support for the tactical level with the various information systems and the Business Warehouse (BW). SAP also supports the strategic level of management through products such as Strategic Enterprise Management (SEM) and the Knowledge Warehouse (KW).

In terms of optimisation, SAP has moved a long way away from stand-alone systems to integrated systems, then to ERP, then to SCM, and now CRM (Figure 6.4).

In terms of collaboration, it has moved from the phone, fax, EDI era into collaborative business scenarios and complete marketplace communities. In terms of personalisation, SAP has moved from employee self-service to sophisticated information delivery, knowledge-based support, and role-based personalised graphical user interfaces. Thus, the current suite of SAP products attempts to provide an optimised, personalised, and collaborative environment.

In a nutshell, in the initial stages SAP, focused on transaction and resource support, and provided modules such as the materials management, sales and distribution, production planning, and financials. This focus shifted to relationship over a period of time, where they started providing business to business support, supply chain management support, customer relationship management, and online businesses. And over a period of time, the focus shifted from transaction to analytical applications, and SAP started providing sophisticated functionality within the context of supply chain management, customer relationship management, and data warehouse tools like the Business Warehouse. From the analytical, the focus then shifted to knowledge, where very sophisticated strategic enterprise management systems are being provided, along with the SEM suite and the knowledge warehouse suite.

While the focus has shifted from resource to relationship, and transactional to analytical to knowledge (Figure 6.5), the shift has always been an inclusive shift. That is, it is not throwing away the old, but keeping the old and building on the old. We cannot have a strategic enterprise management system without having the core resource and transaction-oriented SAP R/3 system. We cannot have the relationship oriented SCM and CRM without having the core resource and transaction-oriented SAP R/3 system. Thus, we need all these systems working together. Each of the systems supports certain aspects of the organisation, certain levels in the organisation. In the following sections, we will look at a couple of representative applications.

Figure 6.5. The inclusive evolution of SAP

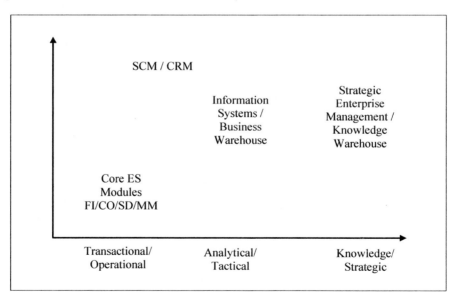

SAP R/3

The core modules of the SAP R/3 system are the financial accounting (FI) and controlling (CO). And depending on the industry, it could be production planning (PP), materials management (MM), sales and distribution (SD), or something that is specialised to that particular industry in which SAP is being implemented. The FI module focuses on the management and reporting of the general ledger, accounts receivable, accounts payable, and specialised ledgers. The controlling module represents the movement of costs and revenue within an organisation, and is used by management as a tool in organisational decision making. And it also supports cost-centred accounting, product costing analysis, and profit-centre accounting. If it is a manufacturing organisation that we are looking at, then we would find the presence of modules such as production planning, materials management, and sales and distribution. The production planning module is used to plan and control all the manufacturing activities that go on within an organisation, and it supports the Bill of Materials (BOM), routings of orders, work centres, master production scheduling, materials requirement planning, production planning and execution, production orders, product costing, and a host of other functionalities. The materials management application module supports functions that are related to the procurement of material and the management of inventory of raw material, work in progress material, as well as finished goods. Specifically, the MM module supports activities such as materials procurement, reorder processing, inventory management, materials valuation, invoice verification, and many other materials management related operations. The Sales and Distribution module supports all the tasks and activities involved in the sales of a product, the delivery of a product, and the billing of the customer. Thus, it has support for quotation processing, sales order processing, delivery processing, billing, and reporting. While there are many other modules in the core SAP R/3 system, it is beyond the scope of this discussion to look at those. Suffice it to say that SAP modules are extensive and provide support for most of the processes and activities that go on in an organisation.

SAP Support
for Making, Buying, and Selling

While we have discussed the SAP modules and their sub-modules and their functionality, it is also interesting to look at the processes that the SAP R/3 modules support. For example, the core SAP R/3 modules support making, buying, selling, and accounting.

The *making* supports the manufacturing, planning, and execution processes. This involves supporting the recognition of demand, the forecasting of demand, the consolidation of the requirements, procurement of the raw materials, planning for production, calculating whether the capacity is sufficient to meet the demand, supporting the execution processes, the order settlement processes and the costing processes. Thus, the modules of SAP support, from the beginning, the demand management to the order settlement phases of the business process. Key modules involved in this process are the master production scheduling, master requirements planning, planned order processing, production order, goods issued and the production order received.

Buying is a process of procurement, and it involves requisitioning a particular product, sourcing of the vendor, purchasing the product from the vendor, receiving the product, quality management, paying for the product and/or service. The key modules in SAP that support these processes are purchasing requisition, purchase order processing, goods receipt, invoice receipt and verification, and payment.

Selling is the process of managing the customers and their orders. It encompasses the processes of taking the order from the customer, checking the availability of the materials, delivering of the material, invoicing the customer, and receiving payment in return for goods delivered. The key modules of SAP that support customer order management are sales order processing, delivery, billing, customer payment, and customer support.

Each of these processes: buying, selling, and making are all supported by the associated information systems. For example, the sales information system supports the customer order management; production planning and procurement are supported by a whole suite of planning, reporting, and analysis tools.

mySAP.com

The key component of SAP is the mySAP.com workplace and marketplace. SAP has evolved in terms of functionality from a very transaction-oriented system like the SAP R/3 to the current mySAP.com system, which is reasonably user-friendly, and supports collaboration. While moving to mySAP.com, SAP was involved in improving the visual design of all the SAP applications. It attempted to improve the interaction with the user. And it provided role based and personalised support for users. The key objective of SAP strategy through the mySAP.com suite of products is to provide personalised and collaborative solutions on demand. There are four mechanisms that SAP uses to deliver this. They provide a mySAP.com workplace primarily for their employees and their partners that is a role-based personalised enterprise portal. SAP also provides mySAP.com marketplace, which is a portal situated at http://www.mySAP.com. Its primary purpose is to enable collaboration across multiple enterprises using the Internet. The third mechanism is the mySAP.com application hosting, whereby the organisation need not have to host the SAP applications in their organisation, but can use the hosting facilities of application hosting centres. To support these three mechanisms — the workplace, the marketplace and application hosting — mySAP.com also has a huge number of business scenarios that support this type of e-community collaboration. SAP, after extensive user analysis and surveys, came up with a solution that provides easy to understand screens, is more friendly to the user, provides extensive mechanisms for searching and retrieving information, and provides personalised applications, that is only those applications that are required by the user, as well as those applications that are appropriate for the roles played by the user. Through its sophisticated security mechanism, it provides a single sign on for all the applications that the user might have to interact with as part of using the system — both SAP and non-SAP systems.

The mySAP.com workplace provides information and services within as well as without the company context. This is provided in a seamless fashion so that the users are unaware of moving outside the boundaries of the organisation. mySAP.com provides support for the variety of roles that people play in an organisation through extensive business scenarios which are implemented by a whole host of components. When a user logs onto mySAP.com workplace, the system provides a launch pad that is personalised and role based, on the left. And using this launch pad, the user can launch many different applications that depend on his or her role. Applications that are within the SAP environment, as well as those that are outside the SAP environment are made available on the launch pad. Once the user selects a particular activity on the launch pad, an appropriate application appears on the right of the screen. Using the launch pad, the user can launch applications such as transactions and reports. The system also uses a push mechanism to push, proactively, alerts and key performance indicators that are relevant to the job of the user.

Intelligence Density

A key concept that helps us to understand the important role that enterprise systems play is *intelligence density*. Dhar and Stein (1997) define *intelligence density* (ID) as the amount of useful "decision support information" that a decision maker gets from using a system for a certain amount of time. Alternately, ID can be defined as the amount of time taken to get the essence of the underlying data from the output. This is done using the "utility" concept, initially developed in decision theory and game theory (Lapin and Whisler, 2002). Numerical utility values, referred to as *utilities* (sometimes called *utiles*) express the true worth of information. These values are obtained by constructing a special utility function. Thus intelligence density can be defined more formally as follows:

$$\text{Intelligence density} = \frac{\text{Utilities of decision making power gleaned (quality)}}{\text{Units of analytic time spent by the decision maker}}$$

Increasing the intelligence density of its data enables an organisation to be more effective, productive, and flexible. Key processes that allow one to increase the ID of data are illustrated in Figure 6.6. Mechanisms that will allow us to access different types of data need to be in place first. Once we have access to the data, we need to have the ability to scrub or cleanse the data of errors. After scrubbing the data, we need to have tools and technologies that will allow us to integrate data in a flexible manner. This integration should support not only data of different formats, but also data that are not of the same type.

Enterprise systems/enterprise resource planning systems, with their integrated databases, have provided a clean and integrated view of a large amount of information within the organisation, thus supporting the lower levels of the intelligence density pyramid (Figure 6.7).

Figure 6.6. Steps for increasing intelligence density (Dhar & Stein, 1997, p.11)

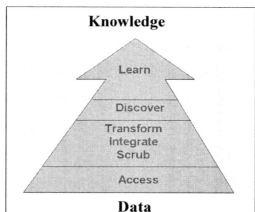

Figure 6.7. ERP and DSS support for increasing intelligence density (Adapted from Shafiei & Sundaram, 2004, p.3)

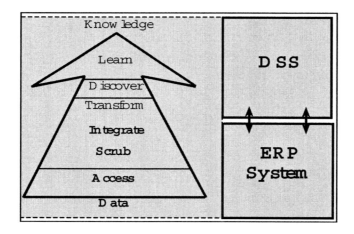

But even in the biggest and best organisations with massive investments in ERP systems, we still find the need for data warehouses and OLAP, even though they predominantly support the lower levels of the intelligence density pyramid. Once we have an integrated view of the data, we can use data mining and other decision support tools to transform the data and discover patterns and nuggets of information from the data.

The Enterprise System Landscape

Shafiei and Sundaram (2004) present a depiction of a Multi-Enterprise Collaborative Framework (Figure 6.8) with respect to the vendors that offer solutions and components to support all levels of intelligence density and collaboration/relationship.

The depiction is a snapshot of the most widely recognised vendors and solutions in the marketplace today. As can be seen, well-known vendors in the marketplace offer a range of solutions that assist firms in their quest to achieve multi-enterprise collaboration using the three components of the framework. Within the Enterprise Management component, vendors offer a range of solutions that assist firms at the operational, management, and strategic levels, such as SAP's R/3 ERP system, JD Edwards' One World ERP system, iBaan Business Intelligence, Siebel Analytics 7.5, PeopleSoft's Enterprise Performance Management (EPM) and SAP's SEM. Similarly, these vendors also offer customer relationship management and supply chain management solutions that allow firms to reach out and conduct a complex range of transactions with their partners along their value chain.

Figure 6.8. Depiction of Multi-Enterprise Collaborative Conceptual ERP-DSS Framework (Shafiei & Sundaram, 2004, p.7)

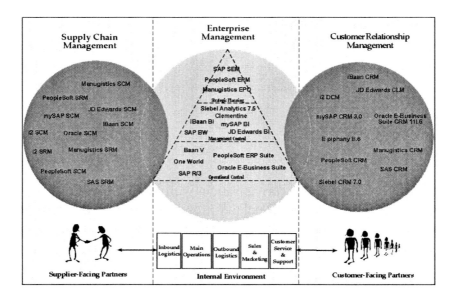

Backward, Forward, Inward, and Upward

Thus, we find that one of the key purposes of enterprises systems is to provide range and reach within the organisation. Enterprise systems enable us to look inward and integrate our internal systems and processes. Integrating the enterprise system backwards leads to extension of the supply chain. Key systems that support this effort are supply chain management, e-procurement, and marketplace systems. Integrating the enterprise system forward towards the customers helps us in meeting their demands and managing them. Key systems that support this effort are customer relationship management and call centre/contact centre systems. Integrating upward leads us toward integrating all the systems that help us in increasing our intelligence density. Key systems that support this effort are executive information systems, decision support systems, data warehousing and data mining, and strategic enterprise management systems.

Costs of Enterprise Systems

The cost of implementation and consulting is much higher than the cost of the hardware and the software licenses. Often, these implementation costs are three to eight times higher than the cost of the software licence. Big systems imply big changes, and one of the biggest costs in putting in an enterprise system is the cost of the changes that have to be done in the organisation. This is generally termed as change management costs. In many organisations, the cost of change management is between 50% to 70% of the total cost of the project. Other costs that need to be kept in mind are costs related with data conversion, training, testing, integration, disruption to the usual processes, reduction in customer satisfaction, and costs of other software that might be required such as process modelling software or testing software.

Problems with Enterprise Systems

Serious problems occur when the philosophy of the enterprise system does not match the management philosophy of the organisation or the culture of the country in which it is being implemented. And these problems get exacerbated when there is a disconnect between the strategic objectives and business practices of the organisation and the enterprise system. Thus, these systems could impose their own philosophy, processes, and procedures, and make organisations to conform, unless they are configured properly.

Even if they were configured properly, such systems used to be quite inflexible, disallowing an organisation to change the enterprise system as their strategy, processes, and procedures changed. This was one of the reasons why the implementation of an enterprise system was likened to *pouring liquid concrete*. That is, enterprise systems are extremely flexible and could be configured to suit many different industry sectors and organisations. But once configured, they used to be quite inflexible. This problem is being overcome through a technical as well as a procedural response. SAP, for example has addressed this problem technically through features such as Application Linking and Enabling (ALE), Business Objects, Business objects Application Programming Interface (BAPI), and NetWeaver. One of the key purposes of these technologies is to allow disparate modules and/or applications to be coupled together as seamlessly and flexibly as possible. SAP has also addressed the problem of inflexibility through procedural responses such as ValueSAP, Accelerated SAP (ASAP), and Solution Manager, in an effort to reduce implementation time and cost. Another key benefit of such procedures is their holistic and life cycle approach, which tries to make the enterprise system into a learning and living environment that can adapt to changes quickly. Key steps in the ValueSAP approach are evaluation, implementation, and continuous improvement of the enterprise system. Another way of looking at it is to identify the problem, define the solution, implement the solution, manage the system, and improve the solution. All these processes have a cyclic perspective, and should hopefully lead the organisation in benign cycles of improvement.

One of the key problems with enterprise systems was the huge commitment to a single vendor. Many organisations had, and still to some extent have, what is popularly known as "vendor lock-in." That is, once you buy the base system from a particular vendor, due to technical, cost, and implementation reasons, it was preferable for most organisations to continue to buy further modules and advanced modules from the same vendor. Many of the recent advances and initiatives in the past few years have attempted to overcome this problem. Notable among these are efforts at standardisation (XML, SOAP, BPEL) that enable diverse systems to talk to each other, and breaking down of monolithic applications into self-contained modules and web services. This has led to the ideas such as the digital nervous system with a backbone onto which multiple modules or applications could be plugged in with ease. SAP's NetWeaver is an initiative that attempts to provide a flexible interorganisational business process composition and orchestration platform that leverages Web services. Once upon a time, it was only the very large firms that had the luxury of selecting the very best modules from the various vendors and implementing a "best-of-breed" (BOB) solution. This was due to the high cost and resource requirements of a BOB approach. But such technologies make the BOB concept a reality for even medium- to large-sized organisations.

One of the major problems that had beset the implementation of most enterprise systems was the very long implementation periods. On an average, most implementations used to take 3 to 5 years, and assembling BOB solutions used to take longer. In this context as well, the vendors had a technical as well as a procedural response. The technical response included systems that were preconfigured to suit the requirement of a particular industry sector. The procedural response included rapid implementation approaches such as Accelerated SAP (ASAP). While the configuration of the enterprise system can be difficult, it was actually changing the business processes and procedures, and people's mind and level of expertise that took the most time in the context of implementation. Apart from these initiatives, some of the key dimensions to reduce the time of implementation, as well as make the implementation a success are management, personnel, software, and project. Key aspects of the management dimension include support from management (especially the CEO/COO and process owners), a strong commitment to change, good communication among the project team as well as throughout the organisation, and empowered decision makers who can take decisions regarding processes and change management. The personnel in the project team need to include a balance of technical and business people from within and without the organisation. The team should have people who will be sorely missed in their regular jobs, that is, the best people in the organisation need to be full time on the project for the project to be a success. Apart from that, the project needs to a champion like the CEO for it to succeed. While the authors themselves prefer a balanced approach in implementation where process and software are given equal importance, many vendors and consultants advise a "Vanilla ERP" implementation. That is, an implementation where the process follows the software; the process is changed to suit the software and the software is left intact with very little configuration. The project dimension involves many aspects, but the key ones relate to phased implementation of smaller chunks of functionality and scope.

Benefits of Enterprise Systems

While the costs of putting in enterprise systems are high and the problems of implementing them are many, the benefits that one can potentially accrue from them are even higher. Some of the key benefits of enterprise systems are, as can be expected, related to information. The idea of single data entry, which results in low data entry error and reduced problems, with respect to communication, gives rise to huge benefits. Availability of system, that is, the uptime of the system is another key benefit. Usually enterprise systems have been architected with a client-server architecture, and optimised for access by people spread out geographically, and usually the access times are much better than in traditional systems. Reliability of enterprise systems, again, is another important aspect which cannot be understated. Since they usually span geographical boundaries and different time zones, it is expected that they are available 24-7, and most enterprise systems do provide that level of reliability. Another aspect is related to language. The ability of enterprise systems to be used by people spread across the world, who speak very different languages and yet are able to use and access the same information in the language that they are comfortable with, truly makes them global. One of the key benefits that enterprise systems bring about is the elimination of fiefdoms and islands of information that exist in almost every organisation. While enterprise systems eliminate fiefdoms, there is also the danger that this centralised, integrated repository of information can be misused if it falls into the wrong hands. Quite often, enterprise systems implementation goes hand in hand with business process reengineering. Most of the benefits that are obtained as a result of putting in an enterprise system are not from technology, but the fact that you have to change your business to fall in line with best business practices. The software enables this change to occur. Another major reason for putting in enterprise systems is the reduction in lead time/cycle time. This is a follow-on benefit from the business process reengineering exercise that one might have conducted. But apart from that, the digitisation of the organisation also results in huge reductions in lead times. For example, Autodesk cut down their shipping time from 2 weeks to 24 hours. Apart from lead time and cycle time reduction, transactions themselves take far less time to process. For example, IBM used to take 5 days to enter pricing information, but after the implementation of enterprise system it just takes them 5 minutes. Some of the core modules that are part of any enterprise system are the financial and control modules, and these modules are some of the first modules to be implemented in an enterprise system. These bring along with them much better financial management leading to savings in all kinds of arenas. Many organisations that put in enterprise systems already have systems that they are perfectly happy with for their transaction processing. But in spite of that, they go in for an enterprise system because they want to use the enterprise system as a foundation, and as an enabler for implementing more advanced systems such as customer relationship management, supply chain management, business intelligence systems, and e-commerce systems. Another benefit that is derived from putting in enterprise systems relates to knowledge management as implemented in the processes and the procedures that are inherent in the enterprise system. Before enterprise systems are put in, much of the organisational knowledge about processes and procedures is tacit and known only to those who have been doing the job for a while. And some hoard this knowledge carefully and do not share it. But once an enterprise system is put in place, the knowledge about processes and procedures becomes embedded into the system and is available to the appropriate knowledge worker. The details of the processes, the decision rules that need to be used and information structures all become transparent. Last but not least, enterprise systems bring in not only standardisation, but also flexibility. The days when people compared the implementation of an enterprise system to *pouring liquid concrete* are long past. Most vendors are aiming toward flexible architectures that enable an organisation to flexibly and dynamically change business processes as their strategy and their external and internal environment change.

Chapter VII

Case of ERP Implementation for Production Planning at EA Cakes Ltd.

This case details the implementation of Systems Applications & Products' (SAP) Production Planning module at EA Cakes Ltd. The market forced the company to change its sales and production strategy from "make-to-order" (MTO) to "make-to-stock" (MTS). The decision to change the strategy involved not only the company's decision to invest much more money in accumulation and keeping stocks of finished goods, it required a complete redesign of its production planning system, which was an integral part of an ERP system that used SAP software.

A team from IT specialists and production planning personnel was formed for designing computer support for the new production planning system business processes. There was no consensus in the design group. IT specialists were sure that existing SAP software could provide adequate computer support. The production planning staff had doubts that SAP modules were relevant to their business processes. They argued that poor fit between the business processes implicit in the software and the business processes of EA Cakes Ltd. would result in failure.

To resolve the problem, the management invited in a consulting company. The consultants suggested designing quickly a rough prototype system. Analysing this system would help the working group to reach a consensus. Apart from giving adequate computer support to the new production planning system, the SAP implementation had to solve several implementation problems identified by consultants. The question is, can a standard software system like SAP give adequate computer support to an individually designed business management system?

Organisation Background

EA Cakes Ltd., New Zealand, is a successful food manufacturing company with a major share of the market in New Zealand and the Asia-Pacific region. It produces over 400 different kinds of fresh and frozen food products.

From a shelf life point of view, the company manufactures three types of products:

1.   Shelf-stable and frozen food with practically infinite shelf life (up to 1 year),
2.   Chilled products with a medium shelf life (from 3 to 6 months), and
3.   Short shelf life products (from 1 week to 6 weeks).

The demand for many products is uneven. Christmas cakes and puddings, for example, are mainly sold during November and December. Generally, the demand for cakes is lower during summer than during winter. Sales are also volatile because they are conducted through numerous channels, including major supermarket chains, route outlets (such as groceries stores), and food service for hospitals, hotels and restaurants. Sales to Australia, the major export market, add uncertainty to demand.

For years EA Cakes Ltd. built a reputable brand name and enjoyed a stable market. Permanent customers, such as supermarkets, shops, and restaurants, placed orders either for the next week, or for longer intervals with a regular delivery, and the company provided good customer service both in quality and delivery time.

The years 1995 to 1996 saw the decline of the market share in many of the traditional markets. The marketing analysis showed that the main reason for the drop in sales was high production costs, and as a result, competitors offered lower prices on similar products. The famous brand name did not attract customers so that they would pay higher prices. An attempt was made to compete on low retail prices with the result of slightly increasing sales volumes, but significantly decreasing profit. An analysis produced surprising results on low-capacity utilisation. Working in volatile market conditions, organising multiple promotions, and catching unexpected opportunities required carrying a significant capacity cushion both in labour and equipment. It was necessary for providing stable customer service while the demand was uneven, sometimes with huge lumps. The company was accustomed to seasonal variations, and Christmas sales lumps, and coped with them by accumulating stock. Daily and weekly variations, though, lead to losses in production time in low periods, and to excessive use of overtime during peak periods. High labour cost variances (as compared to the standards) and low machine capacity utilisation were usual. The ability to perform to any sales staff promises required not only keeping extra equipment and staff, but also using a significant amount of overtime.

The ineffectiveness of production planning was an accepted fact. The company had a two-level planning system (Figure 7.1). The upper level performed sales

Figure 7.1. The old two-level production planning system

SALES PLANNING
ANNUAL BUDGETING

PRODUCTION SCHEDULING

planning as part of the annual budgeting. By default (under the wrong assumption that sales volumes were equal to the production volumes), the sales plan was accepted as a production plan. The objective of this procedure was to reach the sales goals of the company. The sales plan was based on an annual sales forecast, but the forecast was modified by the company's current objectives: usually they were planned sales volume increases or decreases for some products. The forecasting and planning procedures were performed once a year, and resulted in a sales and production plan for the following fiscal year (which in New Zealand is from April to the next March). First, the executive team set the sales goals for the next year, expressed in the total sales revenue. Then the marketing department worked out a sales forecast for products based on sales history, their established connections with customers, and their judgment. These forecasts were accumulated by product groups and sales areas, and finally, the total sales revenue was calculated. When a suitable trade-off between the goal and forecast was reached, it was set as a target for the production. The only difference between the sales and the production plan was the necessity to accumulate stocks for Christmas sales. In order to cope with this huge lump in sales, the manufacturing of Christmas products was spread over the previous 4 to 6 months.

The lower level of the system performed production scheduling. This planning procedure was performed weekly, and produced schedules for all production lines for the following week. The input to this planning level consisted of orders placed during the current week, less current stocks. The stocks of finished goods might exist because of the differences between batch sizes and order volumes in the past. Thus, the volumes of each product that should be produced next week were defined, as a basis for line scheduling. These volumes, rounded by batch sizes, were manually checked against the demonstrated capacity, and if the capacity seemed sufficient, were approved for scheduling. If the capacity was insufficient, then either overtime was added or some of the orders were shifted to the following weeks. The scheduling procedure was concentrated on the development of Gantt-charts according to established scheduling rules, which include:

- Sequencing rules, defining the most economical way of resetting the equipment, and
- Staffing rules, allocating necessary staff to production lines; not all production lines were intended to run simultaneously, and the actual number of stuff was less than the necessary for all the lines to run.

The schedules triggered the supply of raw and packaging materials.

The faults of this production planning were evident:

1. The lack of communication between the sales and marketing staff on the one hand, and operations on the other hand disrupted the operations. The sales department provided the only link between the lower and upper levels. Comparing the current sales (and orders) volumes with the monthly budget, the sales staff tried to compensate insufficient sales by extra promotional activity. The link is not shown at Figure 7.1 due to its insignificance. It was vital that planning levels preserve continuity, both in terms of planning (that is, the plans produced by the lower level had to be detailed plans of the top level) and feedback (that is, the feedback of the top levels was an aggregation of bottom level feedback) — see Beischel and Smith (1991).

2. The time interval for budgeting was too long. Usually, the reliability of long-term forecasts is low, and the effectiveness of the budget by the end of the year was low as well. As a result, there was no continuity in planning: the upper level plan was practically not used in the lower-level planning, and served only as a reference. All the production planning was reduced to the lower level. The company chased the customer's demand, and the chase production strategy caused the excessive use of labour.

3. The supply of raw and packaging materials required a longer time horizon than the one week provided by the production scheduling. The use of monthly budgets (with a time horizon up to 6 months) for purchasing, due to their inaccuracy, led to shortages in some areas, and to accumulation of unnecessary stocks in other areas.

A reputable brand name and a stable market resulted in the fact that the dominant production strategy of the company was MTO (see, for example, Vollmann, Berry, & Whybark, 1997). Permanent customers, such as super-markets, shops, and restaurants, placed orders either for the next week, or for longer intervals with a regular delivery, and the company provided good customer service both in terms of quality and of on-time delivery.

Because of the decline in sales, the company was forced to reconsider its sales and production strategy and to redesign its production planning. Two major faults were identified:

1.   To support its MTO strategy the company was forced to have a significant capacity cushion both in labour and equipment. It was necessary for providing stable customer service while the demand was uneven, sometimes with huge lumps. During Christmas, for example, the company usually tripled their average sales volumes. EA Cakes Ltd. was accustomed to seasonal variations and Christmas sales lumps, and coped with them by accumulating stock. Daily and weekly variations, however, led to losses in production time in low periods and to excessive use of overtime during peak periods. High labour cost variances (as compared to the standards) and low machine capacity utilisation were prevalent.

2.   The MTO strategy implied that the company always quoted lead times to customers, for example, an order placed this week would be promised to deliver next week, or the week after, if there were too many orders. Old traditional customers agreed with this system, and the company was mostly successful in keeping its promises. The market, however, had become much more dynamic. Increased competition from NZ and overseas, and a heavy promotional activity required improved "speed to market." Many customers wanted the product on demand, not next week. The company was unable to exploit such opportunities and lost this significant part of the market.

EA Cakes Ltd. had decided to change its production and sales strategy (as recommended by operations management literature; see, for example, Vollmann et al., 1997) for long and medium shelf-life products, from MTO to MTS. The MTS strategy costs more in inventory than MTO, but it has two benefits:

1.   Increased "speed to market" allows expanding the market share by attracting new customers, and by catching unexpected opportunities; and

2.   Capacity may be utilised more efficiently using the inventory "cushions" instead of capacity cushions (see McNair & Vangermeersch, 1998).

MTS companies hold stocks of all advertised products. The stocks usually are managed by a "min-max" rule: stocks below or close to minimum trigger production until they reach or approach the maximum level. The difference between minimum and maximum is defined by the demand forecast during a planning period. The production process is driven by the current levels of stocks rather than by customers' orders.

The decision to change the strategy from MTO to MTS involves not only the company's decision to invest much more money in accumulation and keeping stocks of finished goods, it requires a complete redesign of its production planning system. There are several major reasons for making significant changes in production planning:

- MTO is driven by customers' orders, MTS is triggered by forecasts; a forecasting system had to be designed and implemented.

- There are no significant stocks of finished goods under MTO, so there is no need for stock management; for MTS, an inventory management system for finished goods had to be developed.

- Under MTO, there are no significant information links between the company planning and shop floor production planning; under MTS it is vital that the planning system preserves continuity. It has to be continuity in planning. That means the plans produced by each level are detailed plans of the top level. Also, there must be feedback continuity: feedback of the top levels is an aggregation of bottom level feedback — for more detail see McNair and Vangermeersch (1998).

The production planning system was an integral part of an ERP system that used SAP software. Its redesign was a part of a major project of the ERP system development, carried out by Ernest Edams Ltd. for 2 years.

Implementation Problems

The implementation of SAP's Production Planning module at EA Cakes Ltd., in order to provide computer support to the MTS production planning system, started from the detailed analysis of the problems.

The production planning system described above carries specific features of production planning at EA Cakes Ltd. Standard software (and SAP by definition is standard software), on the other hand, comprises programmes developed for an anonymous market. The question is, can a standard software system like SAP give adequate computer support to an individually designed business management system?

This class of problems is widely discussed in literature (e.g., Robey, Ross, & Boudreau, 2002; Jacobs & Bendoly, 2003), with rather uncertain results, always pointing at the specific features of the enterprise. Because of this, a team from IT specialists and production planning personnel was formed for designing computer support for the new production planning system business processes.

The concept of a business process is central to many areas of business systems design; specifically to business systems based on modern information technology (see Scholz-Reiter & Stickel, 1996). In the new era of computer-based business management, the design of a business process has substituted for the previous functional design. There are many definitions of a business process (see Davenport, 1993; Rosemann, 2001; Sharp & McDermott, 2001). According to Sharp and McDermott (2001), a business process is a collection of interrelated tasks initiated in response to an event that achieves a specific result for the customer of the process. Thinking in terms of business processes helps managers to look at their organisation from the customer's perspective. Usually a business process involves several functional areas, and functions within those areas. Thus, a business process is cross-functional. Definitely, this is the case of the production planning at EA Cakes Ltd.

The aggregate capacity planning uses sales budget, stock feedback, and available capacity (manpower and machinery). The master scheduling involves forecasting and feedback on stocks. The shop floor scheduling and control absorbs a huge variety of activities from other functional areas such as material control, human resource management, inventory management, and so on.

Quite to the contrary, standard software was initially developed only for certain functions that could easily be standardised. Modern standard software, such as SAP is said to be object oriented or process oriented (see Kirchmer, 2002). However, it is still mostly functional, and the necessary orientation can only be achieved by adjusting the appropriate parameters. Even after the adjustments, the functionality of SAP may not be completely relevant to the business processes of a particular company. Then the implementation team will have only two options (Sawy, 2001):

1. To substitute the business processes of the company for the business processes implemented in SAP, and

2. To create additional special software for providing computer support to production planning.

There was no consensus in the design group. IT specialists were sure that existing SAP software could provide adequate computer support. When the production planning staff got acquainted with the business processes suggested for production planning by SAP, they had doubts that these modules were relevant to their business processes. They were the authors of the new production planning system, and they had a rather firm position that their planning processes were the most efficient for EA Cakes Ltd. No changes would be accepted.

So, the management of EA Cakes Ltd. was presented with the following dilemma:

1.   Believing the IT specialists and continuing to implement the existing SAP modules on comparatively low cost, but facing all the risks of losses due to planning inefficiency; and

2.   Believing the planning staff and ordering high cost computer support in addition to the existing SAP system.

The management invited in a consulting company. The consultants suggested to design quickly a rough prototype system (Hoffer, George, & Valasich, 2002), using ARIS (Scheer, 1999). Analysing this system would help the working group to reach a consensus.

Apart from giving adequate computer support to the new production planning system, the SAP implementation was intended to solve several implementation problems (Hong & Kim, 2002) identified by consultants.

Problem 1

The manufacturing process requires an updated short-term forecast each week. Sales managers must produce the forecast, and then it is automatically processed within the Master Production Scheduling. Sales figures for individual products have to be provided on a weekly basis for the current month and the next month. Actual sales made each week are captured and available for reporting on the following (after actual sales completion) morning. Sales staff compares actual sales with long-term forecasts and using judgement make necessary adjustments. Currently, forecasts are prepared manually and then put into the database. It needs computer support to relieve sales personnel and to eliminate data entry.

Problem 2

The master scheduler has to check the capacity requirements and to change the production volumes according to available capacity. Then he must agree the changes with the Sales Department and the Production Department.

Problem 3

Presently at EA Cakes Ltd., scheduling is only done on finished items. It is desirable to schedule some components production as well.

Problem 4

It is necessary to provide a reliable method for checking inventory availability. The question is: Can the SAP implementation solve all of these problems?

Current Challenges

One of the biggest problems for EA Cakes Ltd. is low capacity utilisation. The company has sufficient regular work force. Nevertheless, the master scheduler sometimes has to schedule overtime production, paying for overtime labour, which results in higher production costs for products. This can also cause shortages or stock-out of some materials for production, further increasing the cost of production. Managers are especially frustrated when an instant need for overtime follows a period of low demand, when inventory could have been built up; for example, in anticipation of an increase in sales following production promotions by marketing.

Another problem was identified in inventory management. Stock control of raw material and finished items needs double-checking. Initially, the line manager records the data about actual production and actual use of raw materials. However, due to possible conflict of interests, this data is not absolutely reliable. The actual amounts of goods produced should be verified regularly. Any variances must be investigated: hence, the necessary data must be kept for a longer time. More thought is required on the handling of rejects/seconds, as some are almost planned by-products. This will also have ramifications with stock control and sales analysis.

There are hopes that these problems could be fixed after the ERP implementation by existing SAP tools.

Case Development

The designer is faced with the initial problem of deciding how many levels to plan with. There is no rule that establishes the ideal number of levels, and the planner is left with a combination of logical analysis of the situation in each company to establish the best estimate, along with experimentation to find the right number. The question of how many plans is answered by the convenient phrase "enough to provide the necessary and sufficient conditions to control production": too many means unwelcome complexity, administration cost, and information overload; too few means a lack of accuracy, instability, and poor control with associated inventory costs.

Every company has at least two levels that are decided by the need to focus on both short- and long-term profitability. The company must make money now, and in the future. However, the plans made for the immediate future cannot be used for the long term, because they rapidly become unreliable as time passes. Likewise, the general and broad nature of the long-term plan is not suitable to plan tomorrow's production. This necessitates intermediate planning levels to bridge the time factor of planning, and strongly suggests that in most cases, the minimum number of levels is three: a long-term company level, a medium-term aggregate level, and a short-term shop level. If more control is needed, then extra levels are added until the ideal balance between control and complexity is found.

In each case, the characteristics of a planning level are unique. This means that every level has its own concept of the production unit, its own planning period and planning horizon, its own view of the flow of materials, and its own planning item to control.

A planner starts with an existing situation that is often determined by the management structure of the company. However, once changes are made in the structure of the planning system, these changes tend to have undeniable consequences on other parts of the business, and may cause the elimination of unnecessary levels of management structures.

The cycle times have significant impact on the planning system and on the inventory levels. Sometimes the cycle time is an unavoidable characteristic of the production type, but in many other instances, the planning design itself sets the cycle time.

Finally the system requires an efficient feedback process that matches the features of the plan that was issued in terms of planning level, production unit, planning period, and planning item.

The new production planning system consists of three levels (see Figure 7.1).

Aggregate Capacity Planning (ACP)

The first (top level) procedure is part of the general budgeting procedure, which starts from sales budget development. There are several other budgets: production budget, capital budget, and so forth. Their development mostly depends on the sales budget, and thus they are secondary. Sales budget is not a simple forecast of the amount of products that could be sold in the future. Budget not only predicts, but also directs the sales and marketing efforts of the

Figure 7.1. The three-level production planning system supporting MTS strategy

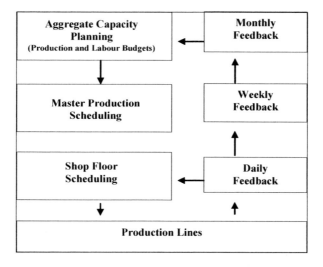

company. Thus, it is more a sales plan than a forecast. This defines the dual nature of the budget: On the one hand it should be realistic and should define what could be sold, on the other hand it should meet the business and financial goals of the company.

The sales budget is a management tool for control of the company's performance by the board of directors. The board provides the inputs to this budget in the form of key performance indicators. The marketing department provides other inputs (launch of new products and other marketing initiatives). The sales budget is developed for the fiscal year, and it is redeveloped every quarter with a 1-year time horizon (a rollover procedure). All the budgets and rollovers are stored in the information system for reference and subsequent statistical processing. At any time, two versions are available for analysis and use in the sales and production planning: a full budget for the current fiscal year, approved by the board of directors and a current rollover budget.

ACP has all the features of a capacity planning procedure. Starting from the sales budget, it produces an aggregate production plan for the following

Figure 7.2. The "level" strategy is not sustainable; negative stocks show this

Month	Apr	May	Jun	Jul	Aug	Sep	Oct	Nov	Dec	Jan	Feb	Mar	Total
Stock	1.65	3.17	3.82	5.48	6.89	3.56	0.85	-3.5	-5.9	-2.9	-0.7	-0	
Sales	3.87	3.99	4.87	3.86	4.1	8.85	8.22	9.85	7.94	2.51	3.36	4.77	66.2
Indicis	0.83	0.85	1.05	0.82	0.88	1.17	1.03	1.39	1.72	0.53	0.71	1.02	12

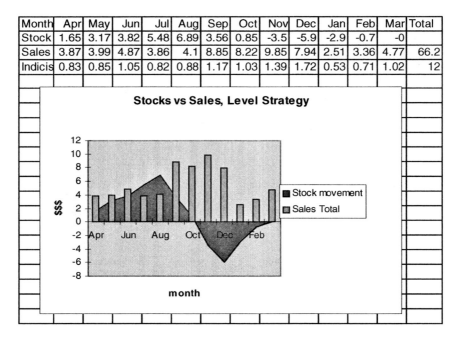

Figure 7.3. Optimum "mixed" strategy

Month	Jan	Feb	Mar	Apr	May	Jun	Jul	Aug	Sep	Oct	Nov	Dec	
Stock	1.51	2.66	2.91	4.56	6.08	6.73	8.39	9.80	6.47	4.26	0.92	0.00	
Production	4.02	4.52	5.02	5.52	5.52	5.52	5.52	5.52	5.52	6.02	6.52	7.02	
Overtime	-1.5	-1.0	-0.5	0.00	0.00	0.00	0.00	0.00	0.00	0.50	1.00	1.50	

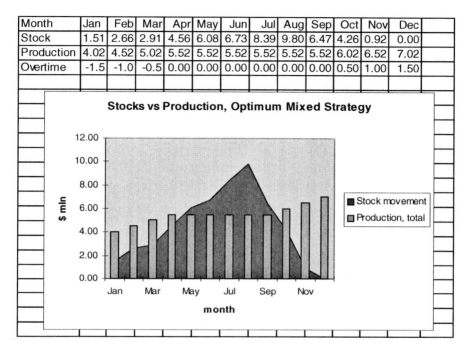

planning periods up to the planning horizon. The plan is balanced against the agreed target capacity, and at the same time meets the production and sales goals of the company. The demand forecast, the financial goals of the company, the target stock levels, and actual stock levels are kept in the budget database.

The planning starts from defining an optimum production strategy. The production strategy that follows the demand pattern month by month ("chase" strategy) is not sustainable here because of high seasonality of some products. Figure 7.2 shows that the "level" strategy, with even production levels is not sustainable as well, because there is not enough time for stock accumulation from the beginning of the year till the start of the peak season. If production starts earlier, then the level of stocks becomes excessive.

The optimum "mixed" strategy that combines stock accumulation with overtime use is shown in Figure 7.3. It plans some overtime at the peak season, and decreased resources utilisation at the beginning of the year to compensate for the effect of increased production.

The optimum mixed strategy, expressed in sales dollars, then is converted to an aggregate production plan. The planner uses:

- Conversion tables, containing unit prices;
- Capacity tables, which show the lines' capacity (units/hour); and
- Labour content tables (labour hours/machine hour), which are necessary because different lines have crews of different sizes.

Here the planner shifts shelf-stable seasonal products to an earlier month, targeting the optimum stock levels, and loading the lines up to their capacity.

The development of an aggregate plan based on the optimum strategy is necessary because:

- The strategy gives total sales dollars, and cannot be used for production planning, while the plan is expressed in units of each product, and
- There is no direct relationship between the selling price and production hours; therefore, the strategy is not balanced against capacity.

Thus, the strategy serves as a goal for ACP. The aggregate capacity plan is developed initially for the fiscal year, and it is redeveloped every quarter, with a 1-year time horizon (a rollover procedure).

Master Production Scheduling

The master production scheduling system is the most important managerial tool for the Operations manager of an MTS company. Master production schedule (MPS) gives the ability to ensure that available capacity is allocated with a customer service focus. The main MPS inputs are:

- The aggregate capacity plan for the following 2 months,
- The actual stock levels, and
- The short-term demand forecast.

The sales team prepares a short-term demand forecast by product for the next 5 weeks each week (a rollover forecast). The sales managers of particular products modify the monthly sales forecasts from the current budget, taking into account changes in demand, planned promotions, and so on.

Starting from the demand forecast for the following planning period, the master scheduler produces a weekly production plan for the next 5 weeks, which is balanced against capacity, and at the same time meets production and sales goals of the company.

The procedure is performed initially at the beginning of the planned month (the main run) in order to work out the MPS for the month. Only the first week of the plan is valid (and frozen). The rest of the plan is necessary for keeping the continuity of planning during the month. At the end of each week, when feedback on actual production and updated demand forecast become available, the procedure is run for the rest of the planning period (a control run). During this run, the updated MPS for the following weeks will be produced. Also, instant changes in demand can initiate a control run in order to react quickly to the market demand.

The primary function of the MPS is to produce feasible assignments for all product lines, which ensure their performance according to ACP with minimum cost. The other functions of this level are:

1.   To keep desirable stock levels, and
2.   To implement a "speed-to-market" principle: react quickly to significant changes in market demand.

Shop Floor Scheduling

This level performs actual scheduling for the next week (with a daily subdivision), specified by production lines and products.

The scheduling constraints (for both men and machines scheduling) were worked out as fixed recommended schedules for different proportions of the output. Set-up times, planned downtime, and average capacity losses due to unplanned downtime were necessary for realistic scheduling. This required a downtime reporting procedure and a schedule for major planned maintenance. The scheduling is performed initially at the beginning of the planned week (the main run) in order to work out an optimal weekly schedule. At the end of each day, when feedback on actual production becomes available, the procedure is run for the rest of the planning period (a control run). During this run, the updated plan for the following days, subject to the same planning constraints, is produced.

Comments

The analysis of EA Cakes Ltd. case is given below in the form of questions and answers.

1.   What is the overall problem(s) in this case?

IT specialists were sure that existing SAP software could provide adequate computer support. When the production planning staff got acquainted with the business processes suggested for production planning by SAP, they had doubts that these modules were relevant to their business processes. They were the authors of the new production planning system, and they had a rather firm position that their planning processes were the most efficient for EA Cakes Ltd. No changes would be accepted.

The management of EA Cakes Ltd. was presented with the following dilemma:

*   Believing the IT specialists and continuing to implement the existing SAP modules on comparatively low cost, but facing all the risks of losses due to planning inefficiency; and

*   Believing the planning staff and ordering high cost computer support in addition to existing SAP system.

Apart from giving adequate computer support to the new production planning system, the SAP implementation was intended to solve several other implementation problems identified by consultants.

2.   *What managerial, organisational, and technological issues are re-
     lated to this case?*

EA Cakes Ltd. had decided to change its production and sales strategy for long
and medium shelf-life products from MTO to MTS. The MTS strategy costs
more in inventory than MTO, but it has two benefits:

- Increased "speed to market" allows expanding the market share by
  attracting new customers and by catching unexpected opportunities, and
- Capacity may be utilised more efficiently using the inventory "cushions"
  instead of capacity cushions.

MTS companies hold stocks of all advertised products. The stocks usually are
managed by a "min-max" rule: Stocks below or close to minimum trigger
production until they reach or approach the maximum level. The difference
between minimum and maximum is defined by the demand forecast during a
planning period. The production process is driven by the current levels of
stocks, rather than by customers' orders.

The decision to change the strategy from MTO to MTS involves not only
company's decision to invest much more money in accumulation and keeping
stocks of finished goods, it requires a complete redesign of its production
planning system.

3.   *How does the change of strategy affect the information technology
     applications?*

There are several major reasons for making significant changes in production
planning and IT applications:

- MTO is driven by customers' orders, MTS is triggered by forecasts; a
  forecasting system had to be designed and implemented.
- There are no significant stocks of finished goods under MTO, so there is
  no need for stock management; for MTS, an inventory management
  system for finished goods had to be developed.

- Under MTO, there are no significant information links between the company planning and shop floor production planning. Under MTS, it is vital that the planning system preserves continuity. That means the plans produced by each level are detailed plans of the top level. Also, there must be feedback continuity: feedback of the top levels is an aggregation of bottom level feedback.

The production planning system is an integral part of an ERP system that uses SAP software.

4.   *What are the possible alternatives, and their pros and cons, facing the organisation in dealing with the problem(s) related to the case?*

The management of EA Cakes had two alternatives:

- To substitute the business processes of the company for the business processes implemented in SAP, and
- To create additional special software for providing computer support to production planning.

The production planning system described in the case carries specific features of production planning of EA Cakes Ltd. Standard software (and SAP by definition is standard software), on the other hand, comprises programmes developed for an anonymous market. The question is, can a standard software system like SAP give adequate computer support to an individually designed business management system? This class of problems is widely discussed in literature with rather uncertain results, always pointing at the specific features of the enterprise.

5.   *What are some of the emerging technologies that should be considered in solving the problem(s) related to the case?*

The concept of a business process is central to many areas of business systems design; specifically to business systems based on modern information technology. In the new era of computer-based business management, the design of a business process has substituted for the previous functional design. Thinking in terms of business processes helps managers to look at their organisation from the customer's perspective. Usually a business process involves several functional areas, and functions within those areas. Thus, a business process is cross-functional. Definitely, this is the case of the production planning at EA Cakes Ltd.

The aggregate capacity planning uses sales budget, stock feedback, and available capacity (manpower and machinery). The master scheduling involves forecasting and feedback on stocks. The shop floor scheduling and control absorbs a huge variety of activities from other functional areas such as material control, human resource management, inventory management, and so on.

6.   *What is the final solution that can be recommended to the management of the organisation described in the case?*

The final solution is to use SAP. The team of consultants provided the proof in the form of a quick prototype system. The business scenarios are given in the following chapters.

Chapter VIII

Core Business Processes in Enterprise Planning:
Choosing the Structure of the System

It was pointed out in Chapter VII that before implementation of an ERP system in EA Cakes Ltd., it was necessary to completely reengineer the production planning process. To change the strategy from make-to-order to make-to-stock involves not only the company's decision to invest money in accumulation and keeping stocks of finished goods. It requires a complete redesign of its production planning system, because:

- There is no forecasting for MTO, it is driven by customers' orders, so a forecasting system had to be designed and implemented.
- An inventory management system for finished goods had to be developed.
- Under MTS, it is vital that the planning system preserves continuity; the plans produced by each level should be detailed plans of the top level. Also, there must be feedback continuity: feedback of the top levels is an aggregation of bottom level feedback — for more detail see McNair and Vangermeersch (1998).

The design of a production planning and control system is unique to each production situation, and there are many considerations that will act to shape the development of an efficient system. However, just as every house built is unique in its own way, and yet is constructed out of common materials, so too are production planning systems constructed from common "building blocks." These "building blocks" will provide the robust foundation on which the uniqueness of the systems design can be constructed.

The Structural Components of a Planning System

The Starting Point

In the EA Cakes Ltd. case study, the management have decided to change the production planning system. While there is evidence that the existing system has faults, it has, nevertheless, been developed to suit the existing situation and the people who manage it. This fact raises the question of where to start when attempting to improve a planning system. It is very rare to be involved in designing the planning system right at the firm's beginnings, and more often, the planning system has evolved over a period of time, and is designed to suit some form of management goals or objectives, or to suit the existing technology and processes. We can assume, in most cases, that the existing system has been designed with the best knowledge and understanding of the existing situation. To improve the situation, therefore, needs new knowledge, or the ability to see something that was missed in the original design phase.

The discussion that follows centres on how to choose the number of levels of production planning, and how to define the production units at each level. Before considering the various factors and influences, however, it will be helpful to get familiar with the basic components of a production planning system.

The Components

To develop a concept of the planning task, we need to understand how the production planning system is built. Just as an architect designs a house with foundations, a frame, claddings, and services of water and power, so a production planner must design the planning system using a variety of planning components that make up the structure of a planning system. A simple diagram of the typical components is shown in Figure 8.1.

From this separated perception of the levels at which the company thinks and operates, we see that production planning cannot be dealt with on only one level, but is in fact a family of planning processes carried out at **different levels**, applied to **different production units** that produce **different outputs**, and are concerned with **different time spans**. The components of the planning system then are:

- Levels of planning
- Production units
- Planning horizons
- Planning periods
- Flow of materials (and associated planning items)

Figure 8.1. The basic levels and components of production planning

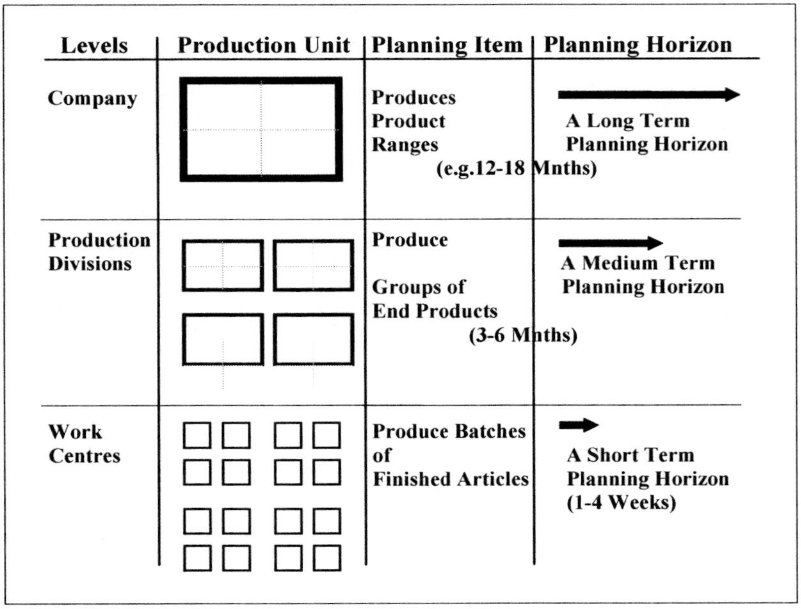

Levels	Production Unit	Planning Item	Planning Horizon
Company		Produces Product Ranges (e.g.12-18 Mnths)	A Long Term Planning Horizon
Production Divisions		Produce Groups of End Products (3-6 Mnths)	A Medium Term Planning Horizon
Work Centres		Produce Batches of Finished Articles	A Short Term Planning Horizon (1-4 Weeks)

The two functions of the production planning system are:

1. To issue work assignments to the production units, and
2. To coordinate the materials flow between production units so as to optimise the balance of capacity utilisation on one hand, and customer satisfaction on the other (on-time delivery).

The Levels of Planning

The starting point in production planning systems design, then, is an examination of what factors provide the support for the existing system. Of particular initial interest are two questions. Firstly, how many levels of planning are ideal, given the nature of production and the companies management structure, and secondly, how should the production units be defined, where will the boundaries be drawn to separate one production unit from another (see Figure 8.1). These two factors are connected. If the focus of the planning task changes from the productive activities of the *whole company* as one production unit, to the productive activities of several *divisions* within the company, then it follows that there will be two levels of planning. Similarly, when production units work to different planning time horizons, it is a strong indication that separate levels of planning are needed.

As the layout in Figure 8.1 suggests, the production planning process begins with an understanding of the structure of levels that are necessary to reflect the characteristics of the company's production environment.

Figure 8.2 shows a structure of five levels, but there is no set ideal number of levels. Rather, the number of levels is governed by the nature of the business and its organisational structure, and the influence of functional areas within the company.

Seven planning levels is the number that is definable by the organisational structure in this example, but commonly it is possible, and often desirable, to amalgamate some of the organisational levels into fewer levels in the planning system. The reduction of levels in the planning system does, however, have one restrictive criterion: the amalgamations will happen in the middle levels so that the system will always be left with the top and bottom levels preserved. It is essential that a top level exists that gives the planner long range direction by

Figure 8.2. An example of a multilevel company structure

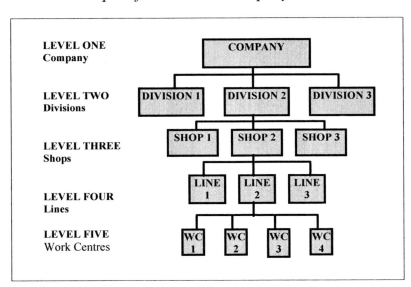

planning for the overall company over a long-term planning horizon. It is also essential that the bottom level be retained to deal with the actual assignments of work to production units for physical production.

When deciding on the number of levels, it must also be considered that there is a trade-off between control, flexibility, and cost that comes as a result of the decision. The more levels that are included, the greater is the degree of control that the planner has over events in the production-planning environment. However, on the down side, more levels mean more cost and less flexibility. Costs will expand in the extra administrative cost to manage the higher number of planning activities. Costs may also rise through the loss of flexibility within each production area. Potential gains in productivity exist in allowing work centre teams or individuals to find the "best" solution to some production scheduling problems. Such solutions can produce more efficient results that would be lost in the case of tighter control from the planning system.

The task in deciding on the number of levels is, therefore, to find the optimum set of characteristics that provide the needed degree of control without loosing the benefits of flexibility and without adding unduly to costs. It must also be remembered that the "control versus flexibility" discussion has another aspect to consider. Control cannot be released indiscriminately or without due caution and regard to the consequences. It is only when the required competency is present within the teams of people concerned that freedoms can be granted to self managing teams within today's ideal of flat organisational structures. Otherwise, delegation of decision making into areas of collective ignorance leads, inevitably, to an *accumulation of chaos* at great cost to productive efficiency, customers, and ultimately, the company. The idea suggested here is not against employee empowerment, but toward a recognition that competence must precede delegation of control if the company is to achieve cost effective outcomes.

The seven-level system, with its many sets of production units, is not unusual in larger companies. However, for the purposes of gaining an understanding of a typical production planning situation we will focus for now on describing a three level system.

The Company Level

The first level of planning deals with the company as one whole production unit and the characteristics of the planning task are broad and general as outlined in Figure 8.3.

This level is usually concerned with long-term forecasts of market demand and plans, broadly for a production planning horizon of 12 to 18 months ahead. The focus of its planning then comes down to production planning of broad product groups for the actual planning period (often 3- to 6-month periods). The plan is assigned to the company without internal operational detail. The company plan will include overall capacity requirements in terms of people, plant, buildings, and distribution, and also the security of supply of materials from external sources.

Figure 8.3. The company as a production unit

Figure 8.4. Production units at the aggregate level

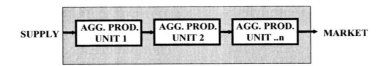

The Aggregate Level

The aggregate level of planning opens up a further level of detail than that provided in the company level. The aggregate level allows us to examine production entities within the company that may be grouped together for planning purposes into production units (see Figure 8.4).

At the aggregate level, the forward planning may go to the 3- or 6-month stage, as received from the company plan, but the planning focus will be detailed typically for 1 month ahead. The focus of the aggregate planning is to coordinate the production at each of the production units and the movement of materials between them, to achieve a smooth flow through the system and to satisfy the market demand. The job of planning at the aggregate level is to create a stable production environment by controlling the flow of materials between the production units, and to optimise the balance of capacity with demand at each production unit. At this level, the task of planning is to both assign plans to the production units and to coordinate the production units and the flow of materials between them.

The Shop Floor Level

If there is need for more detailed planning within a production unit, then more levels of planning are needed to represent that detail. In any event, a shop level will always exist that handles the actual assignment of work-to-work centres. This shop level may be part of the formal production planning system, as shown in Figure 8.5, where shop production units (SPUs) are part of the system. Alternatively, the shop level may be handled outside of the formal system by allowing the production unit manager to control work centre activity.

This third level of planning relates to specific machines or processes, and has a short-term focus of a week, a day, or even shorter time blocks. At this level,

Figure 8.5. Production units at the shop floor level

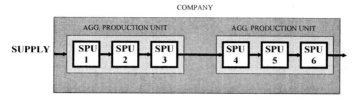

production planning again has the dual role of assigning work to production units, and also coordinating the activities and flows throughout the group. In this diagram, the integrative nature of the planning system is noticeable, as it has a view through all levels of the planning system at once, but also deals with each level individually. The planning system is working at one and the same time *holistically and discretely*.

Production Units

The previous section introduced the idea that production planning is structured on multiple levels, and that at each level the components of the planning system are different and unique to each level. The first of these is the focus of production control, the production unit.

We have seen that as we deal with each level in the planning process, the production unit changes. At the company level, the production unit is the company as a whole, whereas at the aggregate levels, the production units could be manufacturing sections or groups of processes, and at the shop floor, the production units typically are groups of machines or individual machines or processes. When planning and control needs are required for smaller production units such as teams or individual workers, then there is a corresponding need for an associated planning level in the system. Production unit definitions and decisions on the number of planning levels are always interlinked in this way — each subsequent level requires unique production units — or put another way, changes in the type of production units indicate a need for a new planning level. For planning's purposes, these aspects are not predefined, and the issue of definition becomes the task of the planning system designer.

Control Systems

The introduction of production units into the planning system is related to the need for *control* of the production plans within the system. The creation of production units breaks down the whole control problem into subsections that make it easier for the planner to deal with the complexity of the system. Typical problems that the planner has to deal with include: the criteria for accepting customer orders, the supply of raw materials or sub assemblies to various parts of the whole process, and the variety of capacity characteristics throughout the manufacturing process.

A plan without a controlling mechanism becomes ineffective. The production planner must know the outcomes of each plan so that corrective actions and adjustments can be made for future periods. Also, the extent to which a plan for a particular production unit is fully completed will affect all downstream production units. In all cases, the need for control must be balanced against the need for flexibility in the system. Combining more manufacturing steps into the production unit simplifies the overall production control problem and allows more freedom to managers and supervisors within the unit to find optimal internal solutions. At the same time, larger aggregations of manufacturing steps mean a diminished level of control by the planning system over all of the production activities. In reaching for the right balance between control and flexibility, the planner's concept of a production unit does not have to reflect the production reality. For example, a plant may consist of a processing line in one section and a packing department in another. Although the activities are clearly separate in nature, the planner has a choice of also treating them as two distinct production units, or to combine them together into one.

Defining Production Units

Self-contained. The production unit is a definable subsystem within the overall system. This means that the boundaries that describe a production unit will reflect a logical set of activities that can be dealt with as one self-contained entity (see Figure 8.6). The production planner is concerned only with the inputs and outputs from the production unit, and does not intervene in the internal operations.

Figure 8.6. The production unit as a self contained entity within the planning system

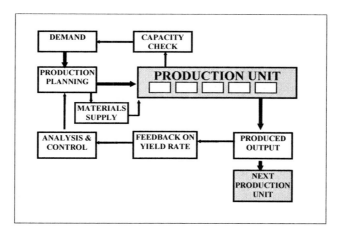

Choosing the Boundary

The choice of boundary may describe one dedicated line that produces one finished product. However, it is more common in companies that the systems boundary will describe a group of manufacturing sections that make a variety of components for a range of finished products. When faced with the task of deciding which activities or processes should be grouped into a production unit, the following factors are considered.

Activities bounded by time and the bill of materials. A natural reason for grouping production activities into one production unit is the lack of freedom in timing within a group. The interdependency of timing — of resources and materials allocation — within a certain group of manufacturing steps, will naturally group these activities together from a planning point of view. It is common in this case that the items involved are all on the same level of a bill of materials for the end item.

Activities bounded by technology or process. The types of technology or processes often determine production unit boundaries. In the steel manufacturing case, as an example, the technology and processes used in slab production are different from those used in rolling, cutting, and surfacing the steel. Likewise, the technology used in the galvanising and painting lines is also different. It may be decided in this case that all slab production activities should be grouped into one production unit, rolling, cutting, and surfacing activities into another, and the finishing lines grouped into a third. In fact, the boundaries would be too broad in this case because the rolling, cutting, and surfacing activities produce a wide variety of end items, and this section would need to be divided into a variety of production units for the purposes of control

Activities that produce for a common end item. Given that the production unit is self-contained from both a planning perspective and a manufacturing perspective, it is logical to expect that the unit will have a specific item of output, a part or subassembly for example. When individual activities collectively produce a common end item, then it is logical that they be grouped together into a production unit.

Production units defined by the management structure. Finally, it can be that the management structure defines the production unit. If a group of production activities are already grouped together under the management of a section manager, then production planning may treat that group as a self-contained production unit. The planner will create production plans for that section, and expect the manager to organise the section so as to produce to the plan.

Bottlenecks as Production Units

Capacity bottlenecks restrict the overall flow of materials to the speed at which the bottleneck can process materials. The bottleneck is, therefore, a critical resource, and production planning must ensure that the capacity utilisation at the bottleneck is maximised by establishing a buffer stock of materials before the bottleneck, to maintain a constant feed. Because the bottleneck production has a dramatic and negative affect on downstream production units, a buffer stock is also required after the bottleneck to minimise its constraining effect.

Figure 8.7. Bottleneck as first operation

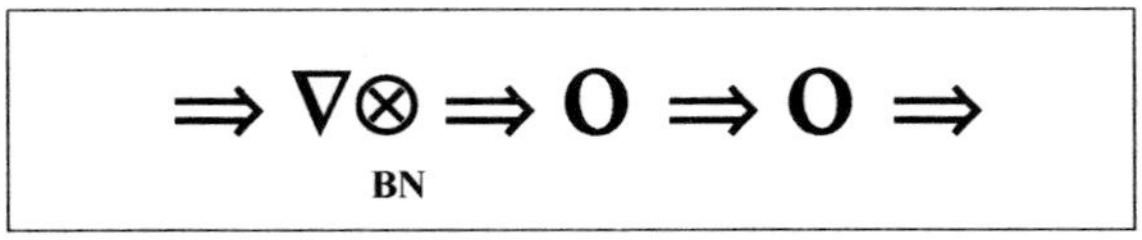

$$\Rightarrow \nabla \otimes \Rightarrow 0 \Rightarrow 0 \Rightarrow$$
$$\text{BN}$$

Figure 8.8. Bottleneck as last operation

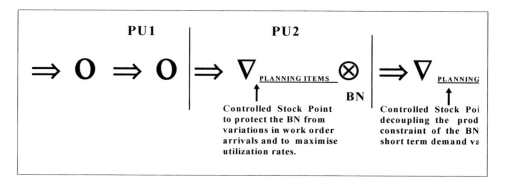

In Figure 8.7, a buffer stock (∇) is held in front of the bottleneck ($\otimes$) just sufficient to maximise the bottleneck utilisation rates. Lead times through the PU will be reliable and short after the bottleneck, and so planning control can release work orders based on the queue size in front of the bottleneck.

If the bottleneck is the last operation with a long series of production lead times leading up to it, then a largely varying queue of released work orders will result in front of the bottleneck and the PU lead times will be unpredictable.

In this case, it is better to split the PU into two parts: PU1 and PU2 as shown in Figure 8.8. This gives the ability to control the queue in front of the bottleneck because this queue is now a controlled stock point. In most cases, it is advisable to define bottlenecks as production units, to provide the necessary control.

Planning Horizons and Planning Periods

The Influence of Time

Two future views of time. The process of planning is not only concerned with the hierarchy of conceptual levels in the planning environment, or the design and description of production units within the system. The planning process is also concerned with **time**. A plan is made for an expected output from a production unit over particular time periods. The planner is concerned both with immediate blocks of time over which a plan can have very detailed output expectations (for example a day's production), through to less detailed expectations for some time in the future. The nature of a company's main goal — to make a profit — means that for all companies there are at least two time zones of interest. The company management must ask itself, "What must we do to make profits *now*?" and at the same time be asking, "How do we make profits in the *future*?"

The need for a medium-term view. This aspect of the time perspective links with the previous discussion on levels of planning and the definition of production units. If management's concern with making profits *now* relates to a time block of 1 week for a production line in a factory, and their simultaneous concern is for *future* profits of the whole company in 18 months time, then there are at least two levels of planning (a shop floor level and a company level), and two production units (the individual production line and the company as a whole). However in this case, the periods of time, 1 week and 18 months, are too far apart for management to achieve any control over the direction of the company, relative to the goals of the future plan. For most companies, this situation means the planning structure needs intermediate stages to bridge the time gap between the immediate and long-term future. If this time factor requires intermediate stages, then it logically follows that there must be intermediate levels of planning and intermediate production units. This concept supports the basic thesis that most planning systems require at least three levels: a company level, an aggregate level, and a shop floor level.

Planning periods and horizons. The time component of the planning system is dealing with diminishing control and certainty as it looks into the future. Each level of planning is faced with the same problem. This means that each time zone should be divided into manageable pieces. In a three-level system, the company level, for example, may have a definite plan for the first 3 months, and less certain forecasts for the following quarters out to 18 months. On the aggregate level, the 3-month horizon inherited from the company plan will be subdivided into a certain planning period of 1 month, and less certain forecasts for months 2 and 3, and finally on the shop floor level, the 1-month plan is taken from the aggregate plan as a horizon to aim for, and then subdivided into weekly segments with fixed details only for the first week.

The rolling plan concept. On each planning level the plan is made up of a number of sequential planning periods stretching out to a particular time horizon. However, only the details of the first planning period will be fixed and used as the absolute information on which production actions will be based. All other planning periods in the set, up to the horizon, will be forecasts only, and used as a general idea of the production intentions for future periods. As each period is completed, a new plan is made that adds one new period to the horizon and drops off the last one. In Figure 8.9, for example, the shop level planning is made up of a group of four planning periods, each a week long. This then provides a planning horizon of 4 weeks in which only the first week is "frozen" while the other three are flexible and can be altered. At the completion of week 1, a new plan is made for a further 4 weeks (weeks 2, 3, 4, and 5 of the original calendar). Now week 2 becomes frozen, while weeks 3, 4, and 5 remain flexible. On completion of week 2, the new plan consists of weeks 3, 4, 5, and 6 with week 3 becoming frozen, and so on. This rolling plan concept is used at every level in the planning system so that the linkage throughout the system is maintained, and so that there is *continuity* of the planning process over time.

Integration of the planning period with the horizon of the level below. The time periods become a set of interlinked stages that are driven from the overall goals of the company down to the detailed daily production plans at the shop floor. Each level has a set of planning periods that reaches out to a horizon that links into the planning period of the level above (see Figure 8.9). In this example, the company has a planning period of 3 months, and an overall planning horizon of 18 months. At the aggregate level, the planning period is 1 month and the planning horizon 3 months, while at the shop level the planning period is 1 week with a horizon of 4 weeks. A fourth level for a particular production line is included in the example that shows a planning period of 1 day and a horizon of 1 week. In some cases, planning periods could be as short as an hour with horizons of one 8-hour shift.

Feedback. Figure 8.10 shows how each planning period must have a feedback loop so that differences between the plan and actual results can be used to modify future plans. The production planner issues a plan for the production unit with the expectation that it will be completed within the allotted time. At the end of the planning period, the planner must have immediate feedback of the production outcome. The results are analysed for variances from the plan (shortfalls or surpluses) and any differences are used to modify subsequent plans at the operative control point.

Interconnected and controlled in this way, the planning system reflects the reality of the business in its patterns of cause and effect relationships that are not necessarily connected in time or space. The further out into the future that the plan reaches, the less reliable and valid it becomes. A forecast for the next three or 4 days of production can be very accurate. To forecast daily production 10 days out will result in very unreliable information because so

Figure 8.9. The inter-level relationship of planning periods and planning horizons

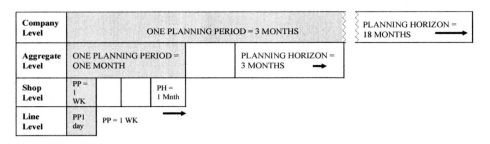

many variables affect the daily outcomes, and the plan quickly becomes obsolete by unplanned events. But if the planner tries to extend that detailed daily planning out to 365 days, the production predictions become completely meaningless. The situation can be controlled only by having the series of connected plans as described in Figure 8.9 and Figure 8.10, which show the integration between levels and the control over the "moving plan" for each successive planning period.

Slack. Figure 8.11 shows the planning period lead time and feedback delay problem in production planning. The ideal of the theory is that the plan is calculated at the exact start of the period and there is instant feedback available to the next period. However, in reality, plans take time to create and are prepared well ahead of the planning period. The most common reasons for this is the lead time associated with the supply of materials, or the advance time needed to alter capacities (organising workers for overtime is an example).

Production plans are also based on forecasts that have the accuracy problems mentioned earlier. Because of the uncertainties, concessions are made in the

Figure 8.10. Operative control for every planning period at every level

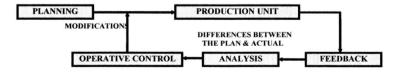

Figure 8.11. The planning lead time and the feedback delay problem

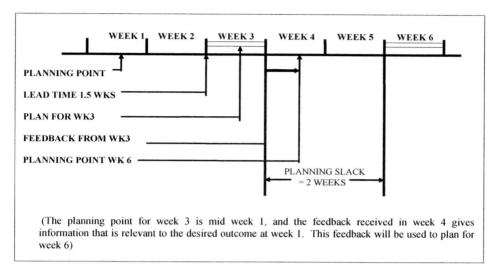

(The planning point for week 3 is mid week 1, and the feedback received in week 4 gives information that is relevant to the desired outcome at week 1. This feedback will be used to plan for week 6)

planning to cover the lack of accuracy. The planner not only works with a forecast of demand, but also with a forecast of yield from the plan. This presence of planning lead times and concessions *adds to the cycle times and the associated inventory costs.* At the other end, there is a delay before the results from the planning period are received in a form that is useful to the planner. The result of all of this, in our example, is that the planner is using information based on a planning point two periods old to make plans for two periods ahead. The planning point for week 3 is midweek 1, but the feedback loop that is feeding into the plan is relevant to planning done 2 weeks previously. Likewise the feedback received from week 3 can only give information that is relevant to the situation as it was in week 1. This feedback information will be used during week 4 for planning the production in week 6.

The example case of planning in Figure 8.11 has a 2-week slack, which has a negative affect on the accuracy, effectiveness and credibility of the plans. Because this situation creates inaccuracies and uncertainty, it is therefore desirable to work as close as possible to real time. This means calculating the plan rapidly and as close as possible to start of the planning period, and receiving feedback instantly at the end of the period. Reduction of planning slack gives greater control and accuracy, and reduces lead times and inventory holding costs. The planning lead time slack remains constant through all levels of planning, and so its impact is reduced at higher levels. A 2-week slack relative to a 2-month planning horizon in aggregate planning is much more dramatic than the same 2-week slack relative to a 1-year planning horizon at the company level. In addition, over the longer planning periods of higher levels, the inaccuracies of overestimating tend to get cancelled out by the inaccuracies of underestimating.

The feedback analysis and control process takes place throughout all of the levels in the system at time sequences to match the planning periods at each level. Each plan deals only with what is controllable at that level. Deciding what is controllable introduces the subject of *planning items* at each level and these will be dealt with in greater depth later.

Planning Periods, Cycle Times, and Inventory

Larger planning periods influence cycle times and result in larger inventories of WIP. If the weekly output of production in dollar value is $50,000, then the average WIP created by a 6-week cycle time is $300,000. If the cycle time could be reduced to only 4 weeks, then the WIP would also reduce — down to $200,000 in this example. Because this concept is clear, the focus must shift to how the planning period decision influences the production cycle. This decision regarding the length of the planning period is made by the planner when designing the planning system, and must be considered along with all of the previously noted factors.

Sequential Processes

The lead time for any process equals the sum of the technology time in production plus the idle time of waiting and queuing. The idle time is an intangible factor that is not set by any technology constraint, but is instead *created* by the company's systems of management including the planning system. At the aggregate level of planning, the planner works with the stacked sequential lead times of each aggregate production unit. The overall lead time is the cumulative total of each and every sequential stage from process beginning to process end. In the previously introduced steel company, the

Figure 8.12. Sequential production, planning periods, and WIP

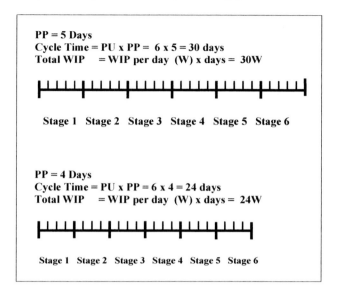

PP = 5 Days
Cycle Time = PU x PP = 6 x 5 = 30 days
Total WIP   = WIP per day (W) x days = 30W

Stage 1   Stage 2   Stage 3   Stage 4   Stage 5   Stage 6

PP = 4 Days
Cycle Time = PU x PP = 6 x 4 = 24 days
Total WIP   = WIP per day (W) x days = 24W

Stage 1   Stage 2   Stage 3   Stage 4   Stage 5   Stage 6

longest physical process in any production unit was 3 days, but the planner allowed a planning period of 5 days per stage to accommodate non-production lead times. With six production units in the process, this created a *planned* cycle time of 6 weeks. (This also included an assumption that each unit would perform to the expected capacity utilisation and productivity). In this example, if the planning period was reduced to 4 days, the overall cycle time would reduce to 24 days instead of the original 30 days, and 6 days of WIP inventory would be saved (see Figure 8.12).

Concurrent Processes

The previous section suggested that cycle times could be reduced through careful planning, by eliminating idle time. In fact, in the case of one job being processed at a time, the cycle time could be reduced to just the technology time, and the idle time thus reduced to zero (the just-in-time (JIT)/line flow concept). However, the reality of the New Zealand and Australian manufacturing environment is that for most companies, a multiple of jobs are processed concurrently in a batch manufacturing style of production. This means that within one production unit and within one planning period a number of jobs are

Figure 8.13. Concurrent processes, planning periods, and WIP

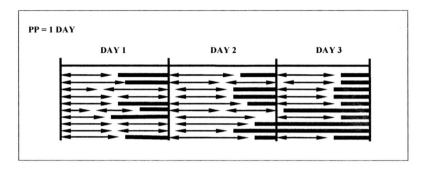

Figure 8.14. An extended planning period with extra WIP

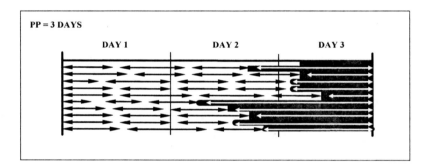

being processed, all with different technical processing times. In Figure 8.13, a plan for a work centre with 10 machines is shown for 3 consecutive days. The planning period is 1 day and all jobs are completed within the period. Fifteen jobs are being processed in the first 1-day planning period. In the second day, 12 jobs are planned, and 7 jobs on the third day. Idle time between jobs done on the same day may be optimised, but the tightly-controlled 1-day planning period also carries a daily capacity cushion of unused machine time represented by the black bars. The cycle time for the set of jobs is about 2.5 days.

In Figure 8.14, the planning period has been extended to 3 days, and freedom to schedule the workload is left to the production unit staff. The jobs are the same in number and length as in Figure 8.13, and the overall cycle time for the

Figure 8.15. Cycle time with planning periods of 1 week

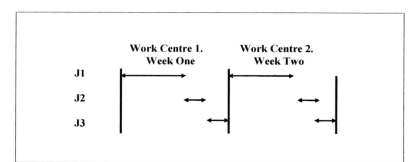

Figure 8.16. Cycle time with planning periods of 1 day

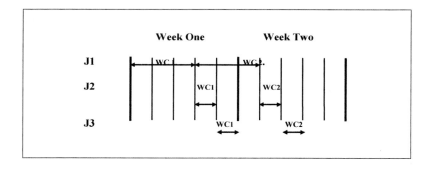

original jobs remains at approximately 2.5 days. The extended planning period has allowed greater scheduling efficiency within the production unit, but now the capacity cushions have been filled with extra WIP (the white arrows). If, however, the increase in scheduling efficiency does *not* occur, the extra complexity of the greater period of time will extend the idle time factor, cycle times will be lengthened, and again the WIP will rise.

To further explain the connection between the planning period and cycle times another example is provided which deals with a simple production situation of three orders: J1, J2, and J3; and two production stages: WC 1 and WC 2. Initially, the planning periods are set at 1 week and the resulting production cycle for the three jobs is outlined in Figure 8.15.

The cycle for the three jobs is 2 weeks (10 days) but this cycle time is set not just by the process time, but also by the length of the planning period designed into the planning system.

In Figure 8.16, reducing the planning period down to 1 day has reduced the cycle time for the three jobs down to 8 days instead of 10, and WIP will be reduced accordingly. The freeing up of extra production time will not lead to additional WIP from new jobs because now order J1 can leave the system at the end of day 6, J2 at the end of day 7, and J3 at the end of day 8. This means that new work *replaces* the original WIP and does not *add* to it, as was the case in Figure 8.16, when work was also condensed into a shorter time, but through an *extension* of the planning period.

As a rule then, with shorter planning periods, the planner gains more control, and idle time per job is minimised. Cycle times are, therefore, reduced in sequential processes, and in concurrent processes, work moves through the production unit quicker. Either of these factors lead to less WIP inventory with short planning periods. In the last example, materials are not required in the system until the day that production is planned, and completed orders can be "sold" out of the system more frequently.

Longer planning periods allow more freedom and flexibility within the production unit that has two possible results:

1. The overall cycle time is increased either by an inbuilt planning lead time cushion, or by an increased complexity in the scheduling problem which increases the amount of idle time.

2. Alternatively, the extra freedom of internal scheduling is more efficient, and a greater workload is accepted by the production unit.

In either case, the longer planning period leads to higher WIP inventory. The planning period question introduces another of the trade-off decisions that must be made in production planning. Short planning periods offer gains in lead-times and WIP, but there is a loss in productivity. Longer planning periods may gain in productivity, but they lose on the lead times and WIP. It must also be noted that the possible gains in productivity are dependent on the competency of the production personnel relative to production scheduling and job sequencing.

Planning Periods and MTS Batch Sizes

In a situation where the production policy is make-to-stock, the length of the planning period may impact on the batch sizing rule. In MTS cases, long planning periods are likely to increase the batch size because the demand factor over a longer period is greater. In Figure 8.17, the difference in planning period length is shown to have a significant influence on the batch size and the accompanying inventory. For the longer planning period, the batch size must be

Figure 8.17. The long planning period and make-to-stock inventory levels

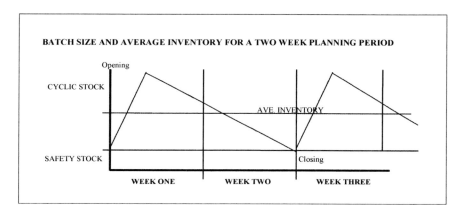

Figure 8.18. The short planning period and make-to-stock inventory levels

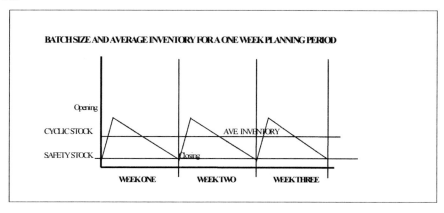

bigger to provide enough inventory to last through to the next production point. With shorter planning periods, the batch sizes are smaller and more frequent. In this second scenario (Figure 8.18) the drop in average inventory is clearly evident.

In make-to-order situations, the same influence is not present because the demand factor is set by the order size, and not by the planning period.

The Range of Planning Horizons and Planning Periods

The choice of planning horizons and periods is influenced by many considerations that range from the influence of the company's existing management system to cost and control goals. Outside of the rule that the planning horizon must cover all of the cycle times, including the tails of long term projects, the range of possibilities is extensive. However, the elements of cost and control do provide guidelines that help in coming to decisions, especially regarding planning periods. Figure 8.19 shows the relationship between planning period control, planning period length, and costs.

Figure 8.19. Planning periods, control, and costs

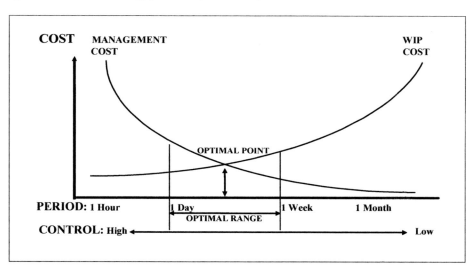

Figure 8.20. Recommended planning horizons and periods for each level

PLANNING LEVEL	PLANNING PERIOD	PLANNING HORIZON
COMPANY	1 YEAR or 1 QUARTER (Sometimes Monthly in the case of very short cycles)	SEVERAL YEARS down to ONE YEAR
AGGREGATE	1 MONTH or 1 WEEK (Sometimes Daily in the case of short cycles)	1 YEAR or 1 QUARTER (Sometimes Monthly in the case of very short cycles)
SHOP	1 DAY or 1 SHIFT	1 MONTH or 1 WEEK (Sometimes Daily in the case of short cycles)

The shorter planning periods provide lower cycles and lower WIP inventory costs, while at the same time giving greater control. However, with shorter planning periods, the administration costs rise. Longer planning periods mean lower administration costs, but also less control. The optimal point lies somewhere within a range that gives the required control at an acceptable cost. The range is unique to each level, and some guides are provided in Figure 8.20.

Synchronising of Planning, Control, and Reporting

It is necessary to ensure that the planning period matches the control period. We can examine two cases to illustrate the point. If a plan based on a planning period of *1 day* is given to a production unit, then it is necessary to the function of the planning process that a *daily* feedback of outcomes is returned to the planner. A return of outcomes for any period more than the relative day of the plan, for example a week, is of no use to the planner because the production department will target the weekly outcome rather than the day's plan. The planner needs to closely monitor every plan issued so that timely modifications and corrections can be made to plans for subsequent events. The alternative case is also undesirable. If the plan is for a period of 1 week, then it is pointless to provide or expect feedback from periods of less than the week because there is no benchmark or goal to compare the results with.

Finally, there is a need to manage the process of reporting dates and close-off dates. The company will have established routines for management and financial reporting that will be tied to specific dates which are likely to be monthly, quarterly, or annually. Because the production planning system (PPS) is likely to be working in integer weeks rather than calendar months, production details will be out of phase with the reporting dates set by these other management functions. There is no rule to handle this situation, but it is advisable that the planner consults with management to establish mutual agreement on what dates will be used as close-off dates for the purposes of management reporting.

To further develop the planning system so that the production system is correctly represented, the planner needs to describe the **flow of materials** between the production units. To represent and control the coordination of materials between the units, the production planner needs to decide what items the flow will be measured in, and how such items will be controlled. This final component of the planning system is the **planning item** or **goods flow control item**. As with the other components in the planning system, the view of the flow of materials and the planning items are unique to each level in the system. Although included here to complete the list of components in the planning system, planning items and the flow of materials is a large topic that is fully covered in subsequent paragraphs.

Conclusion: The Holistic System

In previous sections, the production unit is shown as a self-contained entity with an information feedback loop that allows the planner to receive information on what was actually produced. The planner can then analyse the effects that the production outcome will have on future plans or downstream production units, and make adjustments and corrections to plans as necessary. This information flow with the feedback loops is shown in Figure 8.21.

In this four-level system, the fixed plan for a 3-month planning period provides the planner with the information to draw up the firm *monthly* plan for the level immediately below. The *weekly* and *daily* plans at subsequent levels are set in the same way, taking their information from the level above. When production takes place, the actual output must be compared to the planned output. A daily feedback is used to moderate the next daily plan for the work centre, a weekly result feeds back to allow moderation of the weekly plan for the shop, a monthly report is used to modify the monthly plan for the aggregate level, and finally, a 3-month feedback enables control of the company level plan.

Figure 8.21. The holistic control system for a four-level system

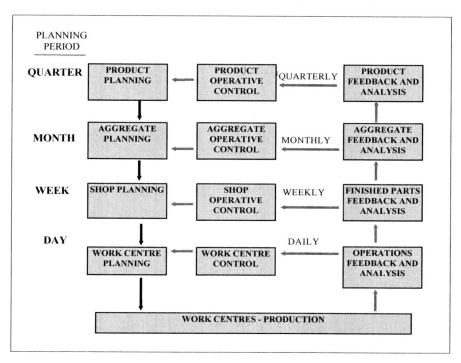

The issue of information linkages and feedback loops exists not only within levels of planning, but also between levels. Production plans for each planning horizon are developed from the first planning period of the level above. There is, in this way, a forward flow of information and planning that provides each level with production expectations. This forward flow must be balanced by an "after-the-event" feedback of information that tells the planner what actually happened. Planned outcomes are compared with actual results, and the differences are accommodated into alterations and moderation of the plans for the next planning period. Production planning systems with missing linkages create a planning environment that rapidly gets out of control, and produces surplus inventory or backorders, or possibly a mixture of both.

Chapter IX

Capacity Management Business Processes

The company is always aware of what it wants to produce because it is defined by the market pressures or by demand. However, what the company wants to make must be rationalised against what it *can* make. The issue of balance between requirements and capacity relates to a type of trade off. On one hand, the company wants to satisfy demand, but on the other hand, it may not have the capital resources to do so. At the senior management strategic planning level, long-range investment decisions are made that can increase the company's capacity resources. Commonly however, the additional capacity lags behind the pressure to produce more product more quickly. In these cases, management must make choices. A company must select carefully how to manage its limited asset of resources to achieve the greatest benefit to the company.

Capacity type investments in plant and people are expensive. In some cases, the management may decide to invest in more productive capacity, but in many others, the emphasis is placed on trying to make the existing capacity do more, through better planning and better management. The approach to this problem starts with a definition at every planning level of:

1.   What do we want to produce; that is, the demand (requirements planning).
2.   What are we able to produce (capacity planning).

The first definition, requirements planning, is therefore never a production plan. It must be modified by the reality of the company's ability to produce, before a production plan is derived. In this balancing and rationalising phase of capacity planning, choices again must be made on how to optimise the use of capacity for the best resulting profitability.

The conclusion is that we must always have two procedures in the planning process: one to establish what the production requirements are, and the other to ensure that adequate capacity exists to carry out the production intentions.

In the following section, we will discuss the situation when only the first procedure, requirements planning, is used.

Requirements Planning

In many companies, the focus of production planning is placed solely on the requirements side of the problem. A full requirements planning system uses a four-level requirements chain that consists of long-range forecasts, shorter-term forecasts, a MRP calculation, and a system of work order releases (see Figure 9.1)

This system effectively tells the company what it has to make so as to satisfy demand. It not only gives the volumes, but also provides the latest start dates for each work order so that due dates can be achieved.

The concept of requirements planning is proven and robust, and so many companies restrict their production planning to just this challenge, without considering capacity. However, to accept orders into a requirements planning system without reference to the capacities available is possible only when a

Figure 9.1. The requirements chain

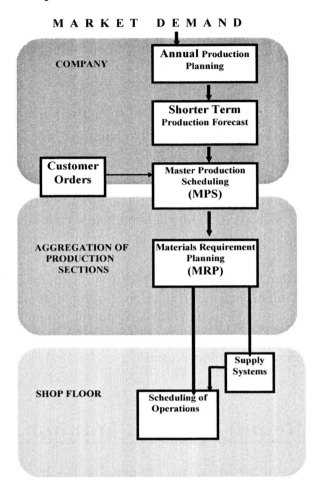

company has a high-capacity cushion. Otherwise, the practice leads to many disruptions to production itself, and a very high chance of regular violations of the production plans.

Demand as the Driver

All companies will focus their productive energies towards satisfying the demand for their products or services. The number one concern is to generate enough sales dollars to cover costs and deliver a return on investment. In a competitive business environment where market share is a key factor of success, the company will commonly be driven towards a sales growth strategy as a means of satisfying the business objectives. A problem then often exists because the effective generation of sales runs ahead of the organisation's ability to satisfy demand on the criteria set by customers and a vigorous marketing department. The problem, however, does not lie in excessive demand. The company will usually have the *physical* resources, *or have access to them*, to be able to satisfy demand. What actually creates the problem is the company's inability to plan and organise its productive resources efficiently enough to handle the market demand pressure put on it. The position of the production planner then, is to accept the level of demand, and to focus the attention on developing a system that has the ability to effectively balance the company's capacity with the demand.

MTS vs. MTO

In consideration of many demand, product, and resource characteristics, a company may decide to base its production strategy on make-to-order or make-to-stock. The most important considerations in the decision relate to the benefits and drawbacks as they affect financial factors and customer service.

The **make-to-stock** strategy provides better supply to customers, but the company must bear the costs involved in carrying finished-goods inventory. Because of the risk of inventory carrying costs, make-to-stock is more suitable for products of reliable demand, and where there is certainty of rapid turn-over of stock. In this case, forecasts can be produced with acceptable accuracy, and the certainty of demand allows longer production runs and better capacity utilisation. Production is carried out ahead of demand, and so the make-to-stock situation depends on forecasts of future demand.

The **make-to-order** strategy may be used when the risk of high inventory carrying costs outweighs the benefits of short lead times on customer orders. For this reason, it is often used for products of long cycle manufacturing and high manufactured cost such as steel, or for products which have irregular demand patterns such as infrequent export orders. With irregular demand, forecasting provides very unreliable short-term production guidance. The requirements planning for make-to-order is based only on actual customer orders, and involves no inventory of finished goods. Market demand is dealt with as it arises, and the planning system does not rely on forecasting to establish the level of demand.

Forecasting for MTS

Forecasting attempts to answer the question, "What can we sell?" The process of planning always takes place before the actual event. To provide the planner with the data on which to base the beginning of the process, a forecast needs to be prepared of what the demand will be for future periods. The marketing department is the common source of the forecast, and it is important that the methods of forecasting are developed concurrently between marketing and the production planning sections so that all assumptions and other criteria for the forecasting technique are agreed between the sections that will use the forecasts. It is not the intention to explain the detail of forecasting techniques in this text, however, the principle methods are time series methods, causal methods, and judgmental models.

The second issue with forecasting is "accuracy." A lack of forecast accuracy, in combination with a lack of correct structure in the planning system will create large "overs" or "unders" in the production quantities for each planning period. This mismatch can get increasingly out of phase until a crisis of some kind (commonly cash flow or backorders) forces the system to return to a restart position from where the cycle repeats. The accuracy of forecasts deteriorates rapidly as the forecasts range into longer term futures. It is therefore critical that the production planner is aware of the forecast accuracy. This is normally expressed as plus or minus ($\pm$) a certain range around the forecast figure. Once the accuracy of the forecast is determined in this way, the production planner can cover the element of uncertainty by planning for safety stock.

Horizontal and Vertical Integration in the System

The balance between requirements and capacity is carried out at each and every level within the planning structure. The sequence is that the requirements are estimated first, and then the available capacity modifies the requirements plan down to a realistic picture of what can be made (see Figure 9.2).

At the same time, each side of the balance has a chain of activities (the requirements chain and the capacity chain) that link from the top, company level through to the shop level planning at the bottom of the structure.

Figure 9.2. Horizontal and vertical integration

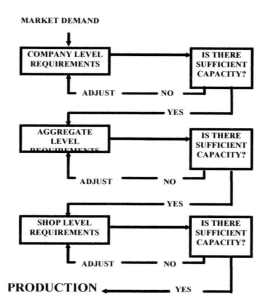

The requirements chain deals with two types of demand - independent and dependent. Independent demand is the demand from the market and typically relates to products or product families. *Dependent* demand depends on the independent demand. A product may be complex in its structure and that structure is defined by the BOM. The BOM will describe the structure in terms of assemblies, sub assemblies, parts and materials that go to make up the end product. It is necessary to calculate how many of each of these components the company has to make or buy, and the amount is defined by the level of independent demand. So in the requirements chain, independent demand changes at some stage into dependent demand. At this point the technique for managing the requirements changes also.

While the demand can be described as independent, the method of management is through forecasting and inventory management. Batching, based on a lot sizing rule will produce cycle stock volumes that form the basis of production planning at lower levels. At the change to dependent demand the management system changes to material requirements planning (MRP).

The capacity plan has no changes in its management system throughout the levels. The process is simply checking the requirements for capacity against the amounts available. The process is universal at all levels. The system must have a method of balancing demand with capacity at every level. If the system is left as just a materials requirement process, the load swings that are part of the natural variation in most production environments will result in failure to produce to plan, long lead times, and poor customer satisfaction, notwithstanding an accompanying poor capacity utilisation. There is then, not a trade-off between customer satisfaction and capacity utilisation, but a lack of either.

MRP

MRP is not a proprietary piece of computer software (although some software is based on MRP). MRP is a time-phased requirements calculator: It is a practical planning framework for calculating the latest possible start dates for dependent demand production items. Doing this calculation is one of the necessary steps in any production planning system. Alone, MRP does not constitute a full planning system because it needs to be integrated with a capacity requirements planning (CRP) function, before the system has full integrity.

We do not see MRP and the JIT philosophy as being in conflict. In fact, MRP with its "latest start date" characteristic, and blended with appropriate capacity balancing in an integrated planning system, provides an effective and workable JIT platform.

In its role as a time-based requirements calculator, MRP is an inherent part of the production planning system as it translates company-level product demand down to shop-level component demand. It therefore has no substitute in any procedure of technology or management, and must be done, either manually, or with the aid of a spreadsheet calculator, or with specialised software.

Because MRP gives the time-phased requirements, it can be considered a production plan, but two points must be noted:

1. The time phasing of MRP gives the latest possible start dates to avoid violation of due delivery dates — there is no forward flexibility. At the same time, there may be earlier start dates that are more efficient, but MRP does not show this information.

2. There is no reference to available capacity in the MRP calculation. Therefore, it is possible for MRP to overload the capacity of the planning

periods which will in turn lead to a series of violations to the plans from the bottom (at production) to the top (product level planning). If, for example, we consider the production of a chair, MRP will take all the chair component lead times into account, and then issue timed work orders for the parts, working backward from the due date. With no reference to capacity, or to the other jobs allocated to the same production time period, it is very likely that an overload may be created, and that some parts will not be made on time (the MRP latest possible start time is violated). Such a delay in component production will hold up final production of the chair, and delivery dates will not be met.

The essential point is that there is no conflict between materials planning and capacity planning. Rather, an effective planning system needs both, and it needs both at every level in the planning system.

In more sophisticated software systems, the basic MRP system can be enhanced to provide solutions to the balance and integration problem in the following ways:

Closed loop MRP provides an expanded information system in software applications that includes the updated delivery dates quoted by upstream production operations and external suppliers. This enables more accurate planning and control by showing if the initial MRP schedules can be performed.

Enterprise Resource Planning (ERP software) takes enhancement another step forward by using the information from closed loop MRP to coordinate the financial budgeting of purchasing, labour, and plant expenditure with the production planning process. ERP allows information integration across various functional areas of the company, and therefore supports the achievement of overall company plans.

Capacity Requirements Planning (CRP) can further augment the basic MRP system by providing a capacity requirements plan that helps planners to avoid underutilisation or overloading of capacity. After the MRP is run, the CRP module can provide a load profile for each work centre. In cases of an imbalance between required and available capacity, the master production schedule is modified, and this in turn creates a revised MRP.

Lot-sizing problems are created by the MRP dependent demand structure that requires specific quantities at every level of the product structure. Economic lot-sizing rules that create minimum batch quantities, especially at higher levels in the structure, can completely upset the balance of component production in multilevel product structures. One method for dealing with this is "lot-for-lot" ordering, whereby orders are released for each period's net requirements as required, rather than being batched.

The period order quantity (POQ) is a variation on the EOQ calculation[1] that divides the EOQ result by the average demand per period to arrive at the number of *periods* (rounded up to the nearest integer) that should be grouped.

MRP takes the information from the MPS and translates that information into a set of time phased releases of work orders to the shop floor production units or outside suppliers. To function well, it depends on an accurate and reliable information system that includes a comprehensive bill of materials and inventory status information for every component in the product structure. In more complex situations, the investment in MRP software must be backed by management commitment to the system, and training for all staff who are users or customers of the system.

The Definition of Capacity

Capacity needs to be identified in many different forms: also for different production areas and for different times. The planner needs to know the upper limits on available capacity at all levels of planning, whether it be at a long-range 3-year plan for the company as a whole, or whether it is the capacity required to complete tomorrow's production.

As the planner works on at least three levels of planning (long-term company planning, medium-term aggregate planning and short-term scheduling planning), capacities also need to be calculated on at least three levels. Within each level the planner is concerned with periods of time: not only the horizon that each level looks to, but also the working blocks or periods of time that lead to the horizon.

The capacity object could be the company as a whole, a division, a shop, a line or machine, or even an individual worker, depending on what level the planner is working. Also, the planner is working with various types of capacity and must use the type that is appropriate to the planning situation. Typically in a production entity, the planner is dealing with machine capacity, but at various planning levels, the planner will also be concerned with the human resource (including knowledge and skills), resources of capital, available space, and, of course, time itself.

Capacity can have a variety of definitions also. The planning system designer therefore needs to set a clear understanding of what definition of capacity is being used: not only for balancing purposes, but also for reporting and controlling purposes. There are three different definitions of capacity that the planner can use:

1. **Design capacity** is the maximum output that the unit has been designed to produce in ideal conditions with no restrictions or interruptions.

2. **Effective capacity** is the maximum possible output given a particular production environment and its accompanying impediments to productivity. These commonly include changeover and set-up requirements, scheduling complexity, the time required for machine maintenance, and other limitations on machine speed, such as when the speed has a negative effect on quality.

3. **Demonstrated capacity** is the rate of output that is regularly produced by a production unit. The demonstrated capacity reflects the "real life" of production environments. It includes all of the undesirable and unplanned interruptions to production such as machine breakdowns, operator variation, scrap, and organisation and planning inefficiencies.

The different definitions give rise to two production ratios that are useful in measuring both production efficiency and capacity utilisation rates.

Efficiency can be measured by comparing what the production unit *could* produce relative to what it *does* produce.

Efficiency = $\dfrac{\text{Demonstrated capacity}}{\text{Effective capacity}}$

Utilisation is measured by comparing the actual output to what the unit is capable of producing in perfect conditions with no interruptions. This gives a measurement of how much of the available capacity is getting used in the normal operation of the unit.

Utilisation = $\dfrac{\text{Demonstrated capacity}}{\text{Design capacity}}$

The world class manufacturing benchmark for utilisation is approximately 80%, but many New Zealand and Australian companies are running at capacity utilisation rates as low as 40% due to a combination of overinvestment in capital plant, small domestic markets, and the social characteristics of the employment environment. The extent to which the actual or demonstrated capacity is less than the design capacity is termed a "capacity cushion." The capacity cushion enables a company to have some flexibility in its ability to respond to demand fluctuations, but the greater the cushion, the less is the productivity from the assets. While it may make the production planner's job more comfortable to enjoy high capacity cushions, the result is a serious erosion of financial return on investment.

The "design" capacity is not useful for planning purposes because it is not an achievable capacity in the real production environment. The ideal capacity definition to work with is the "effective" capacity because it represents an achievable and efficient use of capacity.

However, effective capacity is always an elusive number to capture, as opposed to the others. The design capacity is an engineering calculation with known factors, and the demonstrated is just that: the capacity that is constantly in evidence. Effective capacity lies somewhere in between and is an important number for the planner to know because it represents a more efficient use of

Figure 9.3. Design capacity, effective capacity, and demonstrated capacity

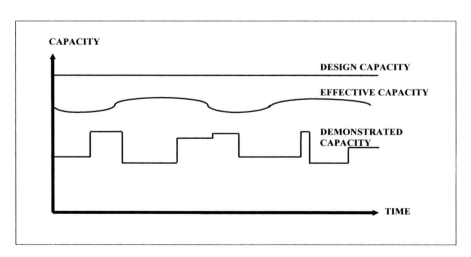

capacity than the demonstrated capacity. It is the best capacity that the plant is capable of actually delivering, given a certain set of product mix characteristics. Figure 9.3 represents the different levels of capacity that are described by design capacity, demonstrated capacity, and effective capacity, and also the nature of their variability.

Left to the natural course of events, the effective capacity will remain concealed. Like the motivational truism, "We will never know what we can achieve unless we try," the planner must push the planning system to its limits to discover the upper range of possible capacities. The planner can experiment by deliberately overcommitting capacities with production quantities that include surpluses of product. If the overall production quantities keep rising while applying this strategy, then the effective capacity has not been reached, and over-commitment of capacity continues. Once quantities plateau is reached and cannot be encouraged upward any further, the surpluses will remain not produced. At this point, the planner has an approximation of effective capacity that is good enough to work with in the planning system.

Methods of Handling a Mismatch of Demand and Capacity

When faced with significant differences between the amount of demanded and the amount of capacity, the production planner has a simple choice: change the demand and/or change the capacity.

Changing demand. The company will face one of three market demand situations relative to its capacity:

1. The demand is constantly above the capacity,
2. The demand is constantly below the capacity, or
3. The demand varies *around* the capacity — sometimes above, sometimes below.

When it is constantly above the company's capacity (the rare case of "infinite" demand), the company can arbitrarily set a level of demand that is comfortable for it to handle. The company is thus able to work with a minimum amount of variation, and has a good chance of producing good capacity utilisation rates and financial returns. The company is also able to manage growth in a controlled way and build capacity as it has the ability to do so, in a financially prudent manner.

If the demand is constantly below the company's capacity, and marketing forecasts show no indication of improvement, then the company must make a decision to reduce the surplus by selling off plant and/or reducing staff levels. Alternatively, the company might knowingly carry the surplus for some future or strategic reason. The cost of such a decision must be known. The opportunity cost can be calculated in unused capacity hours at the normal charge-out rate, and the implications on cash flow should also be considered.

The third situation is the more common of the three, and involves dealing with the dynamic nature of demand in some kind of controlled or controlling manner as follows:

- First, the company may be able to modify the demand using pricing and promotional strategies to either lift or dampen demand as suits the occasion.

- Second, the company can maintain a steady capacity output, and deliberately accumulate inventory during periods when capacity is underloaded, and then feed it out in periods when the capacity is overloaded. The company must monitor the inventory situation carefully because the variation in demand is random and unknown. The company makes stock in the *expectation* that future higher demand will draw that stock down again. If the expectation is unrealised, the company will have a surplus of expensive and wasteful inventory.

- In a third option, the company may follow seasonal patterns, ramping its production up in the high season, and dropping it back down in the lower season. In this case, the company works with known variations in the market demand. Previous years of trading may have revealed a routine pattern of demand that moves through predictable cycles.

- Finally, the company may accept low customer satisfaction by using a backorders strategy to postpone demand to some future point.

Changing Capacity

Capacity can be changed by the decisions made at each level in the organisation.

- At the company level, senior management may make capital investment and staffing decisions that can increase or decrease the company's capacity in the longer term.

- At the aggregate level, the production controller can use factors of flexibility in the capacity environment to make short term changes. These factors of flexibility include moving staff to points of capacity overload, working overtime hours, and subcontracting work to allied producers.

- Finally, at the shop floor level, the production unit operators can work within a flexible range of capacity utilisation, coasting during quiet periods, and working the unit to its maximum rate by using more labour or overtime, when under pressure for output.

Flexibility of Capacity Timing

In production planning systems, various loads on the capacity can also be shifted within a flexible range of dates that will not violate the due date criteria of an order. This concept is similar to what happens in the critical path method of project planning. Once the duration of the project has been set by the critical stages, each of the other various stages of the project are labelled with "earliest start and finish dates" and "latest start and finish dates." This provides the project planner with a useful range of flexibility in the timing of the non-critical stages.

At one end of the range, the requirements planning, in the form of forecasting, and the MRP system provide the *latest* possible start dates for each planning item at each level in the system. Lead times for all dependent items are stacked back from the due date. The MRP system, with known lead times for each part and subassembly, gives the dates at which each work order must be issued to the production units to enable on-time delivery to be achieved.

At the other end the process of capacity planning enables the planner to discover the earlier possible start dates for the production of planning items. The capacity balancing process enables the planner to analyse the capacity situation period by period, and to identify times of underloading. Future orders can then be shifted into earlier time slots to maximise capacity utilisation, and to relieve pressure on overloaded planning periods.

Using time fences for each production unit, the planner can thus move production within the flexibility given by the earliest and latest start dates that are provide by the two systems. This requires no special or additional planning procedures, but occurs as a natural "by-product" of the system itself.

Company Policy on Profit, Capacity Utilisation, and Customer Satisfaction

A well-designed production planning system may have the power to influence management decisions in many areas of the company regarding investment in people and plant. However, for the most part, the planner inherits established structural and infrastructural situations that have evolved from previous management decisions. It is important therefore, to the design of the planning process that clear objectives are set specifically for the planning system. The planning system cannot make strategic decisions that prioritise the inevitable trade-off that occurs between maximising the three key areas of profit, capacity utilisation, and customer satisfaction. The objectives for the planning system must reflect the goals of the company, but in the end, people make situational decisions that prioritise the issues in trade-off cases. Nevertheless, the planning system must be designed to suit and support the policy of the company.

Decisions to maximise short-term profits by reducing staff numbers, for example, may negatively affect long-term profitability because of a loss of service level to customers, and a downstream reduction in demand and sales revenues. Maximising shorter-term profits may also mean lower investments in plant and inventory. Production planning is affected by all of these decisions because they have dramatic influences on capacity resources and the ability to match current demand.

If short-term customer satisfaction is given priority, then the production environment will be highly variable. Specific customer orders may be expedited with associated disruption to the planned schedules, non-standard items may be accepted as orders with resulting high and erratic consumption of capacity, or the product range may be allowed to grow to a size that creates excessive pressure on the production capacities through the multitude of changeovers and setups.

Maximising capacity utilisation means making production decisions that suit production efficiency rather than suiting customers. If the priority is to maximise capacity utilisation, then the planning rule is to have large buffers of work-in-progress inventory so that machines never run out of feedstock. It will also mean a favouring of a make-to-stock policy, with associated planning systems, over make-to-order because the machines will be kept running even without immediate orders for the product. Further to these points, if capacity utilisation is given priority, then the lot sizes of production runs will be very large, and changeovers and setups will be kept to a minimum.

The Need to Balance Demand, Materials, and Capacity

The planning process is about balance and integration as much as it is about control and direction. The planning process must attempt to balance the levels of capacity to meet the demand period by period. At the same time, materials must be moved through the production processes, many of them sequentially, so that each production capacity can be utilised to an optimum level. There is also a need to balance the demand, materials, and capacity at different phases in the planning environment, ranging form the broad, company wide perspective, down to the detailed balancing of a single machine capacity to the hourly work required from it.

While the procedure noted previously addressed the issue of materials requirements, an assessment of the capacity requirements is also necessary at each level. To provide assurance of planned outcomes, demand, materials, and capacity characteristics must be balanced at each level. To ensure continuity of production assurance within each planning level, the balancing must also be carried out for each period of time that is designed into the level.

A company could face the production task with no planning system at all. Incoming orders could just be passed to the production section who would work on them in some order that they might arbitrarily decide on. Putting aside for a moment the fact that customers could not be given any assured delivery dates, the production section would then be dealing with the random arrival of customer orders, and inheriting that variation into the production system. Random changeovers and setups would consume large amounts of productive time, and the effective capacity would be dramatically reduced by the continuous variation and disruption to the production environment. One of the basic tasks of a planning system then, is to create an environment of stability and certainty so that controlled delivery dates can be assured, and so that capacity utilisation can be maximised by practices of aggregation and batching.

The Three-Level View of Systems Design

Standard introductions to production planning provide an outline of how the materials requirements are developed by moving through a series of levels of detail. The levels start from broad forecasts of product group demand, and progress into a master production schedule that specifies in general terms what the production intentions are for a given period. From there, the materials requirement planning calculates specific requirements, and the final stage is a scheduling of work at work centres in the production shops. This progression can be subdivided into at least three levels, one long term, one medium and one short. The benefits of a minimum of three levels is that while the long-term level can deal with general long term production direction, and the short term deals with work assignment and scheduling, the medium term provides a "zone of organisation" that bridges the other two extremes. Careful planning in this zone of organisation creates the stability that is required at the work centre level.

Capacity and Cycle Times

The capacity levels achieved at the shop floor obviously have a large impact on cycle times. If the capacity is less than the planning system allows for, the queue times will rise and the cycle times will lengthen. There is, therefore, an interrelationship between the demonstrated capacity, the capacity balancing and control system, and the cycle times. This interrelationship dramatically affects the efficiency of the whole production system in a more far reaching manner than the technical efficiency of the machinery.

Cycle times also have a strong relationship with planning time horizons and the choice of controllable blocks of time within that horizon (planning periods). The choice of planning period duration in association with cycle times, has a significant effect on the efficiency and utilisation aspects of capacity.

Capacity Planning
at the Company Level

The previous section outlined the nature and characteristics of capacity. The concept of capacity must now be integrated into the overall planning system that extends through the levels and creates a balance at each level. Figure 9.4 outlines the primary functions and balances of an integrated planning and control system. The set of activities at the company level, and the nature of the balances are as follows.

Overall demand forecasts and production planning. Forecasts of demand for future periods are used for company level planning in the longer term — typically from one to several years ahead. The forecasts are expressed in total expected output of product, and serve as the long-term focus for the company's activities.

Resource planning. The required long-term capacity requirements are balanced with the long term expectations of demand. Long-term decisions on investments in plant, buildings, and people are made at this stage.

The shorter-term production forecast. After the annual position is balanced, the annual plan is converted into shorter blocks of time such as 1, 2, or 3 months, so that a general idea of the production goals is arrived at in workable pieces of time. The shorter-term forecast is then balanced with the rough-cut aggregate capacity planning at the aggregate level before producing the master production schedule.

The rough-cut aggregate capacity plan. The overall long-term requirements are converted into shorter periods after being checked through a period by period balancing exercise. This is to ensure that the required capacities exist to produce at the levels and times of the plan. The intended production in product groups is converted to direct labour hours of production for each period. The labour hours per period are then allocated to work centres by historic or estimated ratios, or by more specific methods such as capacity bills or resource profiles for each product type. Because the balancing at this level is still working in the long term, imbalances can be corrected by adjusting capacity decisions, or by altering the shorter-term production forecast.

The master production schedule (MPS). The MPS is developed as a more specific outline of what product groups will be produced in each time period of the long-range production plan. This outline is produced after the balance has

Figure 9.4. An integrated model: balance of demand, materials, and capacity on three levels

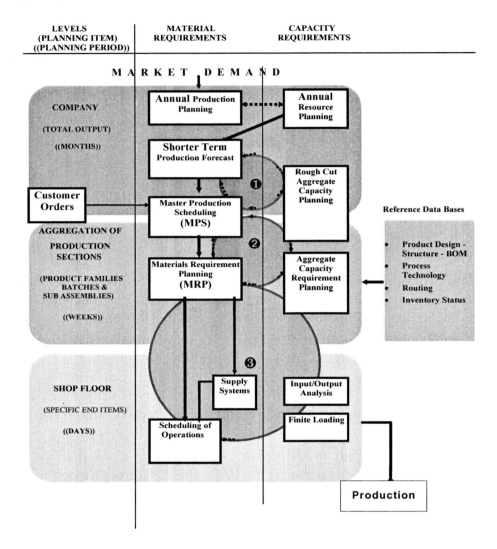

been established between the shorter-term forecast at the company level, and the aggregate capacity planning at the aggregate level. Once produced, the MPS sits outside of the central planning system as a document to be used by all sections of the company as a guide to anticipated production. The MPS is also used by production planning as a feed-in to the MRP system carried out at the aggregate level. The MPS, rough-cut aggregate capacity planning, and the shorter-term production forecast exist in an ongoing iterative cycle ❸ that continuously moderates and balances long range production intentions with aggregate capacity.

Capacity Planning at the Aggregate Level

At the aggregate level, the timing becomes more precise, and the planning issues are more detailed. The planning horizon is subdivided into smaller planning periods such as months or weeks, and actual orders and current inventory levels become part of the calculations. A bill of materials for each product is used to specify the exact component requirements for each product, and a set of time phased requirement plans are developed.

Material Requirements Planning (MRP)

In its basic form, MRP is a requirements calculator for dependent-demand items. It takes the end product quantities from the MPS and breaks them down into their component parts using the information from a bill of materials for each product. The demand for the components is, therefore, a dependent demand in that it is dependent on the demand for the end item. MRP systems not only disaggregate the end item demand into component demand, they also work with lead times to specify when each component will be needed. To work effectively, the MRP method must have feedback of actual performance data. In computerised versions, the MRP is extended to include supplier delivery information, closed loop feedback to the MPS on actual production, and a facility for *capacity requirements*. The most advanced of these systems, MRP II, includes information on the financial resources of the company, and enables complete modelling and simulation of the company's production environment.

Capacity Requirements Planning (CRP)

CRP is the process of balancing detailed material requirements planning with detailed capacity requirements. It therefore includes the time-phased elements of MRP, and takes into account all of the characteristics of the planned order releases including batch sizes, routings, lead times, and current inventory status. CRP also includes an estimate of the yield rate before feeding back into the MRP and MPS parts of the system. In this way, not only is capacity balanced with material requirements within each planning period at the aggregate level, but also the availability of capacity is allowed to feedback into the previous level and moderate the MPS. This then becomes a circular and repetitive relationship between the MPS, MRP, and CRP that runs through many iterations in the course of the planning horizon at the aggregate level. Work orders to the shop floor level are not released until the CRP constraints are satisfied.

The MPS, MRP, and CRP are linked in a second iterative circle that also works on a continuous basis to refer to the capacities, and modify both the MPS and the MRP. The detailed nature of this capacity planning becomes complex in reality because of the many factors and variations that complicate any production environment, such as sequential operations that use different production methods, different production units, and different critical resources. The problem of dealing with this complexity was addressed earlier.

Capacity Planning at the Shop Level

In Figure 9.4 the MRP, scheduling, loading, and input/output analysis are linked in the third iterative circle that keeps the MRP in balance with the shop floor capacities.

The MRP process generates a series of work order releases as seen in the previous example. Produced at the same time are purchase orders for materials that will be sourced from external suppliers. The purchasing element is under the control of a purchasing department, and after generating purchase orders from the MRP, the planner will expect the supplies to arrive in the quantities and at the times specified. The production plans for the shop floor must, however, be balanced with the capacities at each work centre.

Finite Loading and Infinite Loading

Finite loading tightly loads all jobs at all work centres for the planning periods *ahead*, giving specific start and finish times for each operation at each work centre. Full consideration is given to the capacity limit of the operation, and to other jobs already in place. The finite loading can forward-load each future period *vertically* or *horizontally*. Vertical loading fills each period (such as a day) from beginning to end, filling up the available future capacity day by day with jobs, and letting this process set the completion dates. It never schedules more work than the set capacity for each period.

Alternatively, it can load jobs horizontally through sequential operations so that capacity is reserved, at specific times at each machine or operation, for the full set of processes that will complete a job. This means that queuing will be reduced to a minimum, but there is a trade-off in capacity utilisation. Unused machine time may result from horizontal loading because spaces occur at machines that are waiting for a booked job to arrive. The machine operator does not have the discretion to start any other job in the idle space because this will block the progress of the booked job when it does arrive, and therefore all downstream operations will be disrupted.

Infinite loading works differently and disregards capacity, initially. All orders are scheduled backward from due dates with resulting overloads from an

Figure 9.5. Comparison of infinite loading and finite loading

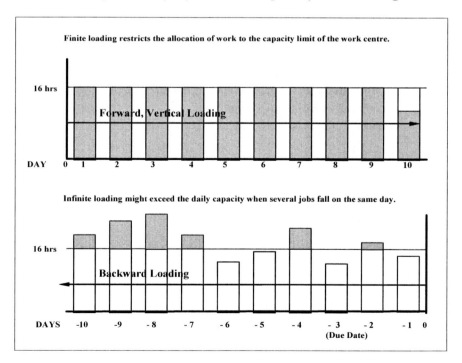

accumulation of orders in some periods, and underloads in others. After infinite loading, the planner must make decisions to add capacity or to shift loadings back or forward. Shifting orders may balance the capacity but it will also disrupt the job sequence, and produce extra lead times, and this in turn leads to extra WIP inventories.

Figure 9.5 shows a work centre profile over 2 weeks, where the daily maximum capacity is 16 hours per day. As the detailed scheduling prioritises the work, each day is loaded. In the top part of the figure, the loading is limited by a finite loading maximum of 16 hours per day and the load is spread forward over the 10 days.

In the bottom part of the figure, the loading is unrestricted, and several days are overcommitted. The planner then makes decisions to add capacity or to shift work in the overloaded periods to either later or earlier periods. The alternatives should be costed, and the lowest cost/least disruption solution selected.

Capacity Analysis

Capacity analysis is a very important function because it allows examination of the relationship between demonstrated capacity and effective capacity. The planner will load the production system with a quantity of work based on an idea of the *effective* capacity level. Observing how the production system then handles that workload provides a view of the *demonstrated* capacity. Earlier in this chapter, we referred to capacity utilisation as being the ratio of actual output to design capacity. In all parts of the balancing problem, the planner works with a given expectation of a capacity utilisation rate to establish what

Figure 9.6. The input/ output control report

Week		1	2	3	4	5
Planned Input		250	250	250	300	250
Actual Input		250	255	255	290	245
Cumulative Deviation			+5	+10	0	-5
Planned Output		250	250	250	300	250
Actual Output		245	245	260	280	260
Cumulative Deviation		-5	-10	0	-20	-10
Actual Input /Actual Output		-5	-10	+5	-10	+15
Actual Backlog	20	25	35	30	40	25

the dependable capacity is at each work centre. As a check on this expectation, an analysis of performance is done using *Input/Output Control*.

Figure 9.6 shows an Input/Output Report that monitors the actual output in hours of work from a work centre, against the expected output set by the planner. Also monitored by the report is the backlog of work hours that build up as a result of less than expected outputs, or from the allocation of work orders beyond the effective capacity of the centre. The backlog aspect is particularly important because the backlog trend is an indicator of the queue size that is waiting in front of a work centre. Excessive queues mean either that the planner is overestimating the capacity of the work centre, or that the work centre is underperforming.

The growth of queue size has negative effects. Excessive queue times mean excessive lead times, and inevitably, excessive WIP inventory. For these reasons, the size of queues must be controlled. The backlog of work hours can be used as a trigger to moderate (or accelerate) the release of work orders from the MRP function in aggregate planning, and thus control the size of the queues. In this example, the backlog has moved from an opening position of 20 hours to a closing position of 25 hours, and may be an indication that work orders should be slowed to this particular work centre. We can also see that something went wrong in week 4. Either the work centre had a technical problem that restricted its capacity in some way, or the planner is working with an unrealistic model of the centre's capacity.

The Connection Between Inventory and Capacity Control

The input/output control also enables the production planner to monitor WIP inventory levels. To achieve good performance in both capacity utilisation and customer satisfaction requires some level of inventory. Inventory held in the system represents stored capacity. Capacity planning and control, therefore, includes a certain amount of inventory in the system, and uses this inventory as a buffer against demand and yield variations.

The idea of this inventory buffer as a reservoir of stored capacity resembles the hydro-electric power generation system. A hydro-lake of stored energy is channelled through the turbines of a hydroelectric power station in a controlled manner (see Figure 9.7). Streams feed water into the lake in a flow that depends on random patterns of rainfall in the same way that orders arrive at production

Figure 9.7. The lake of capacity reserve

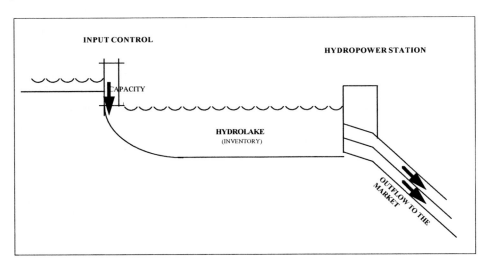

planning in a random pattern. There is a control at the inflow so that water can be diverted when there is too much volume arriving at once. In production planning, this control point is the capacity balancing procedures at the MPS and MRP. At the MPS there is a balance of the level of capacity relative to the demand, and at the MRP, there is control of the release of work orders into the preproduction queues.

The water then is held in a reserve of energy that keeps the turbines working at the desired and controlled rates. In the same way WIP, inventory levels provide a reserve of capacity that can be processed at a controlled rate to maintain a steady flow of capacity output to the market. If the level of inventory drops, more capacity may be added and more work orders released at the MRP "tap." If the inventory levels rise then the "tap" is closed to restrict the input.

The power station turbines equate to the machines and labour in the manufacturing situation.

The hydropower station analogy illustrates how the control of inputs, the size of the inventory reserve, and the rate of throughput, all work in concert to counter the problems caused by irregular demand and irregular yield rates. In this way, a steady and reliable supply to the market is maintained at optimal capacity utilisation.

Endnote

[1]

$$EOQ = \sqrt{2DC_o/C_h}$$

D = Demand per period

C_o = Cost of ordering per period

C_h = Cost of holding per period

Chapter X

Case Solutions

The production planning system described earlier carried specific features of production planning at EA Cakes Ltd. Standard software, on the other hand, by definition, comprises programmes developed for an anonymous market. The question is: Can a standard software system like SAP give adequate computer support to an individually designed business management system?

A team from IT specialists and production planning personnel was formed for designing computer support for the new production planning system business processes.

Thinking in terms of business processes helps managers to look at their organisation from the customer's perspective. Usually a business process involves several functional areas and functions within those areas. Thus, a business process is cross-functional. Definitely, this is the case of the production planning at EA Cakes Ltd.

The aggregate capacity planning uses sales budget, stock feedback, and available capacity (manpower and machinery). The master scheduling involves forecasting and feedback on stocks. The shop floor scheduling and control absorbs a huge variety of activities from other functional areas such as material control, human resource management, inventory management, and so on.

Quite to the contrary, standard software was initially developed only for certain functions that could easily be standardised. Modern standard software, such as SAP, is said to be object oriented or process oriented (see Kirchmer, 2002). However, it is still mostly functional, and the necessary orientation can only be achieved by adjusting the appropriate parameters. Even after the adjustments, the functionality of SAP may not be completely relevant to the business processes of a particular company. Then the implementation team has at least two options (Sawy, 2001):

1. To substitute the business processes of the company for the business processes implemented in SAP, and
2. To create additional special software for providing computer support to production planning.

There was no consensus in the design group. IT specialists were sure that existing SAP software could provide adequate computer support. When the production planning staff got acquainted with the business processes suggested for production planning by SAP, they had doubts that these modules were relevant to their business processes. They were the authors of the new production planning system, and they had a rather firm position that their planning processes were the most efficient for EA Cakes Ltd. No changes would be accepted.

So, the management of EA Cakes Ltd. was presented with the following dilemma:

1. Believing the IT specialists and continuing to implement the existing SAP modules on comparatively low cost, but facing all risks of losses due to planning inefficiency; or
2. Believing the planning staff and ordering high cost computer support in addition to the existing SAP system.

The management invited a consulting company. The consultants suggested to design quickly a rough prototype system (Hoffer & Valasich, 2002), using ARIS (Scheer, 1999). Analysing this system would help the working group to reach a consensus.

Description

The following material details the implementation of SAP's Production Planning module at EA Cakes Ltd. in order to provide computer support to the MTS production planning system.

Similar to most organisations, EA Cakes Ltd. operates on a hierarchical basis. All activities and documents presented here are organised through the Production Planning hierarchy. The hierarchy is organised so that the Aggregate Capacity Planning (ACP) process is at the highest level of aggregation, while, the Shop Floor Scheduling Process is at the lowest level. These levels can be presented using different parameters. Thus, it includes a product hierarchy, time hierarchy, and organisational hierarchy. Each level varies in purpose, time span, and amount of detail (see Figure 10.1).

Figure 10.1. Breakdown of product, time, and production planning system hierarchies at EA Cakes Ltd.

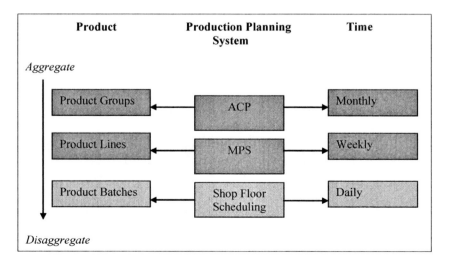

Some Specific Problems

The SAP implementation was intended to solve several implementation problems identified in the process of initial analysis.

Problem:

Currently, in order for the master scheduler to create a master production schedule, there is a need to enter forecast data prepared by the sales department. This can result in data entry errors. EA Cakes Ltd. needs a way to share sales forecast data between the sales department and production automatically (that is, through a computer support system). It must relate its forecasted sales to production capacity and to the time available to make the product, in order to create an accurate MPS.

SAP Solution:

One of the greatest benefits provided by SAP is the integration of data in one centralised database. The data is captured only once and at its source. Once any piece of information has been entered into the system, all authorised personnel are able to access this information from the centralised database. This reduces workload, and most importantly reduces data entry errors.

Problem:

In the current system, the master scheduler has to check the capacity requirements and to change the forecast or production volumes according to available capacity. Then he must agree the changes with the sales department and the production department.

SAP Solution:

The advantage of the SAP system is that the capacity is checked automatically at both the MPS and shop floor levels. This can be done because all capacity data has been entered into the SAP's centralised database in the initial configuration phase of SAP.

Problem:

Presently at EA Cakes Ltd., scheduling is only done on finished items. It is desirable to schedule some components production as well.

SAP Solution:

In SAP sub-modules "routing processing" and "determine WIP" there are functions that enable the scheduling of work-in-process items such as pie fillings.

Problem:

It is necessary to provide a reliable reconciliation method for checking inventory availability.

SAP Solution:

In SAP, availability is automatically checked, and the system can be configured to increase planned production if a shortfall is expected.

Problem:

One of the biggest problems for EA Cakes Ltd. is low capacity utilisation.

SAP Solution:

SAP enables better capacity utilisation because it provides the ability to evaluate and simulate several production plans with different parameters. The master scheduler then can then compare the plans in terms of profitability and costs involved, and select the most satisfying option.

Problem:

The master scheduler sometimes has to schedule overtime production, paying for overtime labour, which results in higher production costs for products. This can also cause shortages or stock-out of some materials for production, further increasing the cost of production.

Managers are especially frustrated when an instant need for overtime follows a period of low demand when inventory could have been built up; for example, in anticipation of an increase in sales following production promotions by marketing.

SAP Solution

SAP offers a systematic approach to production planning:

- Work from a sales forecast to create an "aggregate" production plan for all products;

- Break down the aggregate plan into a more specific production plan for individual products and limited time periods; and
- Use the production plan for detailed scheduling.

Technical Material

Aggregate Capacity Planning

Capacity is the ability to perform a particular task. In SAP, capacities define the available supply of labour and machines within a certain period of time. Several capacities split into different capacity types can be assigned to a production line. Within SAP, the capacity planning process is much more integrated with the other processes, and is therefore much more efficient. By implementing capacity checking procedures at every level, the capacity utilisation is optimised. As a result, EA Cakes Ltd. will not suffer from carrying high capacity cushions in both labour and equipment, resulting in efficient utilisation. Figure 10.2 shows the flow of information that makes up the ACP procedure at EA Cakes Ltd.

ACP at EA Cakes Ltd. looks at the medium-term (monthly) goals and activities of production. Under normal circumstances, the ACP is concerned with the inventory levels of product groups. The planning starts from defining an optimum production strategy by the use of a combination of the "level" and

Figure 10.2. The flow of information leading to the ACP procedure

"chase" strategies. This is because the sole use of the "level" or "chase" strategies does not provide a sufficient capacity plan. The optimum "mixed" strategy combines stock accumulation and overtime.

ACP Business Scenarios

Select Planning Object

- The ACP is produced by comparing the sales budget against the agreed target capacity.
- Under SAP, it is possible to create the ACP automatically (from the sales budget) or manually (entered by the master scheduler). This gives the master scheduler the ability to alter the planning object if required.
- The first step is to select the planning object. The planning object can be a planning hierarchy with various characteristics. For example, at EA Cakes Ltd. the product groups can be divided into product lines (Pies, Cakes, and Puddings, etc.).

Specify Production Planning Version

- Once the planning object has been selected, a production planning version needs to be selected.
- In SAP, it is possible to have several planning versions for the same situation and simulate the effects of each of the planning versions by a few easy commands.
- If several planning versions exist, the version first created is automatically set as the active version, and can also be set to inactive. Versions may be used to test various scenarios.
- In EA Cakes Ltd., these planning versions relate to the creation of capacity utilisation.

Selecting an Appropriate ACP Capacity Balancing Method

- Once the production-planning version has been selected, capacity utilisation balancing needs to be undertaken.

- The utilisation is derived by dividing the production plan by the available capacity and expressing it as a utilisation percentage.
- SAP allows two methods of balancing capacity. These are:
  - ➢ Automatic capacity balancing, and
  - ➢ Manual capacity balancing. The reason for this is that it gives the master production scheduler the opportunity to compare the production plan with the capacity situation interactively.

Balance Capacity to Create Aggregate Capacity Plan

- Once the appropriate ACP Capacity Balancing method has been selected, the monthly ACP can be selected.

Master Production Scheduling

The MPS process is triggered by completion of the ACP process in the previous level of the production planning hierarchy. Planned independent requirements are received from ACP. The aggregate plan provides the general range of operations. The MPS specifies exactly what is to be produced and when. Decisions are made while responding to pressures from various functional areas such as the sales, finance (minimise inventory), and manufacturing

Figure 10.3. The information flow of the MPS process

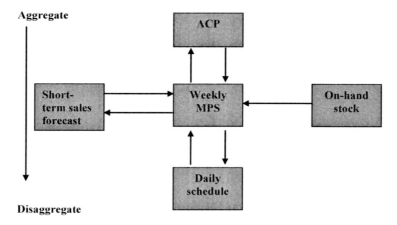

(minimise set-up losses) departments. In master production scheduling, a planning run is produced for all the end items.

Figure 10.3 shows the flow of information related to these three main inputs.

MPS Business Scenarios

Disaggregation of ACP

- The ACP is the basis for subsequent planning levels in production planning.
- The independent items for which capacity requirements were determined in ACP are disaggregated to MPS automatically by SAP.
- When the data is disaggregated from ACP to MPS (from product group to product lines), the material requirements will be generated for the products.
- During the initial configuration of SAP, we must specify a method of disaggregating the results of ACP. SAP will enable the master scheduler to disaggregate the planned data of all the members in a single-level product line. Thus, for EA Cakes Ltd., we have selected the direct transfer of the rough production plan.

Select Product Line

- The inputs for selecting a product line are the disaggregated ACP, rough production plan, and short term sales forecast.
- Upon the initial configuration of SAP, the MTS production planning strategy is set as the default strategy.
- The MPS is to be done on finished items on a weekly basis.
- SAP generates a weekly plan recommending what product lines are to be made every week.
- SAP produces the weekly production plan for the next planning period, which is 5 weeks.
- The weekly production plan is for a specific product line.

Create MPS Using Several Planning Runs

- Once the product line has been selected, SAP calculates the weekly production plan, taking into account the revised short-term sales forecast, the opening stock level, and balances it against the ACP.

- As shown in Figure 10.4, the MPS Process uses the following logic:

  Opening Stock + Production – Sales Forecast = Closing Stock

- The MPS is calculated using several planning runs, and is balanced with the ACP. This can highlight where there are insufficient capacities available to meet the schedule, or insufficient utilisation of capacities that are planned within the schedule.

- The aim is to plan all end items in such a way that cost-intensive resources are used in an optimum way, and production bottlenecks avoided.

Choose Optimum Weekly MPS

- Once the planning runs have been generated, the optimum weekly MPS is selected (for reasons indicated in the previous sub-level).

- The output of the MPS process is the master production schedule, which is a detailed production schedule for the entire product line.

Figure 10.4. MTS production

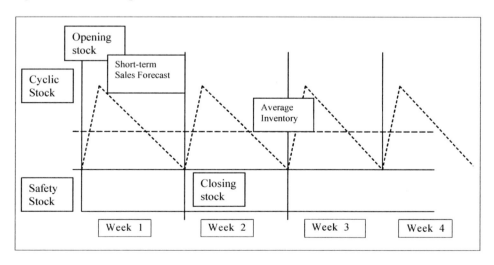

- Other purposes of this level are to keep a desired stock level and to implement the "speed-to-market" principle, in order to react quickly to significant changes in market demand.

- Only the first week of the plan is valid (and frozen). The rest of the plan is necessary to keep the continuity of planning during the month.

This now becomes the input for the shop floor scheduling process.

Shop Floor Scheduling

The shop floor control level at EA Cakes Ltd. looks at the short-term goals and activities of production. Figure 10.5 shows the flow of information with respect to the shop floor scheduling process.

The Shop Floor Scheduling Sub-Levels

- Line scheduling
- Planned order conversion Creation of the production order
- Release of the production order
- Execution of the production order
- Completion and confirmation of the production order

Weekly MPS are received from the upper level in the production planning hierarchy to create the line schedules, with the output being production orders. A production order determines material to be processed, and at which production line. In SAP, disaggregation requires BOM and MRP functionality. The line managers will require the following computer support as part of their production planning process:

- **Fixed schedules:** Predetermined formulae for production of specific products. For example, to make 1000 Type X cakes requires a 0.5-hour set-up time, 8-hour production time, and a 1-hour cleanup time, as well as the appropriate staffing levels. Thus, the total number of hours to create 1000 Type X cakes is 9.5 hours.

- **Shift calendars:** Since Type X cakes require 9.5 hours of production, this is greater than a normal 8-hour shift. So the labour requirements must be calculated to guarantee a smooth production run.

Shop Floor Scheduling Business Scenarios

Line Scheduling

- Once the optimum weekly MPS has been selected, the first step under the shop floor scheduling business scenario is to schedule the production lines.

- The first step in creation of the line schedule is to select a time frame that we can schedule within. For example, let us assume one shift per day consisting of 8 hours. Within this shift we may be able to schedule more than one product (e.g., apricot pies and/or mince pies).

- Once a time frame has been selected, the line manager can select a particular product line from the weekly MPS.

- Having selected the product line, the line manager can now set a batch size. For example, the optimum weekly MPS plan produces a total aggregate number for the production of 1000 apricot pies, the line manager is able to divide this total into minimum batch sizes based upon the maximum mix size (that is, 2 x 500 apricot batches to make the 1000 apricot pies required).

- When the batch size has been set, the line manager checks the fixed schedule against the set batch size to determine if the amount of time in the shift is suitable to run the batch.

- If the amount of time is not suitable, the line manager must reset the batch size. However, if the time is suitable, then the line manager may move on to the next step in the process.

- The line manager is now required to set the labour resources for the shift using the shift calendar. If the line manager sets a labour resource that is not suitable to meet the requirements of the set batch size, the line manager needs to reset the labour resources.

- If the labour resources are suitable, the line manager checks to see if there is any more available time in the shift. If there is, this entire process is repeated until the shift time is full.

Figure 10.5. The information flow of the shop floor scheduling process

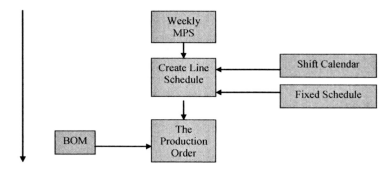

- Once there is no more shift time available, the line manager creates the line schedule for the shift. This process will continue until the line scheduling for the week has been completed.

Planned Order Conversion

- Once the line scheduling has been completed, there is a need to convert the line schedules into planned orders, from which production orders are created. Here a planned order (SAP terminology) is equivalent to a batch.
- For the purposes of automatic conversion of a batch into a production order, the batch requires the following data: required quantity, start and delivery dates of the stock, the material stock keeping number, and the material components.
- When the conversion date is reached, the line schedule is retrieved and the orders are created automatically.

The following steps are specific to SAP (Keller and Teufel, 1998):

- Determining the category of batch conversion. This is a required input for SAP, in order for the system to function properly.
- At this point, the line manager is required to specify a production order type that relates back to the category of batch conversion conducted earlier.
- This leads into the conversion of the batch into a production order.

The Creation of the Production Order

The creation of production orders is the start of activities in production control. It includes the following steps:

- Order information is taken from the database automatically, including due dates, quantities, and routings for the batch.

- Operations data is transferred from the routing of the item to be produced.

- A check is done to ensure that the components of the BOM are actually available. If any component of the BOM is missing, the process stops and must be taken back to the MPS process.

- At this point, the production order status is automatically updated. Once the batch has been converted into the production order, the release of the production order can begin.

Release of the Production Order

- Before production orders can be released for production, a materials availability check must be made to ensure that all the materials needed for production orders are available at the right time and in the right quantity.

- The check is needed to guarantee that the production process is not delayed as a result of missing materials. This would result in an increase in production costs and lead times as a result of the delay.

- If some materials are unavailable, the system will issue an error message and the process will need to be taken back to the MPS process.

- If all the materials are available, then the order is ready to be released.

- Orders can be released using allocated priorities, order status, or dates within the planning horizon.

- The production order is now ready for execution.

Execution of the Production Order

- The execution of the production order is a signal for the production lines to prepare for production.

- At this point, the materials required for production are made available via the materials system; that is, materials are physically issued for the production order.

- The carrying out of the released operation comes next. Once all the operations are carried out, the function of entering the actual data for the production order is triggered.

- This completes the process of execution of the production order, and the production order is to be confirmed.

Completion and Confirmation of the Production Order

- This step serves as a feedback procedure, registering the actual time and cost of production of completed orders.

- This feedback, combined with future planned orders and customer orders, will be used to plan future business processes.

- Various departments such as accounting, personnel management, and plant maintenance, and so forth, may need this completion confirmation data.

The following steps are SAP specific (Keller and Teufel, 1998):

- Once a production order is ready to be confirmed, we need to decide the level at which this confirmation is to be carried out.

- The work process for confirmation needs to be selected; this is done using work process numbers.

- The confirmation data now needs to be entered.

- Completion confirmation data can be split up into the following categories:

  - **Order-related data:** Used to update the order status and statistics.

  - **Labour-related data:** Used to calculate wages and salaries.

  - **Resource-related data:** Refers to the machine times and the amount of time tools were used.

  - **Material data:** Describes the quantity of material used to carry out the production order.

  - Finally, the confirmed production order can now be saved.

Software Specification

The production planning and control (PP) module of the SAP system is used for production planning at EA Cakes Ltd. The PP module deals with the quantity and time-related planning of products to be manufactured, as well as the control of the production process flow. It supports all the quantity and capacity-related steps for planning and control, as well as the corresponding functionality for master data maintenance.

The following sub-modules of the SAP system have been directly used within the redesign of the production planning at EA Cakes Ltd. (See Keller and Teufel, 1998):

- Section 8.17: "Process: MPS — Single-item processing"
- Section 8.31: "Process: Planned order conversion"
- Section 8.32: "Process: Creation of the production order"
- Section 8.34: "Process: Release of the production order"
- Section 8.35: "Process: Execution of the production order"
- Section 8.37: "Process: Completion and confirmation of the production order"

The following submodules of the SAP system have been partly used within the redesign of EA Cakes Ltd. planning system:

- Section 8.15: "Process: Transfer of results to demand management"
- Section 8.16: "Process: Demand management"

Functions within these two sub-modules have been incorporated into the aggregate capacity planning (ACP) solution to disaggregate product groups to product lines.

- Section 8.14: "Process: Routing processing"
- Section 8.40: "Process: Determine WIP"

Functions within these two sub-modules have been incorporated into pie production line scheduling. EA Cakes Ltd. produces pies on two different lines, one of which produces the fillings, and the other makes and bakes the pies. These two sub-modules help to bring the two production processes together.

Finally, the following sub-modules of the SAP system have also been used for the continuous maintenance of the master data file:

- Section 8.13: "Process: Work centre processing"
- Section 8.14: "Process: Routing processing"

A work centre is a physical area within a company. At a work centre, either one operation of an order, several operations of an order, or the whole production order is processed. A routing is a description of the process flow.

Work centres play a central role in production planning. Looking at work centres from a technical point of view, the most important factors are the allocation of work centres to operations in routings and the resulting product costing, lead time scheduling, and capacity planning. Work centres are the main source of data about capacities in production planning.

Work centre processing and routings are used to organise maintenance plans and inspection plans. Events such as new product release, purchase of new machines, and increasing capacity levels of existing production lines will require updating the master data file. Using the functions contained in the above sub-modules can accomplish this.

Solutions Outside SAP

Not all the necessary solutions can be provided by SAP. The functionality of line scheduling in the shop floor scheduling, for example, is not sufficient. In order to provide this solution, the following three options were considered:

1. Hire outside developers to programme a separate system specific for EA Cakes Ltd., which will then have to be integrated into the SAP system.
2. Purchase third-party software that will meet EA Cakes Ltd.'s line scheduling requirements and integrate this solution with the SAP system.

3.   Hire SAP developers to add additional functionality into the programming code under the current SAP system.

Due to the limited financial resources available to EA Cakes Ltd., we recommend option number three. That is, the line scheduling process be directly programmed into the production planning module of SAP.

The advantages and limitations of this choice are as follows:

Advantages:

1.   It is the most cost-effective choice of the three available options;
2.   There will be less integration problems than using third-party software; and
3.   SAP developers will have a greater level of understanding of the SAP system, and thus can embed the functionality with greater confidence.

Limitations:

1.   Because the additional functionaltiy is being "hard-coded" into the SAP system, there is a possibilty of issues arising when updated versions of SAP are released; and
2.   If in the future, EA Cakes Ltd. decide to change their line scheduling process in any way, shape, or form, the SAP developers have to be called in to reprogramme the necessary areas.

Chapter XI

Production Planning Redesign:
Special Topics

Competitive Advantage
from Production Planning

For manufacturing companies, competitive advantage is ultimately measured in terms of financial results, and the key financial result is usually a margin of profit from sales, which then translates into a margin of return on investment.

How then does production planning and control (PPC) have a significant influence on this outcome? It is our contention that efficient production planning is one of the three *crucial* and *vital* driving factors that enables the other functional areas to be effective. Figure 11.1 displays the driving position of PPC in a causal relationship layout.

Efficient *PPC* has a direct and beneficial influence on both *customer satisfaction* and *capacity utilisation*. The first leads to greater sales volume, and the second to lower costs, both of which have a major impact on *profits*.

Figure 11.1. The linkage of production planning and control to profits

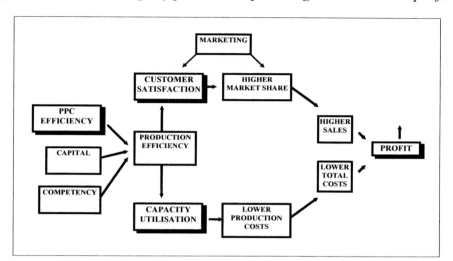

It is the role of production planning to set up a regime of production situations that are achievable, controllable, and best utilise the available capacity. This last point brings us to the unique position of PPC in today's business environment. For many years companies have seen marketing as the main pathway to competitive advantage. However, the potential to gain significant competitive advantage has now been opened up to operations areas through the revolution in information technology. Initial major cost and efficiency gains have been made in inventory management through production philosophies such as just-in-time (JIT).

However, capacity is more expensive than inventory, and it is in this area (capacity management) that companies, especially in New Zealand and Australia, have the largest potential to gain competitive advantage.

The current performance in capacity management is very low, but because most companies are at a relatively equal position, low performance has become an accepted norm. The development of information technology will change this, however, and it is our belief that the next big wave of competitive advantage will come from managing capacity more efficiently. For this to occur, companies need skill-based competencies in production information systems and production-planning systems design.

Capacity Management: A Matter of Balance

The planning system is expected to support company policy by creating stability and control at all levels within the system, and by converting demand factors for product into efficient production outcomes. The planning process, therefore, includes many factors of balance and integration.

It is also helpful to understand what production planning is *not*. It is not about just-in-time production philosophies, nor is it about the engineering task of reducing set-up times. It is not about flexible manufacturing, integrated teams, or the management of quality. Although all of these and various other operational strategies, policies and practices, are part of today's production environment, they are not the concern of the production planner who has the right to expect that all such factors are developed to their optimum by others. In contrast, the production planner starts with what is there, and attempts to represent the real production world in a conceptual model of the production dynamics. The model will not always reflect the exact physical nature of the production flows and movements, but nevertheless, provides the ability to plan and control production so that stability is achieved at the shop floor level, and certainty of regular supply can be offered to customers. It is the production planner's job to find an optimum balance between capacity utilisation rates and customer satisfaction rates (measured in on time delivery of orders). Finally, it is the production planner's job to achieve this optimum balance without the waste of excessive inventory. Despite the fact that the planning system represents what is physically already in place, changes to the production planning system sometimes have far reaching consequences to the existing structures and procedures within the company. Because of this factor, there can be resistance by company personnel and managers to the introduction of changes to the system.

The company is always aware of what it wants to produce, because this is defined by the market pressures or demand. However, what the company wants to make must be rationalised against what it *can* make. The issue of balance between requirements and capacity relates to a type of trade-off. On one hand, the company wants to satisfy demand, but on the other hand it may not have the capital resources to do so. At the senior management strategic planning level, long-range investment decisions are made that can increase the company's capacity resources. Commonly however, the additional capacity lags behind the pressure to produce more product quickly. In these cases, management must make choices. Just as an individual person has many ambitions for material possessions and lifestyle but can only have an optimal balance of items that their income allows, so too a company must select carefully how to manage its limited asset of resources to achieve the greatest benefit to the company.

Capacity type investments in plant and people are expensive. In some cases the management may decide to invest in more productive capacity, but a more effective strategy is to place the emphasis on trying to make the existing capacity do more, through better planning and better management.

Associated Philosophies and Factors

Lower investment in inventory: JIT. The emphasis on operational efficiency over the last 20 years has been on management of quality, and a minimisation of resources (mainly inventory) committed to production. An underlying idea of JIT is that inventories provide capacity cushions that hide inefficiencies and waste. They therefore should be reduced so that the inefficiencies are exposed and remedied, enabling the firm to outperform competitors. Lean manufacturing is strongly associated with JIT in that it seeks total elimination of waste through making only what customers want, and producing at the last possible point in time that still provides customer satisfaction.

The implementation case studies, however, have shown an important fact. The successful implementation strategies do not come from inventory reduction. Instead, they come from working at *improving the infrastructural systems and processes* that are connected to inventory levels in a cause and effect relationship. The message is do not attack the inventory levels. Search instead for underlying factors that cause the inventory level to be where it is — remedy the underlying cause and allow the inventory to drop naturally to a new lower level.

We believe that one of the main drivers of high inventory levels is poor production planning and control systems, and recommend that this is a rewarding area to seek improvement.

Lower investment in capacity: Lean manufacturing. As with the previous goal of achieving effective productivity through reduction of wasteful investment in inventory, there is also room in most firms for critical analysis of the capital investment in plant and technology. In both cases (inventory and plant) there is a tendency to create cushions of capacity so that customers can be satisfied in terms of quality, flexibility, and delivery.

Part of the drive towards lean manufacturing is a focus on investment in manufacturing equipment. The aim is to have simple, reliable equipment with the flexibility built into the tooling design. This runs contrary to some philosophies that seek competitive advantage through automated mass production systems with dedicated machines. Such equipment is capital intensive and inflexible, and requires a set staffing level regardless of productive output. Typically a "forward thinking" management has made the investment decision based on expected future volumes of demand, and they work on the principle of "patient money," expecting downstream returns. Unfortunately, in many cases, the expected demand levels are not realised, and the result is an excessive and wasteful capacity investment.

The true extent of this waste may be hidden by inefficient systems. The company finds that it needs the highly productive and expensive equipment just to maintain basic levels of customer satisfaction. If this is the case, can we follow the equipment policy of lean manufacturing, whereby equipment purchasing is typically based on only 80% of the expected demand, with overtime and incremental capacity increases covering the shortages? The short answer is "yes," but only when the underlying production planning and control systems are robust and efficient.

Material requirements planning (MRP) as a planning tool. MRP was designed as an inventory management tool for dependent demand items that occur within the makeup structure of end products. In this respect, MRP performs very well, and produces a time phased set of orders for each assembly, subassembly, part, or quantity of raw material that is required to make a product by a particular due date. There is, however, some debate regarding the value of MRP as a planning tool and this relates to the use of MRP in its most basic and simple form: as a requirements calculator. In this original role, there are some limitations on its ability to supply a comprehensive workable production plan. These limitations relate primarily to issues of capacity balancing and lot sizing.

This text promotes MRP as an integral part of any production planning system. It assumes an integration of MRP with capacity balancing and lot sizing procedures.

The development of "post mass" batch manufacturing. As companies seek the most efficient and effective ways of producing goods, they are working with three dynamic business environmental factors: the continuing balance of variety, volume and process; increasing demand for greater flexibility and faster delivery; and the new and evolving information technology.

Figure 11.2. The variety/volume/process matrix

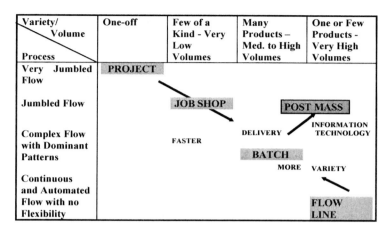

In the variety/volume/process decision, variety and volume were inversely related, so that if variety was high, volume was low, and vice versa. This relationship between variety and volume then led to a logical decision on process design (project for one-offs, job shop for few of a kind, batch flow for lower volumes of many products, flow lines for high volumes of one product). However, market and technological forces are changing traditional paradigms of manufacturing. Figure 11.2, shows how the traditional diagonal pattern of process design is being changed by influences from the two other environmental factors.

The market demand for flexibility and wide ranges of niche markets means that the rigidity of flow line production is less suited to today's environment: There is pressure for more variety and a resulting trend towards batch manufacturing. At the low volume end of the diagonal, there is competitive pressure for faster delivery. This drives companies towards adopting modular design concepts that allow increases in volumes of standard component production - a further trend towards batch manufacturing.

Historically, the factor that had restricted batch manufacturing's ability to perform economically at points above the diagonal was the complexity of the planning and organisational task, and the relatively slow speed of the somewhat jumbled flow. With the current development of production information systems, however, all of that is changing. At the same time that pressure has built for more variety and faster delivery, the new information systems give batch manufacturing the ability to perform well in both respects. Using the machinery of the mass production flow line in combination with principles of flexible manufacturing (group technology, multitask machinery, and interchangeable tooling for very fast set up times), the new, integrated information technology has leveraged batch manufacturing to a new status as the high-variety/high-volume post mass ideal.

Again our call is reinforced. The benefits available in the area of operations management have never been greater. The new manufacturing philosophies and strategies offer great opportunities for competitive advantage and growth for companies operating in what is now a global market. *However, these advantages will remain as potential only, unless the underlying production planning and control systems have been developed as integrated, robust platforms on which to build the new competitive advantages.*

Balancing Capacity Vectors

The previous material has emphasised the issue of balancing the demand requirements of the market with the available capacity. The concept is simple, logical, and appeals to intuitive common sense. Why is it then that so many companies carry out requirements, planning but not capacity planning?

The answer, we believe, is that although the *concept* of balance is simple, the *practice* of capacity planning is not. There are a number of reasons for this. One that has already been dealt with is the definition of capacity. Many firms may know the design capacity of their plant, but have no reliable measurement of their effective capacity, and therefore have no measurement of the efficiency that the demonstrated capacity represents.

However, this is the least of the difficulties in working with capacity. Not only is effective capacity a "mystery" number in many companies, but it is also a dynamic and elusive number. It is dependent on the mix of products and setups in the planning period, and therefore varies over time. There are also different capacities at different production units — and different capacities in different planning periods.

The complexity is even greater still. There are also different resources used by different products, any mix of which may influence the effective capacity. Take, for example, a simple form of furniture component production that is continuous and makes only one product such as a drawer side. If the set of machines can process raw material at $30 \, m^2/hr$, then the capacity for an 8-hour run is $240 \, m^2$. But what happens when a different size and design of drawer side is introduced to the situation that consumes capacity at a different rate: What quantities of each should be run, and how do you balance the capacity? Further complexity arises when the process is not continuous, but works with batches. If the capacity for the period does not match with an integer of batches, should the planner underload or overload the capacity?

So the general idea of balance between requirements and capacity is not enough. The issues are more complex, and that complexity is the problem of capacity planning. This chapter provides some guidance on how to deal with the initial levels of complexity through a process of balancing the vectors of capacity with the planned workload.

The Capacity Planning Problem

It is useful to define what we mean when we discuss the capacity planning problem (CPP).

A capacity planning problem is usually solved for a particular production unit and for a certain planning period (PP). On different planning levels, the PU may be a company, a shop, a work station, a team, or even a complex machine.

As follows from its name, the focus of the CPP is the correct planning of capacity utilisation. Though there may be several different types of constraints associated with the problem, such as product quantities, technology, material flow, and so forth, the core of the problem is always the balance between required capacity and the available capacity.

A Simple Problem: One Resource

Here we assume that there is only one kind of resource in the PU, for which the capacity planning procedure is performed. This case looks simple, but covers many important practical applications. The examples of such situations are cases where:

- A PU is a line operated by a crew of workers;
- A PU is a technologically oriented area, performing similar jobs, such as turning area, drilling area, assembly area, and the work force consists of

individual workers with similar qualifications, or organised in teams, and any job can be done by any worker or team; and

- A PU is a flexible manufacturing unit.

The most widely used capacity characteristic of such a PU is the number of working hours per planning period (if the resource is labour), or the number of machine hours (if the resource is a machine or a group of machines). Let us denote this number as P. For example, in the case of the furniture company, the planning period for the press is equal to 2 weeks. Given that the press works for three shifts 5 days a week, the capacity characteristic of the press is equal to:

$$P = 2*3*5*8 = 240 \text{ hours/planning period}$$

The capacity characteristic may be interpreted as a capacity constraint as follows: The planned workload for a fortnight's operation of the press cannot exceed 240 hours.

Usually an overload is possible for some resources and capacity can be increased. In this case, extra capacity should be planned and organised. Let us denote the possible extra capacity reserve as a surplus (P').

Changing the capacity and capacity use of a PU may incur costs, or sometimes changes may not even be possible at all in the short term. In our example, it is impossible to increase the capacity of the press during weekdays. But if we assume that, if necessary, the press also can be operated on every Saturday (three shifts), then

$$P' = 2*3*8 = 48 \text{ hours/planning period}$$

The additional cost is equal to the difference between overtime pay rate and normal pay rate to the crew of operators for 48 hours.

We shall call P "regular capacity," and P' "capacity surplus."

The planning procedure defines a set of planning items (PI) to be produced during a planning period, which we shall call "a production programme." Let PI: $i = 1, 2, ..., m$, be included in the programme. The standard volume of resource required for production of item i is assumed to be known, and we shall denote it as t_i. Then, the total volume of resource, which is necessary for the whole programme, is equal to the sum of resources required for each PI:

$$T = \sum_i t_i$$

The Cost Structure

The capacity planning is always associated with comparing costs and choosing a plan with minimum costs. The cost items are different for different levels of planning. On the top level, usually the possible costs are:

1. The cost of the capacity increase: investment in equipment and staff increase (wages, training, etc.); and
2. The cost of losing possible market share: lost profit.

On the aggregate level, the possibility of capacity increases is limited to working in overtime, or the use of extra casual labour, and the possible losses include inventory accumulation, backlogs, and loss of customers' goodwill. So the costs under consideration are:

1. The cost of any capacity increase: The difference between overtime and casual costs, and the regular cost of labour.
2. Inventory carrying cost, and possible backlog discounts. It is difficult to express loss of customers' goodwill in monetary value. This defines the limits of its application: If its monetary value cannot be defined precisely enough, but can be assumed to play a significant role in the decision regarding capacity, then company management will make the final decision on changes to capacity.

On the shop floor level, the possibility of capacity increase is usually limited to overtime only, and possible losses include the violations of the aggregate plan, which are very hard to evaluate. These losses are specific to the aggregate planning system, and basically are evaluated in terms of loss of yield (or diminished performance-to plan), which may result within a PU.

It may seem strange that the cost of regular capacity is not included in costs at any level. The reason is that the cost of regular capacity is constant during the planning period, that is why it is not evaluated when selecting alternatives in the capacity plan (this regular cost is included in any plan). The only possible cost that may be considered is the cost of capacity underutilisation. In this case, the production programme could be implemented by a lower capacity of resource. Because we cannot decrease the regular capacity during a short period, the result is that we incur underutilisation losses. Whether or not we can justify these losses depends on the production conditions.

Example:

The master production scheduler of the furniture company is in the process of working out the fixed pressing schedule for the next planning period (fortnight). Filling up the time slots (shifts) with customer's orders (CO1, CO2, ...), the following results shown in Table 11.1 were found.

It is clear that regular capacity (30 shifts) is not sufficient for this programme implementation, but it can be implemented with the use of overtime.

Table 11.1. The first draft of the fixed pressing schedule

1	2	3	4	5	6	7	8	9	10	11
16 mm	16 mm	20 mm	20 mm	20 mm	25 mm	25 mm	32 mm	32 mm	40 mm	40 mm
CO1	CO2	CO5	CO5	CO6	CO7	CO9	CO8	CO8	CO4	CO10
CO1	CO2	CO5	CO5	CO6	CO7	CO9	CO8	CO3	CO4	CO10
CO2	CO2	CO5	CO6	CO6	CO9	CO9	CO8	CO3	CO10	CO10

The available capacity for the planning period was calculated earlier in the chapter.

$P = 2*3*5*8 = 240$ hours $= 30$ shifts

$P' = 2*3*8 = 48$ hours $= 6$ shifts

The capacity necessary for the programme given in Table 11.1 is:

$$T = \Sigma\, t_i = 33 \text{ shifts (3 shifts for 11 days)}$$

What options does the scheduler have in this situation?

Option 1. To accept all the orders, and to schedule an additional Saturday. This variant should be accepted if the gains from this order exceed the additional labour cost. (If the planner cannot calculate the gains in monetary value — as is the case with customers' goodwill — then the decision must be based on opinion from the appropriate section of management).

Option 2. To shift one of the customers orders to the next PP. As most of the orders take more than a day of pressing, shifting an order forward will leave the press under-loaded. The value of lost capacity is equal to the loss of crew wages plus the cost of machine hours.

Option 3. To shift only part of a larger order to the next PP, thus increasing the lead time of this order by 2 weeks. The losses, described in Option 2, may therefore be avoided, but only at the expense of additional inventory carrying costs and other losses associated with the delays in delivery.

The Vector Balancing Criteria and Step-by-Step Procedure

No matter what solution is adopted, the goal is to match the following criteria:

1   The total planned workload should not exceed total available capacity;

2   If the plan includes the use of capacity surplus, the extra cost should be justified; and

3   The ideal solution results in the total planned workload matching the total planned capacity use as closely as possible.

.

This example shows the capacity planning procedure step-by-step:

Step 1. Define the capacity and the possible capacity surplus with its associated cost.

Step 2. Define the possible workload for a planning period.

Step 3. If the workload is less or equal to the regular capacity, the programme is accepted.

Step 4.   If the workload is more than regular capacity, but less than maximum (the sum of regular capacity and capacity surplus), then either accept the workload, or cut it to the regular capacity, whichever brings the cost to minimum.

Step 5.   If the workload is more than the maximum capacity, then choose a set of customer's orders which add up to workload which is less than or equal to the maximum capacity. At the same time, the mix should be selected to arrive at the optimum cost structure. It is not so easy to solve this problem, and the correct answer is achieved only by using a linear programming model.

More Complexity: Several Resources

Frequently, several resources of a PU need to be considered. Examples of this situation include:

- A PU consists of several lines working sequentially (producing and packing, making parts and assembling, etc.),
- A process-oriented PU has several different machines or several specialised teams, and
- A PU of an upper level (a company or a division) frequently is represented as several resources.

When dealing with the situation of multiple resources, it is important that the planner works in measurements of the same planning items. Only then can they be considered simultaneously. If these resources are used separately, for example, one set of PIs is produced by resource 1, the next set is produced by resource 2, and so on, then the situation is the same as for the simple one-resource case already presented. When we have multiple resources, then the capacity characteristic of a PU is a vector (which means an ordered sequence of numbers):

$$P = (P_1, P_2, ..., P_n)$$

where P_j is the capacity characteristic of the resource j (j = 1,2, ..., n).

Table 11.2. Capacity characteristic of a PU for a week (40 hours)

	Turning	Drilling	Grinding	Milling
N of workers	12	7	6	5
Regular capacity Vector P (hours)	$P_1 = 480$	$P_2 = 280$	$P_3 = 240$	$P_4 = 200$
Capacity surplus Vector P' (hours)	$P'_1 = 48$	$P'_2 = 28$	$P'_3 = 24$	$P'_4 = 20$

For example, a PU performs different operations, and there are workers of four specialist types in the PU. Each worker can perform only his specialist work. Then the capacity characteristic of the PU consists of four numbers, each giving the capacity of the PU to perform operations of one kind. The capacity is not interchangeable.

In the same manner, the possible capacity surplus is also characterised by four numbers. The regular capacity and the possible capacity surplus of the PU may be presented in the form of Table 11.2.

In the planning process, a programme is developed, which requires resources. Let planning items (jobs) $i = 1, 2, ..., m$, be included in the programme, and the volume of resource j required for processing the item i be t_{ij}. Then, the total volume of resource j, which is necessary for the programme, is

$$Tj = \sum_i t_{ij}$$

and vector

$$T = (T_1, T_2, ..., T_m)$$

is a capacity characteristic of the programme in the same way as vector

$$P = (P_1, P_2, ..., P_n)$$

is a capacity characteristic of the PU. The elements P_j and T_j with the same index j denote the available capacity of the resource j and the projected workload of the resource j correspondingly. The capacity balance condition here means that for every resource j,

$$P_j \text{ should be no less than } T_j.$$

T_j may exceed P_j only if there is a possibility of overloading the regular capacity, and then by no more than the value of the capacity surplus. The capacity surplus costs, of course, also have to be considered.

Continuing the example given in Table 11.2, let us assume that five jobs are to be included in the production programme of this PU. The data about the jobs is given in Table 11.3.

The problem is solved in the same manner as in the single resource case, but the additional difficulty is evident: If a job is removed from the production programme, than the workload of all the resources decreases.

The current programme is feasible because we have sufficient amounts of resources of each kind, but it may be rather costly. Turning and drilling are overloaded, and overtime should be used. However, at the same time, the grinding and milling sections are being underutilised, so there are losses from both sides. It is important to understand that these losses could be incomparable: while the overtime represents an out-of-pocket cash expense, the unused capacity is loss of opportunity to make additional profit.

For simplicity, let us assume that the losses are comparable: the loss of unused capacity is equal to the pay for the unused hours (with the rate $10/hour), and

Table 11.3. Production programme

	Turning, hours	Drilling, hours	Grinding, hours	Milling, hours
Job 1	100	50	43	25
Job 2	27	32	45	36
Job 3	123	45	38	35
Job 4	144	132	37	26
Job 5	122	32	54	65
Vector T (hours)	$T_1 = 516$	$T_2 = 291$	$T_3 = 217$	$T_4 = 187$
Regular capacity Vector P (hours)	$P_1 = 480$	$P_2 = 280$	$P_3 = 240$	$P_4 = 200$
Capacity surplus Vector P' (hours)	$P'_1 = 48$	$P'_2 = 28$	$P'_3 = 24$	$P'_4 = 20$

Table 11.4. Cost of the programme

	Turning	Drilling	Grinding	Milling
Overtime, h	36	11		
Unused capacity, h			23	13
Cost, $	720	220	230	130

the overtime is paid at a double rate. Then the monetary evaluation of the plan can be made (Table 11.4).

The total losses in overtime pay and unused capacity from Table 11.4 are equal to $1,300 (the sum of the last line costs).

To relieve the workload in the turning and drilling sections, we can remove, for example, job 2. This will also cut the capacity utilisation of grinding and milling. The results of this alternative plan in financial costs are given in Table 11.5. The losses in the modified programme are equal to $1,560. This shows that the initial programme was better.

If the five jobs given in Table 11.3 are the only jobs currently available for this PU, we can stop the solution process and accept this plan. The situation frequently is much more complex, because the set of available jobs may be much larger, and even with all possible overloads the capacity could be insufficient. In this case, the "try and fit" process may be computationally very difficult. In these cases, it is necessary to use special mathematical techniques and computers.

Now we can see why the single-resource capacity planning problem is easier than the multiple-resources problem. The solution procedure of the second problem follows the pattern of the first problem solution, but it is necessary to balance all the resources simultaneously.

Table 11.5. Cost of the modified programme

	Turning	Drilling	Grinding	Milling
Overtime, h	9			
Unused capacity, h		21	68	49
Cost, $	180	210	680	490

The main goal of both procedures is to develop a production programme with a workload not exceeding capacity, but as close as possible to it. This "closeness" is the measure of efficiency in planning.

More Complexity: Several Stages, One Resource at Each Stage

Frequently, the production process consists of several production stages, and there are several PUs taking part in the process, in a fixed sequence.

This situation always occurs when the production cycle is long. Although commonly the case is one of multiple resources at each stage, in this section, we will limit the case to one resource at each stage for the sake of simplicity.

This situation has some similarities with the case of one stage with several resources, but it also has its own peculiarities that add complexity.

The example in Table 11.6 reflects a job shop environment in which there are three PUs specialised in turning, drilling, and grinding. The jobs, which are to be produced by the PUs during the planning horizon, and the capacity characteristics of the PUs are given in Table 11.6. The planning period is equal to 1 week, and the cycle time for each operation is also 1 week.

The similarity in procedures between the "multiple resources — one stage case," and the "multiple stages — one resource case," lies in the fact that the

Table 11.6. Production programme and capacity

	Turning, hours	Drilling, hours	Grinding, hours
Job 1	100	50	43
Job 2	27	32	45
Job 3	123	45	38
Job 4	144	68	37
Job 5	122	32	54
Job 6	90	50	51
Regular capacity Vector P (hours)	$P_1 = 200$	$P_2 = 100$	$P_3 = 90$
Capacity surplus Vector P' (hours)	$P'_1 = 24$	$P'_2 = 8$	$P'_3 = 8$

Table 11.7. Production plan: Part one

	Week 1, PU 1	Week 2, PU2	Week 3, PU3
Job 1 (hours)	100	50	43
Job 5 (hours)	122	32	54
Vector *T* (hours)	$T_1 = 222$	$T_2 = 82$	$T_3 = 97$
Regular capacity Vector *P* (hours)	$P_1 = 200$	$P_2 = 100$	$P_3 = 90$
Capacity surplus Vector *P'*(hours)	$P'_1 = 24$	$P'_2 = 8$	$P'_3 = 8$

planning must be performed for the whole job at once. So, we have to plan for 3 weeks simultaneously, as shown in Table 11.7.

This is the end of the similarity in procedures between the "multiple resources —one stage" case, and the "multiple stages—one resource" case. Table 11.7 gives only a fragment of the production plan, because the plan caters only to jobs one and five, and therefore, covers only 1 week for each PU. To complete the planning, several more plans have to be developed (see Tables 11.8 and 11.9).

Tables 11.7, 11.8, and 11.9 give the plans for the six jobs to be completed over a period of 5 weeks. Still, the picture is incomplete because the plans for each of the PUs in all of the 5 weeks are not provided. The missing plans at the start are for PU2 (week 1), and for PU3 (weeks 1 and 2). At the other end, there

Table 11.8. Production plan: Part two

	Week 2, PU 1	Week 3, PU2	Week 4, PU3
Job 2 (hours)	27	32	45
Job 4 (hours)	144	68	37
Vector *T* (hours)	$T_1 = 171$	$T_2 = 100$	$T_3 = 82$
Regular capacity Vector *P* (hours)	$P_1 = 200$	$P_2 = 100$	$P_3 = 90$
Capacity surplus Vector *P'* (hours)	$P'_1 = 24$	$P'_2 = 8$	$P'_3 = 8$

Table 11.9. Production plan: Part three

	Week 3, PU 1	Week 4, PU2	Week 5, PU3
Job 3 (hours)	123	45	38
Job 6 (hours)	90	50	51
Vector *T* (hours)	$T_1 = 213$	$T_2 = 95$	$T_3 = 89$
Regular capacity Vector *P* (hours)	$P_1 = 200$	$P_2 = 100$	$P_3 = 90$
Capacity surplus Vector *P'* (hours)	$P'_1 = 24$	$P'_2 = 8$	$P'_3 = 8$

are no plans for PU1 (weeks 4 and 5), and no plan for PU2 (week 5). These plans would be present, if the planning were performed according to the roll over concept in a continuous process. If the plans were made every week for 5 weeks ahead, then the set of plans for weeks 1 and 2 would always be complete, and the "tail" of the plan would grow correspondingly.

What is the specific rule for this planning procedure?

All three plans should be developed in one planning run, because they compliment each other. However, this adds difficulties to the planning process.

Balancing Vectors for Each PU

The plans developed in Tables 11.7, 11.8, and 11.9 are working documents. The real production plan is composed for every PU for a given PP. For example, the plan for PU1 is presented in Table 11.10.

Let us see how the main features of capacity planning are implemented in this case by examining the three vector balancing criteria specified previously.

1. The total planned workload should not exceed available capacity.

The plan in Table 11.8 is not overloaded in any PU. However, suppose we have an additional small job (job 7), which is grouped with jobs 2 and 4, as shown in Table 11.11.

Table 11.10. Production plan for PU1

	Week 1	Week 2	Week 3
Job/hours	Job 1/ 123	Job 2/ 27	Job 3/ 123
Job/hours	Job 5/ 90	Job 4/ 144	Job 6/ 90
Vector *T* (hours)	$T_1 = 213$	$T_1 = 171$	$T_1 = 213$
Regular capacity Vector *P* (hours)	$P_1 = 200$	$P_1 = 200$	$P_1 = 200$
Capacity surplus Vector *P'* (hours)	$P'_1 = 24$	$P'_1 = 24$	$P'_1 = 24$

Table 11.11. Production plan

	Week 2, PU 1	Week 3 PU2	Week 4, PU3
Job 2 (hours)	27	32	45
Job 4 (hours)	144	68	37
Job 7 (hours)	35	15	15
Vector *T* (hours)	$T_1 = 206$	$T_2 = 115$	$T_3 = 97$
Regular capacity Vector *P* (hours)	$P_1 = 200$	$P_2 = 100$	$P_3 = 90$
Capacity surplus Vector *P'* (hours)	$P'_1 = 24$	$P'_2 = 8$	$P'_3 = 8$

It is very tempting to add this job to the plan, because the resulting overload on PU2 (7 hours) seems insignificant — it is only 7% of the regular capacity. We may think that PU2 is flexible enough to cope comfortably with the extra load, and therefore expect the extra 7 hours to be covered in the normal hours of the week's work. The benefit of this decision then will be an increase in output.

But think about possible consequences if there is no increase in the performance, and PU2 fails to complete the workload.

Note that under the properly structured planning system we give an assignment *before* the start of the PP, and ask for feedback on the actual performance *after*. That is why if job 7 is not completed by PU2 during week 3, it would:

1. Overload the week 4 assignment of PU2. Currently, the week 4 assignment of work in PU2 (see Table 11.9) uses all the regular capacity, and there is no overtime planned, so this work assignment would be disrupted as a consequence of the overflow from week 3.

2. Make a gap in capacity utilisation of PU3 in week 4 (see Table 11.11). We plan full use of regular capacity plus 7 hours overtime, and the overtime would be organised. However, job 7 will not arrive at PU3 in week 4. The expensive overtime capacity will be wasted, and we can also expect workers' dissatisfaction with the disorganised state of affairs.

There is further potential for disruption. The plans do not indicate the order of sequence for the jobs. As a result, the PU2 manager may decide to start the week from job 7, and then to work on job 2. Thus, it would be the large job 4 that was not completed in week 3, resulting in more severe violations of the plans. These are the possible consequences of the wrong capacity planning.

2. If it is planned to use the capacity surplus, then its cost should be justified

In the last section, we did not pay enough attention to the choice of the plans from point of view of their cost characteristics. The true and exact costs would require many calculations, and should be done fully in a real situation. For the purpose of demonstrating the concept here, the pattern of calculations is similar to the one described in the "single stage — single resource" case, and so the calculations have only to be expanded for the total plan (see Tables 11.7, 11.8, and 11.9; and the missing plans for the PU2 week 1, and for PU3 weeks 1 and 2).

If for simplicity, we reduce our evaluation to the existing plans (see Tables 11.7, 11.8, and 11.9), then the cost of the production programmes is shown in Tables 11.12, 11.13, and 11.14. The cost per hour is the same as it was earlier: $10/hour regular time, $20/hour overtime.

The total cost of this programme is equal to $1,470. Another set of programmes may be derived by a different coupling of jobs in time periods: This will change

Table 11.12. Cost of the programme in Table 11.7

	Turning	Drilling	Grinding
Overtime, h	22		8
Unused capacity, h		18	
Cost, $	440	180	160

Table 11.13. Cost of the programme in Table 11.8

	Turning	Drilling	Grinding
Overtime, h			
Unused capacity, h	29		8
Cost, $	290		80

Table 11.14. Cost of the programme in Table 11.9

	Turning	Drilling	Grinding
Overtime, h	13		
Unused capacity, h		5	1
Cost, $	260	50	10

the total cost. The set of programmes that gives the minimum total cost is the one the planner should use.

3. The closer the total planned workload is to the total planned-capacity use, the better is the efficiency of the plan.

The correct solution of this problem is computationally very difficult. A simple rule, named "the greedy heuristic" rule, may help. The rule is, "Try to compose sets of jobs which complement each other by loading different resources as fully as possible." Thus, you can compose several "good" plans. Though the last plans may be really "bad," the total cost might be reasonable.

The problem is difficult only with small and moderate numbers of jobs in the assignment. The larger is the scope of the problem (the more jobs to be allocated to each programme), the smaller is the resource consumption by individual jobs, as compared with available resources. This may not be intuitively obvious. However, the difficulty in composing a programme goes down due to the effect of averaging. So with hundreds of jobs to allocate, the rule becomes very simple: Load to the limit, and the load swings will be relatively minor.

Extremely Complex: Several Stages with Several Resources at Each Stage

The problem of comprehensively solving the full complexity of this situation is beyond the scope of this text. However, a brief introduction is given to outline some general approaches that a production planner might take as an initial step.

If the planning is to be performed for a multistage multi-resource facility, first the planner should try to reduce the complexity of the problem. The possible way of reduction is looking for bottlenecks, and focusing the balancing issues on those points in the production system. There may be two types of bottlenecks:

1. A bottleneck PU; then the problem is reduced to the single-stage multiresource case, where the planner concentrates on balancing the resources with demand, just at the bottleneck.

2. Each PU has a bottleneck resource; then the problem is reduced to a multistage single resource case where the planner concentrates on balancing just the bottleneck resource with demand in each PU.

Another possible reduction of complexity is to ignore non-scarce resources: any resource in any PU which is definitely not a bottleneck may be dropped off the problem. Any resource left out in this way may be scheduled using simple rules, after the plan for the other resources is composed.

If after all possible reductions the problem still remains multistage and multi-resource, then the planner must look to the use of special mathematical tools to solve the complex balancing issues.

Summary

The practice of efficient production planning involves balancing the production requirements with the capacity that is available. In most companies, the requirements side of the problem is calculated without too much difficulty because the systems of requirements planning are well-developed and standardised. There is so little variation to the requirements problem that "off-the-shelf" systems will suit most companies.

This is not so with capacity planning, however. The issues are complex and unique to each type of production, and in many companies there is a combination of different types of production used to make a particular product. At the early levels of complexity the production planner can use vector balancing as a tool to solve the problem, but with increasing numbers of variables, the situation may require the use of more sophisticated algorithmic solutions which are outside the scope of this text.

Even if the complexity issue is overcome, the production planner is invariably faced with a mismatch of demand and capacity. The natural tendency is towards the demand. If the capacity is lower than demand, the capacity is lifted, if there is an excess of capacity over demand, then capacity is reduced. The methods of harmonising the mismatch can be summarised as:

1.   Changing the speed of the process,
2.   Changing the resource of labour,
3.   Changing the resource of plant and technology, and
4.   Changing the whole process.

The development of an effective planning system depends on the word *system*. The design must reflect an integrated system with fully working linkages and balances that occur at all parts of the structure.

Earlier, we discussed the vertical nature of the requirements planning beginning with market demand at the company level, and flowing down to dependent demand for product components at the aggregate and shop levels. Then, we developed the concept of capacity, and discussed the need for horizontal integration at every level to create a balance between requirements and capacity.

Finally, we dealt with a higher level of complexity in the balancing problem, and introduced capacity vectors as a method of analysing the balancing problem and evaluating the cost of various options.

The conclusions from this discussion can be summarised in four points that have relevance to the business environment.

1. The requirements chain is a well-established and unavoidable structure that establishes production requirements at each level in the planning system. In simple situations, the planner can manually compute the requirements, while in more complex situations, MRP software is used to do the calculations.

2. In contrast, the capacity chain is rarely implemented by companies. The widespread result of this disregard for capacity planning is poor delivery performance, low capacity utilisation, and a reduction in profits. We must ask why, then, do so many companies ignore capacity in their planning systems?

3. The answer stems from the difficulty in defining capacity in the first place. This difficulty is then compounded as the issues of measurement become very complex. There is no off-the-shelf generic solution to this problem. Every production environment is unique and requires unique solutions. Using the systems design and methods recommended in this text may help a company overcome many of the problems; however, in more complex situations, special mathematical tools will be required to solve the capacity problem.

4. It is evident that capacity management represents a major field of potential competitive advantage for companies in today's business environment. The revolution in information technology is creating the ability, for the first time, for people to deal with the complex issues of capacity management, and those companies that involve themselves in this science will have the ability to create significant cost, flexibility, and delivery advantages.

The Factors of the Production Planning Environment

A question arises as to how to design the production planning method for a particular company. Is there a generic design that covers the needs of most companies, or is each situation totally individual and unique? The question is important because there are many aspects and factors that influence and regulate the development of the method of planning.

If we suppose that there is a typical situation and generic problems to be solved, then there will be "off-the-shelf" software, and standard methods and procedures. The planner could then just transfer those standard systems to the company and implement them.

On the other hand, if we suppose that there is no standard or typical situation, then no software will be useful and no working systems can be transferred from another company. In this scenario, previous industry experience can be transferred only on a philosophical level, and it will be relative to broad issues such as inventory control and setup time reduction, or the benefits of using quality teams, and so forth

The truth lies somewhere in between. The planner typically is drawn to look at other cases in the same industry, but this is the wrong approach. Some elements of the structure (e.g., planning horizons, planning periods, and planning items) might be transferable, but the method of planning is not industry dependent. The starting point is to analyse the production characteristics and to be able to describe the nature of the production planning environment for which a solution is sought. Then look for examples of production planning design in other companies that are effective in solving the same set of problems. The nature of the set of production variables is the determinant of the planning method: The industry they come from is irrelevant. Once the type of production has set the criteria for the method, the whole system must be developed to suit each level in the planning structure.

In the following material, we deal with how different volumes, variety, and processes of production (flow shop, batch manufacturing, job shop, and project) relate to and affect the planning method. Four variables (type of production, production strategy, cycle time, and planning level) can provide 48 different possible blends of the key environmental factors impacting on the design of the planning method.

Then, we complete the subject by discussing the problems of aggregation and dissaggregation, and the need for a fully integrated system that not only is connected between and within all levels, but also that uses the same language and methods of inter-level translation throughout the system

The Types of Production

Most texts on operations management define "type of production" in terms of variety vs. volume, but from a production planning perspective this is not enough. Instead, a set of three criteria variables are used to define the type of production, and this set then determines the nature of the appropriate planning and control method. Therefore, in looking for examples of model systems, the right approach is to examine planning systems that work with the same sets of variables. Production planning methods are unique to each situation, and so they change not only between industries and companies but within companies as well. The three main factors that describe the type of production and influence the method of planning that is used are:

- The production variety/volume characteristics,
- The production strategy of make-to-stock vs. make-to-order, and
- The cycle time relative to the planning period.

After these three criteria have determined the design, the production planning and control system also needs to be shaped to suit each level in the planning structure. These four factors are now discussed in detail.

1.   **Variety/Volume/Process.** Although there are many variations and degrees within production process types, the range is reduced here to the main four types: flow shop, batch manufacturing, job shop, and project (see Figure 11.3). Each one has distinctive characteristics that shape the design of the planning system.

- **Flow shop.** The flow shop production environment is one where one or very few products are processed in highly specialised equipment. The emphasis is on low cost and high volume production, where the pace of production is set by the design of the equipment and the process. Set up costs are high, and the production runs are long with very few changeovers. In the flow shop, the dominant production policy is make-to-stock, and although WIP inventory is very low, stocks of finished goods are often high. There is therefore a trend to reduce inventories of finished goods, and an associated trend to make-to-order instead, by way of strong supply relationships with customers, and indent or forward ordering.

Because the scheduling and capacity factors are designed into the process, production planning and control is simplified to issues of productivity improvement through eliminating down time, and issues of process control to avoid waste.

Capacity can be adjusted only by running the process for more or less hours. Because of this the normal procedure is to aim for the market demand, and adjust the capacity to suit. A bottleneck in the process is a fixed constraint in the technology that the planning system must work with.

- **Batch manufacturing.** This production process has evolved in recent years as a sequel to mass production. As markets required more variety, the restrictions of mass production reduced the suitability of high volume, one-product flow lines. A new style of production emerged which we call batch manufacturing, but which is also referred to as "post mass" production in some literature. Batch manufacturing attempts to gain the benefits of the flow shop production by using similar high-volume machinery, but this time in combination with a modest variety of product.

Figure 11.3. The variety/volume/process matrix

Variety/ Volume Process	One-Off	Few of a Kind - Very Low Volumes	Many Products - High Volumes	One or Few Products - Very High Volumes
Very Jumbled Flow	PROJECT			
Jumbled Flow		JOB SHOP		
Complex Flow with Dominant Patterns			BATCH	
Continuous and Automated Flow with No Flexibility				FLOW SHOP

In this production type, multiple products are manufactured on the same machines. WIP inventories can be large if cycle times and planning periods are allowed to extend too far beyond the technical cycle time. Batch manufacturing is commonly associated with a make-to-stock production strategy, and lot sizes are decided by an appropriate, economic lot sizing model. Despite the fact that make-to-stock is the dominant production policy, many make-to-order situations are also available in the form of house brands or infrequent export orders, for example. The two strategies can successfully be used in combination so long as the difference is understood and mirrored in the production planning methods

Demand is random, but stable. Forecasting is based on steady, historical data, and the short-term variation in demand is smoothed by a "level" production strategy. There is a high potential for variability in the production outcomes, however, because expediting jobs is possible and indeed probable due to attempts to satisfy particular customers ahead of others. This is disruptive to the focus of production planning and control, which is on coordinating materials flow on the aggregate level, and maintaining stability and certainty at the shop floor level.

In comparison to flow shop manufacturing, there is much more complexity in the planning process because of the many possible stock mix combinations, their affect on setups, and the competition by many products for the same resources. Lack of integrated planning creates capacity bottlenecks that tend to shift from one location to another in the production system.

Technology capacity can only be altered in the longer term, and so any capacity adjustments tend to be made by adjusting hours of work or by rescheduling work to quieter periods.

- **Job shop.** The job shop production type is typified by short-run, custom designed jobs of very small volumes. Machinery and processes are general-purpose and flexible using less automation and lower utilisation rates. Setup costs are low, but the labour content is high, and generally costs are high in association with the uniqueness of the work.

  Because each order is new and different, the complexity in the planning process is also high, and each planning design may have unique characteristics. Complexity also exists in the many unique planning items and jumbled flow of work. The cycle is usually long because there are often long breaks between the jumbled process stages. The dominant production strategy is make-to-order. However, market pressure for shorter lead times, and financial pressure for better capacity utilisation mean that job shop companies look more today for opportunities to modularise and standardise many components. They then make these components as stock and assemble-to-order at the final stage.

Job shop production is characterised by a strong focus on coordination of the workflow. To keep a continuity of work, there is often very high WIP inventory that waits, ready to feed into the production system when required.

Bottlenecks are harder to avoid due to the unknown randomness and variability in the work itself, and it is harder to balance capacity accurately. The shop floor environment is uncertain with frequent changes. The challenge to production planning and control is to be flexible and able to respond quickly to bottlenecks arising in the production system.

- **Project.** Projects introduce the greatest complexity of all the production types. Each project is a one-off task with totally unique characteristics. The work will commonly extend over long periods, years in some cases, and all stages tend to be long cycle planning problems. Variability an uncertainty is very high.

At the aggregate level of planning, the various stages of the project are separated out and time estimates are calculated for each one. Stages that have sequential relationships are identified and the longest sequential path through the project becomes the "critical path." The cumulative times of the stages on the critical path determine the length of the project. All stages not on the critical path then have some flexibility between an earliest possible start date and a latest possible finish date. The scheduling of all stages is then displayed on a Gantt chart to enable management and control of progress of the project against the planned times.

Capacity adjustments are made through the addition of workforce, or by subcontracting, so that milestone checkpoints are reached along the life of the project. The variety of complications is great and the task of managing the complexity of workflow, capacity, and costs is often best handled by proprietary computer software designed especially for project management. The key requirement of the planning system is to know, at any point in the life of the project, how various stages of the project are progressing relative to planned levels of completion, planned capacity usage, and planned cost.

The basic production strategy is make-to-order, but for the same reasons as for the job shop case (shorter lead times), the modern trend is to find ways to standardise many parts, and to make these parts on a make-to-stock basis (e.g., Kit-set house construction).

Each production style favours a dominant strategy of either make-to-stock or make-to-order, but there is no clear-cut or absolute alignment that rules the decision.

2. **Production strategy.** The production strategy is developed in response to two considerations:

- MTS vs. MTO benefits and drawbacks, and
- The cycle time of the production.

    A company is faced with many different product demand situations and characteristics and many factors must be taken into account when deciding on MTS/MTO. The decision can be described as making a choice between investing in stocks or investing in capacity.

    Investing in stock (MTS) provides benefits of rapid supply to customers (e.g., 24-hour delivery assurance) good capacity utilisation from the ability to plan ahead, and smooth production over the forward planning horizon. On the downside, MTS means accepting the cost of carrying inventories of finished goods on a regular and permanent basis.

    Investing in capacity (MTO) enables very low- or nil-finished goods inventories, but on the negative side, the irregular production results in low capacity utilisation rates, and the lack of inventory means longer lead times for customer orders, and less reliable delivery dates.

    Often the decision is influenced by the nature of the product. If it involves long lead times in production and high WIP inventories, then there is a high risk of high carrying costs, and so the bias is towards MTO. In all other cases, the trend is towards MTS, except when the product has a short shelf life or chance of rapid obsolescence.

    Some companies have achieved a blended strategy that takes the best of both types. To do this requires a JIT type relationship with customers, so that a steady pre-ordering regime is developed enabling the company to MTO ahead of time.

- The **make-to-stock** strategy provides better supply to customers, but the company must bear the costs involved in carrying finished-goods inventory. Because of the risk of inventory carrying costs, make-to stock is more suitable for products of reliable demand, and where there is certainty of rapid turn over of stock. Production is carried out ahead of demand, and so the make-to-stock situation depends on forecasts of future demand. In this case, predictions of what to make can be forecast with some accuracy, and the benefits are a better delivery performance and higher capacity utilisation than achievable by the make-to-order strategy.

When making-to-stock, the correct method of calculating the lot size must be decided. With independent production facilities and immediate replenishment, the model used is the Economic Order Quantity (EOQ). When replenishment is not instantaneous, the correct model is the Economic Production Quantity (EPQ). However, it is more common that production facilities are shared among many products and production is not immediate. In this case, the correct model is the Economic Lot sizing and Scheduling Problem model (ELSP), which uses a more complex algorithm to calculate the right lot sizes. The ELSP requires software application for solutions, but the EOQ and EPQ are widely known.

• The **make-to-order** decision provides a better strategy when the financial burden of carrying inventory is too great, or with certain products where there is risk of high inventory carrying costs. Such risks are high when the product value is very high and demand is not reliable, meaning that high cost inventory might be carried for long times. At the same time, under this strategy the level of capacity utilisation is lower, because of the shorter runs. Also, because no inventory of finished goods is held, lead times on customer orders become extended by the stacked sum of all sequential stages, and BOM levels in the product structure. In make-to-order situations the lot sizes are set by the order size. This often creates poor capacity utilisation and extra costs that must be recovered from differential pricing. Make-to-order is common in long cycle production situations, where accumulating value becomes high for extended periods in WIP inventory. Project work always uses make-to-order because everything is a "one-off" situation.

3. **Cycle time.** The common definition of cycle time is the time taken by a production unit to complete the work allocated to it. The cycle time is made up of a technical component and a system component. The technical component consists of setup time, run time, and the travel time between work centres. The system time is created by organisation of the work, and is represented in the development of queues in front of work centres.

- **Short cycle.** A short cycle exists when the production cycle time is less than the planning period. In this case, the production unit can complete the planning items allocated to it within the planning period, and each event completes an independent part of the production.

  To give more flexibility within the production unit, the planning system may give longer planning periods and allow for queues so as to provide better capacity utilisation through more efficient scheduling. However, as mentioned before, excessive queues create extended cycle times, delay delivery, and add significantly to WIP inventory.

  Ideally, the cycle time will be less than the planning period because that simplifies the planning and control process. A cycle time of greater than the planning period means that production will spread over more than one time unit. Situations where the production time is longer than a planning period are termed "long cycle." The long cycle provides a more complex set of production planning problems and is undesirable in manufacturing environments.

- **Long cycle.** As pointed out earlier if the cycle is longer than the planning period, many complexities are introduced to the planning task. A plan is made for the planning period, but very few of the production stages fit within the planning period. Some stages start and finish either side of the planning period, some start inside the period but finish outside, while others start outside but finish inside. To manage the planning and control task, a large amount of technical information must be added to the planning system to enable it to be effective. Production types that have very long stages, but still need to have control over short blocks of time are the usual cases that generate long cycle situations. If the planning designer cannot expand the planning period enough to encompass the cycle times, they may try to "squeeze" the cycles into the planning period to avoid the complications of long cycle production.

4. **Planning level.** The three essential levels of planning are company level, aggregate level, and shop floor level. Other levels may exist, but because these will be variations on the basic three, only the three are described here.

- **Company**

  - ➤ *Components.* The planning horizon will be long term and may extend for 2 or 3 years into the future, with at least the first year divided into shorter planning periods such as quarters. The production unit is the company as a whole, and the planning item is expressed in end products or volumes of product groups.

  - ➤ *Process.* The requirements planning process begins with market demand that is then converted into forecasts for the future periods. Capacity requirements are checked against available capacity, and a balance is planned between the company's desire to satisfy customer demand and its ability to add or subtract capacity to suit. The output of the company planning process is the MPS that is used to drive the aggregate planning level

- **Aggregate**

  - ➤ *Components.* The planning horizon is derived from the planning period of the company level above and typically is 3 months, but may extend to 1 year in some cases. The planning period is commonly 1 month, but may drop to shorter periods such as a week (or even daily when the production cycle is very short). The production unit in dependent demand situations governed by the BOM will be a self-contained production section, the planning item will be assemblies or subassemblies. For non-BOM situations the production unit will be a complete stage in the production sequence, and the planning item will be stages of the product.

  - ➤ *Process.* Requirements planning consists of running an MRP calculation manually in simple situations, or with MRP software in more complex situations. Aggregate capacity planning must also be carried out to balance the production unit capacities with aggregate requirements. The MPS provides the inputs for aggregate planning, and the output is planned-order releases. The relevance of production type and cycle time becomes more important at the aggregate level because of its job of converting market demand into shop floor activities, and its pivotal role in feedback and disaggregation. The aggregate level also has the task of planning and coordinating materials flow within the system and between production units.

- **Shop Floor**
  - ➤ *Components.* The planning horizon will be a month or a week, depending on what planning period the aggregate level above uses. The planning period is typically 1 day or one work shift. For BOM controlled situations, the production unit will be a machine or group of machines and the planning item will be a batch of parts. For non-BOM controlled situations the production unit will be a complete operation within the aggregate stage and the planning item will be the single operations on the batches of parts.
  - ➤ *Process.* The requirements planning is set by the order release, and capacity planning is a matter of scheduling and capacity loading. Input/output analysis monitors the workload throughput and controls the release of new work orders to the shop floor from the MRP process on the aggregate level.

    Planning and control is deeply influenced by process type, cycle times, machine capacity, and man-hours capacity. Efficiency is affected by lot sizes and number of setups, and the shop floor requires controlled stability in the work order flow, so that it can maximise capacity utilisation, and produce to plan within the planning period. In some situation, it is appropriate to lengthen the planning period in order to grant flexibility within the production unit to find optimal scheduling solutions. However, longer planning periods and greater flexibility come at the expense of higher WIP inventory costs.

The Production Type Possibilities

The factors just mentioned provide a range of possible combinations that are found in the manufacturing business environment. Each mix of production factors calls for a special design of the planning process. The following section summarises the common mixes, and identifies some of the planning characteristics.

Four process types, two production strategies, two cycle times, and three planning levels, give: 3x2x2x4 = 48 possibilities.

There are variations to the rule of 48. For example, there are no flow shop situations with a long cycle and no projects with a short cycle. This reduces the possibilities to 36. However, there are other possible hybrid production types which could expand the number beyond the original 48.

The Different Types of Planning

The production planning system design has two parts:

1.   The *structure* as described earlier, and
2.   The *method of planning*.

The nature of the structural choice is not complex and consists of building the recommended components as specified in the early chapters, into the design of the system.

In contrast, the choices of method of planning are many and care must be taken to develop the right one.

This chapter has developed the concept that each production situation requires a different method of carrying out the production planning. The factors that determine the nature of the planning task are contained in the type of production, and each planning design then needs to be tailored to fit each level in the planning system.

Every company is unique, and systems are not easily copied from one company in an industry to another in the same industry. It is not industry type that governs the design of the planning system but rather the type of production, and this changes from one company to another.

The flow shop type of production requires a disciplined and regimented initial design of the process. Because the production type has so little flexibility, many of the production planning and control issues are designed into the process, and so the planning problem is somewhat simplified.

Batch manufacturing is a very common production type in New Zealand and Australia, and when the system works in a short-cycle planning environment, the complexity remains at a manageable level. The key factors are accurate integration of the planning levels, using appropriate lot sizing models, balancing materials requirements with capacities in each production unit and planning period, and providing accurate feedback loops to the higher levels at the end of each planning period.

Job shop production commonly involves long-cycle planning characteristics that add significant complexity to the planning task because all stages of the production extend beyond the planning period. This makes the planning task more difficult because there is not the opportunity for accurate feedback information at the end of each planning period. The jumbled flow of the job shop also adds to the scheduling and sequencing problem at the shop floor, and it is common that the optimisation complexity must be handled by using computer software solutions. The project type of production shares many of the job shop characteristics.

Finally, it should be noted that in many companies, several production types might be used at various points in the manufacturing process. When this is the case, a different planning method should be used in each new situation.

Coordination and Integration

Implementation of integrated databases was intended to unite all OM activities in a company, and to link them to other activities like strategic planning, human resource management, and so on. This unification promised to resolve the problem of efficient interfaces between different management groups, the existence of multiple copies of the same data, and the necessity of their regular and simultaneous update. A slow interface between managers diminishes such business capabilities as flexibility, quick response to the market demand, reduced inventory, reliable delivery performance, and competitive quoted lead times.

The necessity for operations management database integration is so widely addressed in literature that a comprehensive survey is impossible. By now, practically every book on operations management contains a chapter describing the necessity and possible benefits of an integrated database.

To solve this problem sometimes it is recommended to develop a modelling tool that can integrate an information flow of a firm (sometimes such tools are called "workflow management"). This software develops a description of the united information system, analysing diagrams drawn by the user of the system.

Another approach is proposed here. In this approach:

- The model of information flow is derived from the flow charts of the operations management,
- The model is used as an input to a scheduling model, which schedules the business processes, and

- A system clock is introduced to organise the scheduled business processes.

The management information system of a manufacturing company consists of several business processes. Each business process represents one or several managerial problems, which are being solved regularly at given intervals of time. The input to a problem solution algorithm consists of a predefined set of data elements from a database, which should be up to date. The output of a problem solution algorithm updates a predefined set of data elements in the database.

For example, a MRP type planning system (combined with capacity requirements planning) uses as inputs updated information from the following business processes:

- **Forecasting:** Forecast demand
- **Customer order servicing:** Customer orders
- **Inventory management:** Field warehouse demand, current inventory
- **Human resources management:** Workforce available

After a planning run, it updates the databases of the following business processes:

- **Customer order servicing:** Delivery promises
- **Inventory management:** Purchase orders
- **Manufacturing activity planning:** Order releases

The information management problem, as addressed here, may be stated briefly as follows:

At certain points of time in an indefinite interval some information is produced that should be conveyed to other business processes. The information in the originating business process is used for problem solving, which is performed regularly at given intervals of time. Therefore, the information transfer can begin only after completing a certain problem solving procedure, and should be completed before the problem solving in the corresponding business processes begin. So the information management is characterised by a typical scheduling problem in which the exact time of each transaction should be defined.

The solution of the scheduling problem should be represented as a scheduling algorithm. This algorithm forms a basis for the organisation of the workflow management.

Scheduling Model

We shall begin with the formulation of an adequate scheduling model, using scheduling terminology. We have a set of jobs (business processes) to be processed.

There are several types of constraints in the problem:

1. **Precedence constraints:** Certain subsets of jobs must be processed in a given order and with given time lags between the jobs;
2. **Ready times:** The jobs may not become available before a given time; and
3. **Due dates**, or the times by which it is necessary to complete the processing of the jobs.

The problem is to find a schedule, within which the jobs are processed, that is

1. Compatible with the constraints, that is, a feasible schedule, and
2. Optimal with respect to some criterion of performance.

The model described is rather well known in scheduling literature. Let us discuss how to define the above elements of the model.

Precedence Contstraints

These constraints basically might be derived from the management flow chart (Figure 7.21, Chapter VII). The objects of scheduling, which are the information flows between business processes, are shown in the flow chart by means of arrows.

BP1 < BP2 (T) will denote, that business process 2 (BP2) should be performed after business process 1 (BP1) with a time lag no less than T.

As an example we can write down a precedence constraint:

BP1 (FORECAST DEMAND);
BP2 (MASTER PRODUCTION SCHEDULING);
BP1 < BP2 (T1),

where T1 is the given time of the solution of all master production scheduling problems.

The main pitfall of this definition of the precedence constraints is that in a real system there is no start and no finish time for its functioning. This is why the precedence constraints would be formulated as infinite chains of BPs. To clarify this problem, we need an understanding of timing organisation inside the management system.

A fragment of a planning system of a manufacturing enterprise is given in Figure 7.21, Chapter VII. Three levels of planning are presented: aggregate planning, shop scheduling, and operations planning of work centres. The functioning of the system is as follows:

Before the beginning of every month, an aggregate plan is derived for a planning horizon of 3 months. The plan is defined in aggregate planning items (API, for the definition see Chapter VII). Following this, the plan for the first month is transferred to the shop planning business process. There it is transformed into shop planning items (SPI), which may be, for example, finished parts. Then scheduling is performed, and the part of the schedule for the nearest week is considered to be an operations plan. This plan is transferred to the work centres' planning business process, where it is transformed into work centre planning items (WCPI), which may constitute operations, and it is used for daily operations planning.

The daily plan is sent to every work centre at the beginning of the day. At the end of the day, feedback on completed operations is collected and is put into the work centres' planning business process. At the end of the week, feedback that has accumulated for a week is sent to the shop planning business process, where it is transformed into SPIs, and is used in operations planning for the next week. At the end of the month, the feedback accumulated for a month is sent to the aggregate planning business process. There it is transformed into APIs and is used for correcting of the aggregate plan for the next month.

This is only a brief description that includes only routine data exchange between business processes. There may be other transactions, for example, instant calls for feedback in case of sudden plan changes, evaluation of work-in-process, and so on.

It can be seen from this description that the majority of data exchange form infinite cyclical chains. This is why the chains can not be used as precedence constraints.

An obvious solution of this problem is to restrict the schedule by a certain planning horizon, which will cut the chains into finite parts. Though the parts might be rather lengthy, nevertheless, they would give a true precedence picture. *We introduce here another approach that is based on a system clock concept.*

System Clock

From the description of management system functioning we can draw two conclusions:

1. The management system functions within a number of managerial cycles. The shortest cycle may be an hour, or even smaller. The longest may last a year or more.

2.   The majority of the transactions between business processes should be made in a very small time interval at the end of each cycle.

Now we can introduce the system clock. The system clock, like a physical clock, should have a timing mechanism related to the current calendar. But instead of physical time units, some system time units should be introduced, that reflect those existing in the production system managerial cycles. In our example, it is a month, consisting of 4 or 5 weeks, depending on the current calendar month, and a week, consisting of 5 or less days, if there are holidays during the week. The clock should generate an alarm signal shortly before the end of each time unit, thus launching corresponding transactions. The exact meaning of "shortly before" will be addressed below.

The right ordering of events in the system is also based on the description of the managerial system dynamics (Figure 7.21, Chapter VII).

As it was shown earlier, we can not perform direct ordering, because the functioning process, in reality, is indefinite and cyclical. That is why the ordering of events will be considered not for the whole time scale, but only during a definite managerial cycle. As the transactions should be performed only at the end of each cycle, only the last time period in each cycle is of importance. Consequently, we shall have a number of different orderings, equal to the number of managerial cycles plus the number of all their intersections.

For simplicity, we shall set the duration of the time unit equal to the duration of the smallest cycle. Then we shall have time units that are end time units of one cycle, two cycles, and so on. It is evident that all end time units for all different combinations of managerial cycles are inside one largest cycle. These time units can be easily defined and numbered.

Let us consider the example (Figure 7.21, Chapter VII), in which:

- The work centre cycle is equal to a day (cycle 1);
- The shop planning cycle is equal to a week, consisting of 5 days each (cycle 2);
- The aggregate planning cycle is equal to 4 equal-length weeks (cycle 3); and
- The time units (which are days) are numbered from N1.

Then we shall have three different orderings:

1.   For cycle 1, which is used in periods 1, 2, 3, 4, 6, 7, 8, 9, 11, 12, 13, 14, 16, 17, 18, 19;
2.   For cycles 1 and 2, which are used in periods 5, 10, 15; and
3.   For cycles 1, 2, and 3, which are used in period 20.

The actual ordering for a given time unit is specified for the described managerial conditions.

We assume that our distributed system consists of a collection of processes. We shall define a process as a sequence of managerial problems that uses the same business process. An event is represented by the execution of a particular programme on a computer.

There is no need for ordering events inside a process: we assume that the ordering was performed earlier, when the process had been created. The same reason does not apply to the ordering of events of different processes, though once a data element is updated, it can be used for all events in any sequence. Nevertheless, the sequence of events inside a process has an influence on the sequence of transactions. For example, in Figure 7.21, Chapter VII, there are two connections between aggregate planning and shop planning business processes, both reflecting transactions in period 20. But the up-going arrow represents the feedback data, which should be updated before aggregate planning, and the down-going arrow represent the plan, which is sent to the shop business process after planning. So there is not only a precedence relation between these two transactions, but there is also a time lag between these two events. This time lag may be derived from the process structure, and may be stored as a system characteristic.

The same difficulty should be considered if there are several consecutive connections between different business processes in one time unit. While the order of transactions is defined by the arrows in the management flow chart, the time lags must also be computed and stored as system characteristics.

Summing this all up, the ordering process will be as follows:

1.   The ordering of transactions between business processes is defined by arrows in the management flow chart;

2. All the incoming transactions are performed prior to the outgoing transactions; and

3. Time lags between the consecutive transactions are constants depending on the process between them.

As a result, all the transactions in a given period of time will form chains of consecutive transactions, and every individual transaction will be defined by the period of time, its place in the chain, and business processes, from and to which the transaction should be made. There may be at least two levels of description of the information flow:

1. **Business process level**, which reflects the interconnection between the business processes (as shown in Figure 7.21, Chapter VII); and

2. **Data element level**, which includes the inputs and outputs of each problem-solving programme and their further usage.

The more detailed is the level of description, the more information is involved in analysis and problem solving. That is why it is natural to restrict the description to a sufficient level. The timing and ordering problems are mainly connected with the logical description of business processes, and for these problems the business process level appears to be sufficient. Actual organisation of transactions needs a more detailed level of description, because we need to know which data elements should be transferred from one business process to another.

Other Constraints and the Criterion

There are two more sets of constraints in the scheduling model: ready times and due dates.

The ready times and due dates are necessary in the model because all the transactions should be performed in a certain period of time. If the schedule is feasible, and all the transactions in the schedule are performed at the right time, then it really does not matter what order of transactions is assigned in the schedule, provided the precedence constraints are satisfied.

But if we cannot find a feasible solution, we must violate either ready times, or due dates. Then they form a set of "soft" constraints, which may be violated, but a penalty is incurred for this violation.

The penalties for violation of the ready times come from moving the solution of some functional problems to an earlier time. Then the quality of the solution could worsen, because it would be performed on incomplete data. The penalties for violation of the due dates are connected with moving the solution of some functional problems to a later time. The structure of the penalty function may be rather complex. For example, there may be a time lag between the end of one managerial cycle and the beginning of the other cycle (a night or a weekend). If the transactions are scheduled to be late, the lateness inside the time lag may incur only inconvenience and overtime payments to the personnel. The lateness outside the lag may be followed by losses in production.

The structure of the criterion in the model will be as follows: If a job is scheduled to start prior to its ready time, its earliness (E) is equal to the difference between the ready time and scheduled time. If a job is scheduled to be finished after the due date, its tardiness (T) is equal to the difference between scheduled time and due date. Associated with each job is a unit earliness penalty and a unit tardiness penalty. Assuming that the penalty functions are defined for each job separately, the objective function for the E/T problem will represent the sum of penalties for all the earliness and tardiness.

It is quite easy to define a due date for the end job of a chain. Logically, it is the end of a corresponding managerial cycle. However, the due dates for other jobs should be defined too.

There are two ways of assigning due dates to the jobs, which are not end jobs in a chain:

1.   The due date is equal to the due date of the end job in the chain; or
2.   The due date is equal to the due date of the end job in the chain less the sum of time lags, which are necessary for execution of the part of the chain from the current job to the end of the chain.

The first way is easier, but the second gives a more complete description of the quality of the solution.

Not so easy to define are the ready times. The jobs that constitute the beginning of a chain should be determined by the corresponding managerial staff.

Logically, their ready times represent the instances of time when the data is ready to become transactions. The instance, for example, may be the conclusion of feedback data collection. It is clear that the later we stop to collect the feedback, the more complete is the feedback report. However, if it is too late for planning, than the report will be useless. So certain times should be defined in the system when initial transactions of every chain could start.

The ready times for next jobs in every chain could be computed as early start times just by adding the corresponding lag times to the ready time of the previous transaction.

The implementation of this model requires a scheduling algorithm, which depends on a chosen scheduling model, particularly on its set of constraints and on its criterion.

While the precedence constraints are practically always present in the model and are similarly formulated, the means of introduction of ready times and due dates may differ significantly. For example, either ready times or due dates may be introduced as "firm" constraints. Ready times may be equal for all the jobs in one cycle, or they may be different. The same applies to due dates.

The criterion has the most important influence on the scheduling algorithm. The way the penalty functions are formulated defines the necessity for creating of algorithms with a wide complexity range. Nevertheless, both the theory and practice of creation of such algorithms are extensively developed, but experience in implementation of similar algorithms in production scheduling would be of help.

Chapter XII

A Tutorial Case Study:
Pasta Company

This case study is intended as a tutorial. The case solution is given up to the end of the business process redesign stage. The SAP implementation (quite similar to that described for EA Cakes Ltd.) is left to the readers of the book (or to the students, if the book is used in education). The main lesson of this case is the following: though the company does not look like EA Cakes Ltd., and the goals of the production planning systems are different, nevertheless, analogous SAP solutions can be used to give computer support to the production planning staff.

Case Description

Tasty Pasta is a company that produces a range of products for wholesale, retail and restaurants. While the previous Cases one and two relate to more complex

Table 12.1. Product range information

PRODUCT	PACK WEIGHT, gr	PRICE, $/ton
1. Egg noodles (Large)	200	3000
Egg noodles (Small)	50	3500
2. Spaghetti	500	2000
3. Salad pasta (Large)	200	3500
Salad pasta (Small)	50	4000
4. Short pasta (Large)	500	2500
Short pasta (Small)	200	2800

production and organisational situations, the Tasty Pasta situation has only one production line and seven products. The case, therefore, provides a good example from which to calculate fully developed solutions to production planning problems.

The marketing policy is that all orders are accepted. For permanent customers the shipments are performed once or twice a week. For casual customers the shipment is performed within 24 hours, if necessary. Otherwise, the shipment is performed within a week, and the date of shipment is agreed with the customer. If for some reason the company cannot ship the order in the agreed time, it offers a 2% discount per day on the part of the order volume, which has been shipped after the due date.

Products and Prices

The company produces the following products shown in Table 12.1.

Capacity

The production facilities of the company are detailed as follows:

- Production line, productivity 1000 kg/hour (PL)
- Buffer storage, 1600 kg (BS)

- • 3 automatic programmed packing machines (PM), which together have different maximum productivity for different pack sizes:
- • Pack size 50 gr: 200 kg/h
- • Pack size 200 gr: 400 kg/h
- • Pack size 500 gr: 600 kg/h

The packing machines can be programmed and reprogrammed in very little time. That is why the set-up time for them is negligible. The machines can be programmed to work at less than the stated productivity, and any combination of the machines can be used for packing at a time. The flow of materials is shown as follows in Figure 12.1.

The line is working continuously for a planned number of hours starting from the set up time on full capacity, feeding the products either to the buffer storage and/or directly to PMs. The maximum run is equal to 8 hours, after that a stoppage is necessary for cleaning, and the duration of stoppage is equal to 1 hour. Cleaning may be combined with the next setup. The packing from the buffer storage may be combined with cleaning and setting up of the production line. A cleaning and set up time of 1 hour is necessary after each stoppage, either planned for a changeover, or other stoppages. The line should not be stopped between shifts, but is always stopped at the end of the day.

All the facilities are staffed for two shifts per day, 5 days a week. If necessary, a Saturday shift (not fully staffed) with an overtime payment is allowed. The Saturday shift (8 hours) also includes 1-hour set up time, thus expected output from the Saturday shift is only 7 tonnes.

Figure 12.1. The flow of materials

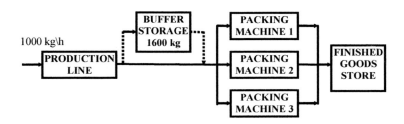

Demand and Safety Stock

The marketing manager prepares a demand forecast based on historical data. He also uses his experience and judgement to adjust the forecast. The forecast is prepared for the next month, and is given in weekly volumes as per Table 12.2.

The traditional point of view (which in this company represents rough-cut capacity planning), is that 20% of the capacity will be enough for setup and cleaning of the line. The normal capacity use is 80% (80 hours/week*0.8 = 64 hours/week). The planned month has a growing demand in week 3 and 4 because of school holidays, but the overall demand is balanced by the average 64 hours per week.

Further details regarding the rough-cut capacity planning are found in the forecasting procedure. The marketing manager runs a long-term forecast (1 year, with monthly buckets), which shows that the demand is highly variable. Not only are there seasonal variations, but also random spikes of demand occur due to wide competition. The variability in demand is one of the reasons why rough-cut capacity planning is necessary. To do the rough-cut planning, the planner must have an understanding of the production capacity of the company.

It is clear that the designed capacity of the company, which is 80 hours/week, cannot be the loading target. The effective capacity, which can be used as a loading target, is variable because it depends on the mix of products. The mix of products, however, is difficult to forecast accurately. The long-run statistics of demonstrated capacity show that it is equal to 80% of designed capacity on average. This is why the marketing manager smoothes the production plan for

Table 12.2. Weekly production volumes by product for 1 month

Product	Week 1, t	Week 2, t	Week 3, t	Week 4, t	Large: Small, %
1. Egg noodles	22	23	26	25	50:50
2. Spaghetti	12	12	15	15	n/a
3. Salad pasta	14	14	18	17	50:50
4. Short pasta	10	11	11	11	50:50
TOTAL	58	60	70	68	

Table 12.3. Safety stock volumes

Product	Safety stock, t	Large:Small, %
1. Egg noodles	24	50:50
2. Spaghetti	13.5	n/a
3. Salad pasta	15.75	50:50
4. Short pasta	10.75	50:50
TOTAL	64	

the next 4 weeks to 64 tonnes/week (80% from 80 tonnes). Basically, he or she uses demand modification for smoothing. When the demand is lower than capacity, he or she either plans stock increases or plans major maintenance of the facility. When the demand exceeds capacity, he plans either to postpone or even reject some orders. He never plans overtime utilisation, which instead is reserved to cover unplanned downtime, or excess of downtime due to complexities in production.

There is no visible trend (either positive or negative) in the sales forecasts, and so there is no planned capacity increase during the planning horizon.

The company's production policy is *produce-to-stock*. There is a safety stock to satisfy the anticipated demand, which is equal to the average weekly forecast (64 tonnes) and has the same proportion of different packs. It is assumed that after week 4, the closing stock will be sufficient to cover demand for the next week. The safety stock volumes before the beginning of week 1 is as follows in Table 12.3.

Cost Structure

Normal operational costs (including materials, safety stock carrying costs, and overhead costs) account for 60% of the sales revenues. Other costs that must be included in production planning decisions are:

- Labour Cost
- In regular time: $1,100 per shift, and
- In overtime $1,400 per shift.

Extra Inventory Carrying Cost

There is enough space in the company's warehouse to carry a volume of safety stock of finished goods equal to the average weekly demand (safety stock). The cost of carrying this stock is included within fixed costs. This limits the storage capacity of the company. Any other stock is being stored outside at a cost equal to 1% of the sales value per day. The difference in cost for using the off-site storage is explained by the differences in the weight and physical volumes for different products. For example, a standard carton has much less weight when it contains small packs, than when it is filled with large packs.

Current Difficulties

Currently, the company has difficulties in balancing its line. These difficulties are connected to the recent introduction of small product packs (50 gr packs in particular). Initially, the small packs were met by the customers with caution, and their volumes did not exceed 20% of total sales volumes.

When this product was introduced, the problem of balancing was immediately recognised. The problem is that the balancing of the line is impossible, even using all the three packing machines to full capacity. The line output is 1000 kg/hour, and the total packing capacity on small packs of the three packing machines is equal to only 600 kg/hour. The simplest way to overcome this difficulty was to buy two more packing machines. But the machines are very expensive, and the company is not prepared to meet this investment. That is why the engineer suggested two ways to overcome the difficulty (two new production regimes):

Regime 1. Combined packing, when one packing machine is producing small packs, and the rest are producing large packs. Then the output characteristics are:

- Output, large packs: 800 kg/h, or 80%, and
- Output, small packs: 200 kg/h, or 20%.
- The production time between setups is limited to 8 hours, that's why the most economic duration of this regime is 9 hours. Thus, we have the

Figure 12.2. Gantt-chart of Regime 1

TIME, h	1	2	3	4	5	6	7	8	9
PRODUCTION	Set -up	Run	Run	Run	Run	Run	Run	Run	Run
Packing mach 1		Pack	Pack	Pack	Pack	Pack	Pack	Pack	Pack
Packing mach 2		Pack	Pack	Pack	Pack	Pack	Pack	Pack	Pack
Packing mach 3		Pack	Pack	Pack	Pack	Pack	Pack	Pack	Pack
Output (Small packs)		0.2 t	0.2 t	0.2 t	0.2 t	0.2 t	0.2 t	0.2 t	0.2 t

smallest set up capacity loss per hour. The schedule for this regime is given in Figure 12.2.

- This regime was successfully used while the demand for small packed products was modest. Then these products became unexpectedly successful in the marketplace, and the demand for them began to grow so quickly that it reached 50% of all output.

- The engineer suggested that the company still could cope with the demand for small-packed products without adding packing capacity.

Regime 2. Use of the buffer storage, where the output of the line (1000 kg/h) is directed partially (600 kg/h) to the packing machines, and partially (400 kg/h) to the buffer storage, as shown in Figure 12.3. After the buffer storage is filled up, the production line should be stopped, while the packing machines continue to pack from the buffer storage. This is represented in Figure 12.3. The time and production characteristics of this regime are:

- **Setup:** 1 hour;
- **Production:** 4 hours; the production time is limited by the capacity of buffer storage (1600 kg:400 kg/h = 4 hours);
- **Packing off the product from buffer storage:** 2.75 hours (1600 kg:600 kg/h = 2.75 h);
- **Total time:** 1+ 4 + 2.75 = 7.75 hours; and
- **Total output:** 4 tonnes.

Figure 12.3. Flow of materials using the buffer storage

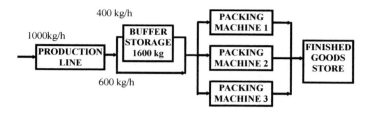

The capacity loss as compared with large pack production is:

$(6.75 - 4)/6.75 = 0.4$, or 40%.

The losses might be less, because the last hour can be used for subsequent setup and cleaning. Then the production looses:

$(6.75 - 4 - 1)/6.75 = 0.26$, or 26% of production time.

The Gantt chart of this regime is given in Figure 12.4. We shall call "Regime 0" the usual production regime, when only large packs are produced, and the line is balanced. Then the most economical run for any product is to set up the line in the first hour, and then to produce for the following 8 hours. The schedule for Regime 0 is given in Figure 12.5. Note that for some products it is not necessary to use all packing machines, and the packing capacity is not specified in the schedule.

Figure 12.4. Gantt chart of Regime 2

TIME, h	1	2	3	4	5	6	7	8	9
PRODUCTION	Setup	Run	Run	Run	Run	Run	Run	Run	Run
Packing mach 1		Pack	Pack	Pack	Pack	Pack	Pack	Pack	Pack
Packing mach 2		Pack	Pack	Pack	Pack	Pack	Pack	Pack	Pack
Packing mach 3		Pack	Pack	Pack	Pack	Pack	Pack	Pack	Pack
Output		1 t	1 t	1 t	1 t	1 t	1 t	1 t	1 t

Figure 12.5. Gantt chart of Regime 0

TIME, h	1	2	3	4	5	6	7	8	9
PRODUCTION	Set up	Run	Run	Run	Run	Run	Run	Run	Run
Packing mach 1		Pack	Pack	Pack	Pack	Pack	Pack	Pack	Pack
Packing mach 2		Pack	Pack	Pack	Pack	Pack	Pack	Pack	Pack
Packing mach 3		Pack	Pack	Pack	Pack	Pack	Pack	Pack	Pack
Output		1 t	1 t	1 t	1 t	1 t	1 t	1 t	1 t

Case Assignment

The case presents several problems for the production planner that are interconnected. The object is to arrive at an optimal product mix week by week for the 4-week period that satisfies demand, maximises profit and leaves the safety stock replenished to its opening levels.

1. **Work out all schedules for the production line and packing machines for week 1.**

    After week 1, actual sales for period will be known (Table 12.4). Adjust the stock levels according to feedback from Table 12.4.

    Work out all schedules for week 2 and so on. Note that at the end of week 4, the safety stock should be as close as possible (volume and structure) to the opening safety stock.

2. **At the end of week 4, make a statement of the cash flow for the 4 weeks in the form of:**

    *   Total sales revenue,
    *   Total cost (labour plus inventory plus expenses), and
    *   Profit.

Table 12.4. Weekly sales for the 4-week period

Feedback on Actual Sales

Products	Week 1 sales, t	Week 2 sales, t	Week 3 sales, t	Week 4 sales, t
1	Egg noodles, 22	Egg noodles, 25	Egg noodles, 26	Egg noodles, 26
2	Spaghetti, 10	Spaghetti, 14	Spaghetti, 15	Spaghetti, 15
3	Salad pasta, 13	Salad pasta, 17	Salad pasta, 18	Salad pasta, 17
4	Short pasta, 9	Short pasta, 11	Short pasta, 11	Short pasta, 11
TOTAL, t	54	67	70	69

Case Solution

The obvious way is to begin the scheduling, using Regimes 0, 1, and 2 as blocks. This is a useful exercise, but unfortunately it will get us nowhere, which will be clearly shown in the subsequent analysis.

The recommendation is to start with the analysis of the real production capacity, which we call *effective* capacity.

Effective Capacity Analysis at the Shop Floor

When an assignment is given to the production line, the immediate question is whether or not the assignment is realistic. This question is equally important to the line manager, who is responsible for the assignment implementation, and to the company's planner, who has to be sure that the assignment is realistic and is implemented with reasonable reliability.

We know the traditional point of view is that the normal capacity use (effective capacity) is 80% of the designed capacity (80 hours/week*0.8 = 64 hours/week). This number can be explained as follows. With the maximum run of the line set at 8 hours, there needs to be at least 10 setups during an 80-hour week. This leaves no more than 70 hours for production.

We also know that due to the current increase in small-pack packing, there will be inevitable capacity losses due to the use of Regime 2. This leaves no more than 6 hours/week for these losses. The question is whether it is enough or not to cover the losses?

Table 12.5. Capacity required to produce the safety stock

Product	Safety stock, t, lge pks	Safety stock, t, sml pks	Regime/ times	Production + set-up time, h	Volume produced t, lge pks	Volume produced t, sml pks
Egg noodles, 200 gr	12		1	15+2	12	3
Egg noodles, 50 gr		12	2 /3	20.25		12
Spaghetti	13.5		0	13.5+2	13.5	
Salad pasta, 200 gr	7.875		1	9.85+2	7.85	2
Salad pasta, 50 gr		7.875	2/2	13.5		8
Short pasta	10.75		0	10.75+2	10.75	
TOTAL	44.125	19.875		82.85+8	44.1	25

Consider the case when the assignment consists of the reproduction of safety stock that is equal to the average weekly assignment. Then the necessary capacity (production time and volumes) is shown in Table 12.5.

The table shows that such an assignment is not implementable, because it requires approximately 91 hours, with all capacity losses included. Even with the use of a Saturday overtime shift, we have only 88 hours.

However, our goal was to satisfy all the demand, and following this goal strictly, we planned a significant overproduction (over 5 tonnes of small packed products). If we decide to exclude from 1 week a run of 50 gr egg noodles under Regime 2, and on the other week to exclude a run of 50 gr salad pasta, (Regime 2), then we will have at the same time the production balanced for 2 weeks, and the capacity balanced without overtime. Alternatively, we can use Regime 0 instead of Regime 1 for large-pack production, but this is not always logical, because Regime 1 produces small packs without capacity losses.

Now we can see where the 64 tonnes of capacity limit comes from. The capacity analysis shows that with the product structure at 50:50 large to small packs, at best we can produce about 68 tonnes of products, using all overtime allowed. Without overtime, we can produce only about 64 tonnes.

Note that it is not yet a sufficient condition, because actual scheduling may decrease the effective capacity. So, shall we start scheduling?

Aggregate Capacity Planning

The answer is definitely "no." Just a quick return to the demand forecast (see Table 12.6) will be enough to understand the simple fact that was proved earlier: the demand forecast is not a production plan.

According to the capacity analysis in Table 12.6, we can probably schedule successfully the production of the volumes forecasted for weeks 1 and 2. Next comes week 3, when even with the overtime we will be short about 2 tonnes of products, which will decrease our safety stock. We shall carry on the shortage through week 4, still using overtime, and we will not catch up with this shortage, causing the risk of backlogs in the next week.

This is the price of a "chase the demand" production strategy: two overtime shifts plus possible backlog costs. In weeks 1 and 2, we will have idle times instead, which also may be qualified as losses.

As an alternative, we can consider a "level" strategy, shown in Table 12.7.

This strategy is characterised by high inventory costs. Even though we have chosen the product with the lowest carrying costs for building up stocks, under this strategy we shall nevertheless carry 20 tonnes of it over a week.

Conclusion: We should perform the regular aggregate capacity planning procedure in order to work out a production plan, based on the demand forecast.

Table 12.6. A repeat of the demand forecast

Product	Week 1, t	Week 2, t	Week 3, t	Week 4, t	Large: Small, %
1. Egg noodles	22	23	26	25	50:50
2. Spaghetti	12	12	15	15	n/a
3. Salad pasta	14	14	18	17	50:50
4. Short pasta	10	11	11	11	50:50
TOTAL	58	60	70	68	

Table 12.7. The level production strategy

Product	Week 1, t/ stock volume	Week 2, t/ stock volume	Week 3, t/ stock volume	Week 4, t / stock volume	L:S, %
1. Egg noodles	22	23	26	25	50:50
2. Spaghetti	18/6	16/10	9/4	11	n/a
3. Salad pasta	14	14	18	17	50:50
4. Short pasta	10	11	11	11	50:50
TOTAL	64	64	64	64	

We have the following means to work out the most cost-effective plan, when the demand is uneven:

1. To build up stocks in advance to cover the lumps in demand that occur later on; the additional cost will be the outside storage cost.

2. To use overtime at overtime shift's cost.

3. To use backlogs, selling the products at discounted price.

The recommended straightforward way to work out an optimal plan is to construct all possible plans. This will reflect the two extreme strategies ("chase" and "level"), and all variations of mixed strategies. Then the task is to evaluate the cost of each plan and to choose the one with smallest cost. Technically, this is impossible because of an indefinite number of mixed strategies. A mathematical linear programming model, implemented in proper software, can help. So, let us see "what the computer says." (See Example 1.)

The cost definitions in the computer programme are as follows:

•   The periods are weeks with regular time effective 64 hours (actual 80 hours), which enables the production of 64 tonnes of product. The overtime effective is 7 hours (7 tonnes maximum production).

Example 1. Computer report

Computer Report: Problem Title: PASTA

*** Resource Section***

Period	Capacity		Cost Per Unit	
	Regular Time	**Over Time**	**Regular Time**	**Over Time**
Period 1	64.0	7.0	0.0	200.0
Period 2	64.0	7.0	0.0	200.0
Period 3	64.0	7.0	0.0	200.0
Period 4	64.0	7.0	0.0	200.0

Demand Section

Period	Prod 1	Prod 2	Prod 3	Prod 4
Period 1	22.0	12.0	14.0	10.0
Period 2	23.0	12.0	14.0	11.0
Period 3	26.0	15.0	18.0	11.0
Period 4	25.0	15.0	17.0	11.0
H-Cost	227.50	140.00	262.50	185.50
S-Cost	455.00	280.00	525.00	371.00

Production Schedule

Period	Reg-Time	Over Time	Demand	Invent.
Product: Prod 1				
1	22.0	0.0	22.0	0.0
2	23.0	0.0	23.0	0.0
3	24.0	2.0	26.0	0.0
4	21.0	4.0	25.0	0.0
Product: Prod 2				
1	12.0	0.0	12.0	0.0
2	16.0	0.0	12.0	4.0
3	11.0	0.0	15.0	0.0
4	15.0	0.0	15.0	0.0
Product: Prod 3				
1	14.0	0.0	14.0	0.0
2	14.0	0.0	14.0	0.0
3	18.0	0.0	18.0	0.0
4	17.0	0.0	17.0	0.0
Product: Prod 4				
1	10.0	0.0	10.0	0.0
2	11.0	0.0	11.0	0.0
3	11.0	0.0	11.0	0.0
4	11.0	0.0	11.0	0.0

Example 1. Computer report (cont.)

*** Cost Report: By Product ***

Product: Prod 1	0.00
Regular Time Production Cost	1200.00
Over Time Production Cost	0.00
Inventory Carrying Cost	0.00
Back Order Cost	0.00
Product Subtotal Cost	1200.00
Product: Prod 2	0.00
Regular Time Production Cost	0.00
Over Time Production Cost	0.00
Inventory Carrying Cost	560.00
Back Order Cost	0.00
Product Subtotal Cost	560.00
Product: Prod 3	0.00
Regular Time Production Cost	0.00
Over Time Production Cost	0.00
Inventory Carrying Cost	0.00
Back Order Cost	0.00
Product Subtotal Cost	0.00
Product: Prod 4	0.00
Regular Time Production Cost	0.00
Over Time Production Cost	0.00
Inventory Carrying Cost	0.00
Back Order Cost	0.00
Product Subtotal Cost	0.00
Regular Time Production Cost	0.00
Over Time Production Cost	1200.00
Inventory Carrying Cost	560.00
Back Order Cost	0.00
Overall Total Cost	1760.00

*** End of Report ***

- The regular time cost is set to zero, because in our labour environment we should pay to workers a full shift pay, whether they are producing, or setting up, or just having a planned maintenance downtime. That is why every plan has the same fixed component for the regular labour cost. This is equal to the crew wages for 4 weeks at 10 shifts per week: 4*10*$1,100 = $44,000.

- For a similar reason, the overtime hour cost per hour is set to $175 = $1,400:8, because it includes the payment for setup of the line.

- H-cost stands for holding costs. The holding costs are calculated at the basis of 7% of the price per week (because the storage management charges for weekends as well), or 1% of the price per day. If there is a mix of products (small:large), then the price is averaged.

- S-cost stands for backorder costs. They are calculated in the same manner as H-cost, with the rate of 2% of the price per day.

- The optimum capacity plan is summarised in Table 12.8.

It may seem strange that the computer does not use the regular time in week 1, and uses instead overtime in periods 3 and 4. This may be explained by the large inventory holding costs. If we produce the extra 6 tonnes of product 1 in the regular time of period 1, we shall save $200*6 = $1,200 on overtime, but we shall pay the following holding costs:

$$*\$227.5*2*2 + \$227.5*3*4 = \$2,730.$$

For a similar reason, if we produce 4 tonnes of product 2 in advance (in period 2) and use it in an overloaded period 3, the holding cost $140*4 = $560 is less than the overtime cost $200*4 = $800.

Table 12.8. The optimum capacity plan

Product	Week 1, t/ stock volume	Week 2, t/ stock volume	Week 3, t/ stock volume	Week 4, t / stock volume	L:S, %
1. Egg noodles	22	23	24	21	50:50
1. Egg noodles (overtime)			2	4	50:50
2. Spaghetti	12	16/4	11	15	n/a
3. Salad pasta	14	14	18	17	50:50
4. Short pasta	10	11	11	11	50:50
TOTAL	58	64	66	68	

The actual minimum cost of the aggregate plan is equal to the sum of:

regular time cost : $44,000
overtime cost : $1,200
holding cost : $560

Total : $45,760

One last comment should be made about the eternal problem of the relevance between the production planning and the software we use for production planning. This example is also affected by this problem. It can be easily observed that the plan does not reflect one important feature of the production situation: You can either use a Saturday shift and pay for this in full, or not use it at all. At the same time, the optimum plan recommends to use two shifts, 2 hours in the first one and 4 hours in the second one. This unreasonable suggestion was made only because we used software, which implemented a linear programming model. To solve the problem in full, we should have used an integer programming model, which requires many more calculations.

However, there is a simple way to make the solution more reasonable: to use only one Saturday shift, and to concentrate all the 6 tonnes of production in that one overtime shift. The decision, whether to do it at week 3 or 4 depends on the actual sales at week 2. If we are at risk of running out of stock, then we will produce in week 3, because the backlog cost is twice that of the holding cost. Otherwise, produce at week 4 and save on the holding cost.

To finalise the aggregate planning, we shall project the financial outcomes of the plan's implementation. This is done in two parts as follows in Table 12.9 (a) and (b).

Production Planning System Functioning

Now is the time to recall that the actual functioning of the company is going on under the production planning and control system guidance. Therefore, the scheduling will be performed not at once, but at the beginning of each planning period, when the feedback from actual sales will be known and analysed.

The structure of the system is assumed to be as follows in Figure 12.6, (for simplicity we show only the capacity chain).

Table 12.9.(a). Revenue from sales

PRODUCT	SALES	PRICE, $/ton	Revenue, $000
1. Egg noodles (Large)	48	3000	144
Egg noodles (Small)	48	3500	168
2. Spaghetti	54	2000	108
3. Salad pasta (Large)	31.5	3500	110.25
Salad pasta (Small)	31.5	4000	126
4. Short pasta (Large)	21.5	2500	53.75
Short pasta (Small)	21.5	2800	60.2
TOTAL	256		770.2

Table 12.9(b). Costs and profit, $000

Fixed cost (60% from revenue)	462.12
Labour cost	45.2
Inventory holding cost	0.56
Total cost	507.88
Taxable profit	252.32

The system is functioning in cycles. The lower is the daily cycle. The schedule is worked out up to the end of the planning horizon, but its frozen part is only the first day. The actual output of this day may be affected by unplanned downtime, material shortages, and so on. When feedback on actual production is collected at the end of the day, it may be not exactly equal to the planned output. Then the schedule for the rest of the week may be changed in order to reach the planned weekly production.

The weekly cycle is the next. At the end of each week, both actual sales and output are known. The actual sales may differ from the forecast, and the actual output may be affected by unplanned downtime. That is why the next weekly plan should be amended with the goal to be as close as possible to the monthly plan. The monthly cycle works in a similar way.

In this example, there is no information for monthly cycle analysis. In the daily cycle the main cause of variation is possible yield uncertainty. As we assume

Figure 12.6. The production planning and control system

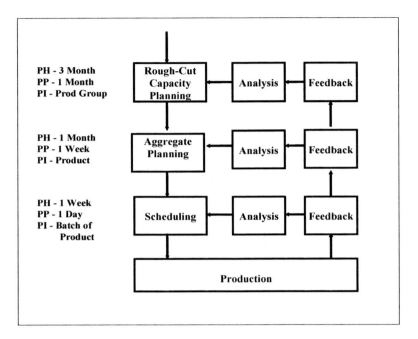

(for simplicity) that the yield is stable, then in the daily cycle nothing unexpected will happen. That is why the main attention here is given to the weekly cycle. In order to understand the complex interaction between aggregate planning and scheduling, we shall go through this cycle week by week.

Planning and Production Interaction

Week 1 Scheduling

We start from the week 1 production plan. The schedule is given in Table 12.10. Then we schedule using the Regimes 0, 1 and 2 as scheduling modules. If we do not need the full economical run, we can cut it to the necessary length. This is done, for example, on Wednesday, Shift 2.

It is easy to see that we did not use all the regular time. The second shifts on Wednesday, Thursday and Friday are short, and some time is left for planned

Table 12.10. Schedule week 1

	Shift 1	Shift 2
Monday	Prod 1, Regime 2 (8 hours)	Prod 1, Regime 1 (8 hours)
Tuesday	Prod 3, Regime 2 (8 hours)	Prod 3, Regime 1 (8 hours)
Wednesday	Prod 1, Regime 2 (8 hours)	Prod 1, Regime 1 (6 hours)
Thursday	Prod 2, Regime 0 (9 hours)	Prod 2, Regime 0 (5 hours)
Friday	Prod 4, Regime 0 (9 hours)	Prod 3, Regime 2 (3 hours); Prod 4, Regime 0 (2 hours)

Table 12.11. Production week 1

Product	Open stock, t	Wk 1 plan, t	Mon, t	Tue, t	Wed, t	Thu, t	Fri, t	Actual produced
1. Egg noodles (Large)	12	11	6.4		5.6			12
1. Egg noodles (Small)	12	11	5.6		5.4			11
2. Spaghetti	13.5	12				12		12
3. Salad pasta, (Large)	7.875	7		6.4				6.4
3. Salad pasta (Small)	7.875	7		5.6			1.4	7
4. Short pasta	10.75	10					10	10
TOTAL	64	58						58.4

maintenance. Note that the last hour of Regime 2 production may be used for the next setup. The production is summarised in Table 12.11.

The actual volumes produced are not exactly equal to the plan. Product 1 is overproduced by 1 t, and at the same time product 3 is produced 0.6 tonnes less than planned. As generally we do not expect the actual production be 100% accurate either, we can agree that the schedule is within the limits of planning accuracy.

In this example, we do not consider any yield variations: that is why we expect that the actual output will equal the scheduled output. Therefore, at the end of week 1, we shall have the following changes in the stock.

Table 12.12. Week 1 closing stocks

Product	Opening stock, t	Sales, t	Actual produced	Closing stock
1. Egg noodles (Large)	12	11	12	13
1. Egg noodles (Small)	12	11	11	12
2. Spaghetti	13.5	10	12	15.5
3. Salad pasta (Large)	7.875	6.5	6.4	7.775
3. Salad pasta (Small)	7.875	6.5	7	8.375
4. Short pasta	10.75	9	10	11.75
TOTAL	64	54	58.4	68.4

Week 2 Aggregate Planning

The actual picture is not very inspiring. Due to inaccurate demand forecast, we overproduced 4.4 tonnes of product, and we should pay additional inventory holding costs at a rate 7% of the price, which totals to:

$$\$3000*0.07 \ + \ \$2000*2*0.07 \ + \ \$3500*0.1*0.07 \ + \ \$4000*0.05*0.07 + \$2650*0.07 = \$840$$

Now the question is: Is the monthly forecast generally inaccurate, or have the sales not picked up the forecasted growth in demand at this stage?

If we believe that the forecast is inaccurate, then we must change our aggregate plan. If, on the contrary, we believe that the monthly sales volumes will eventually be according to the forecast, then we will continue with the current aggregate plan. Suppose that we choose the last option.

Remember, that the aggregate planning is a roll over procedure. Every week it produces an aggregate plan for the next 4 weeks. The limits of our case study do not allow us to do this. These limits also affect the possibility to change the aggregate plan only for the current month.

Table 12.13. Schedule week 2

	Shift 1	Shift 2
Monday	Prod 1, Regime 2 (8 hours)	Prod 1, Regime 1 (8 hours)
Tuesday	Prod 3, Regime 2 (8 hours)	Prod 3, Regime 1 (8 hours)
Wednesday	Prod 1, Regime 2 (8 hours)	Prod 1, Regime 1 (8 hours)
Thursday	Prod 3, Reg 2 (3 h); Prod 2, Reg 0 (8 h)	Prod 4, Reg 0 (5h)
Friday	Prod 2, Regime 0 (9 hours)	Prod 4, Reg 0 (7h)

Table 12.14. Production week 2

Product	Opening stock, t	Sales, t	Actual produced	Closing stock	Safety stock	Inventory cost +
1. Egg noodles (Large)	13	12.5	12.8	13.3	12	
1. Egg noodles (Small)	12	12.5	11.2	10.7	12	
2. Spaghetti	15.5	14	16	17.5	13.5	112
3. Salad pasta (Large)	7.775	8.5	6.4	5.675	7.875	
3. Salad pasta (Small)	8.375	8.5	7	6.875	7.875	
4. Short pasta	11.75	11	10	10.75	10.75	
TOTAL	68.4	67	63.4	64.8	64	

Week 2 Scheduling

The production is summarised in Table 12.14. We can now see that we used all regular time, and still, with this ratio of small to large packing, the maximum output is 0.6 tonnes short from the 64 tonnes target. We are also not up to the planned structure: product 1 is produced over the plan, and product 4 is under-produced. But all in all, the schedule gives enough safety both against shortages and extra stock accumulation. At the end of week 2 we shall have the following changes in the stock.

Table 12.15. Closing stock week 2

Product	Opening stock, t	Sales, t	Actual produced	Closing stock	Safety stock	Inventory cost +
1. Egg noodles (Large)	13	12.5	12.8	13.3	12	
1. Egg noodles (Small)	12	12.5	11.2	10.7	12	
2. Spaghetti	15.5	14	16	17.5	13.5	112
3. Salad pasta (Large)	7.775	8.5	6.4	5.675	7.875	
3. Salad pasta (Small)	8.375	8.5	7	6.875	7.875	
4. Short pasta	11.75	11	10	10.75	10.75	
TOTAL	68.4	67	63.4	64.8	64	

Table 12.16. Schedule week 3

	Shift 1	Shift 2
Monday	Prod 1, Regime 2 (8 hours)	Prod 4, Regime 0 (8 hours)
Tuesday	Prod 3, Regime 2 (8 hours)	Prod 3, Regime 1 (8 hours)
Wednesday	Prod 1, Regime 2 (8 hours)	Prod 1, Regime 1 (8 hours)
Thursday	Prod 3, Regime 2 (8 hours)	Prod 3, Regime 1 (8 hours)
Friday	Prod 1, Regime 2 (8 hours)	Prod 1, Regime 1 (8 hours)
Saturday	Prod 2, Regime 0 (8 hours)	

Week 3 Aggregate Planning

As we can see, the forecasted sales growth has now appeared. We were prepared to meet it, and even quite unexpectedly, we saved on holding costs against the planned level. Following from the results, we shall carry over the week only 0.8 tonnes of product 2 instead of planned 4 tonnes at a cost of $560. Certainly, there is no need to change the aggregate plan.

The main problem now is when to plan the Saturday shift, either at week 3 or at week 4.

Table 12.17. Production week 3

Product	Open stock, t	Week 3 plan, t	M, t	T, t	W, t	T, t	F, t	S, t	Actual produced
1. Egg noodles (Large)	13.3	13			6.4		6.4		12.8
1. Egg noodles (Small)	10.7	13	4		5.6		5.6		15.2
2. Spaghetti	17.5	11						7	7
3. Salad pasta (Large)	5.675	9		6.4		6.4			12.8
3. Salad pasta (Small)	6.875	9		5.6		5.6			11.2
4. Short pasta	10.75	11	7						7
TOTAL	64.8	66							66

Just to be on the safe side, we should plan a Saturday shift at week 3, and if the demand differs from the forecast significantly, we shall still have a capacity reserve at week 4. But this security will cost the company at least the payment for off-site storage of 4 tonnes of product 1.

Week 3 Scheduling

The first days of the week are scheduled for products that have stocks lower than projected sales, in order to minimise the backlog risk. The production is summarised in Table 12.17.

The aim of the week 3 schedule is to produce, as much as possible, small-packed products. For this we pay by losses in production: the total volume is only 66 tonnes produced during 88 hours. As a compensation, we are 2 tonnes above safety level in small packed products.

Table 12.18. Closing stock week 3

Product	Opening stock, t	Sales, t	Actual produced	Closing stock	Safety stock
1. Egg noodles (Large)	13.3	13	12.8	13.1	12
1. Egg noodles (Small)	10.7	13	15.2	12.9	12
2. Spaghetti	17.5	15	7	9.5	13.5
3. Salad pasta (Large)	5.675	9	12.8	9.475	7.875
3. Salad pasta (Small)	6.875	9	11.2	9.075	7.875
4. Short pasta	10.75	11	7	6.75	10.75
TOTAL	64.8	70	66	60.8	64

At the end of week 3 we shall have the following changes in the stock, as seen in Table 12.18.

Week 4 Aggregate Planning

As we can see, the forecasted sales growth continues. We were prepared to meet it, but still, due to the excessive sales in week 2, our closing stocks are well beneath the target of 64 tonnes.

Now is the time for aggregate planning decisions. The main problem at this stage is the validity of the demand forecast for week 4, and for the total month. The sales by now have exceeded the forecasted demand by 3 tonnes. Will the tendency hold, or will the demand drop to the month's expected total of 256 tonnes?

If the demand in week 4 is lower by 3 tonnes, then we will not need to produce the planned 68 tonnes. To do so will mean carrying the extra 3 tonnes of stock, to say nothing of the cost of the extra Saturday shift needed for production of this volume. On the other hand, if the actual demand in week 4 is up to the forecast, which is rather probable (after all this is the second week of school

Table 12.19. Schedule week 4

	Shift 1	Shift 2
Monday	Prod 2, Regime 0 (8 hours)	Prod 4, Regime 0 (8 hours)
Tuesday	Prod 3, Regime 2 (8 hours)	Prod 3, Regime 1 (8 hours)
Wednesday	Prod 1, Regime 2 (8 hours)	Prod 1, Regime 1 (8 hours)
Thursday	Prod 3, Regime 2 (8 hours)	Prod 2, Regime 0 (8 hours)
Friday	Prod 1, Regime 2 (8 hours)	Prod 1, Regime 1 (8 hours)
Saturday	Prod 4, Regime 0 (8 hours)	

Table 12.20. Production week 4

Product	Open stock, t	Wk 4 plan, t	M, t	T, t	W, t	T, t	F, t	S, t	Actual produced
1. Egg noodles (Large)	13.1	12.5			6.4		6.4		12.8
1. Egg noodles (Small)	12.9	12.5			5.6		5.6		11.2
2. Spaghetti	9.5	15	7			8			15
3. Salad pasta (Large)	9.475	8.5		6.4					6.4
3. Salad pasta (Small)	9.075	8.5		5.6		4			9.6
4. Short pasta	6.75	11	7					7	14
TOTAL	60.8	68							68

holidays, and our customers still need to feed the children on vacation), then we will consume part of the safety stock. This will bring a danger of possible backlogs in the following weeks.

The decision of the aggregate planner is to go for safety, and to schedule the 68 tonnes for production using one more overtime shift.

Table 12.21. Closing stock week 4

Product	Opening stock, t	Sales, t	Actual produced	Closing stock	Safety stock
1. Egg noodles (Large)	13.1	13	12.8	12.9	12
1. Egg noodles (Small)	12.9	13	11.2	11.1	12
2. Spaghetti	9.5	15	15	9.5	13.5
3. Salad pasta (Large)	9.475	8.5	6.4	7.375	7.875
3. Salad pasta (Small)	9.075	8.5	9.6	10.175	7.875
4. Short pasta	6.75	11	14	9.75	10.75
TOTAL	60.8	69	68	59.8	64

Week 4 Scheduling

The production is summarised in Table 12.20. The aim of the week 4 schedule is to produce more large packed products. The total volume is 68 tonnes produced during 88 hours.

At the end of week 4 we shall have the following changes in the stock. (See Table 12.21.)

This ends the work. Though the safety stock is lower than we started by 4 tonnes, this is not the fault of production planning. Due to the inaccuracy of the forecast (which cannot be accurate by their nature), we sold more products than planned for. This brought additional profit to the company, even though an additional overtime shift was used. The financial results of the company are summarised in Table 12.22.

Conclusion

The main idea of the case study was to show the proper functioning of the production planning system, in particular, the role of aggregate capacity

Table 12.22. Revenue from sales

PRODUCT	SALES	PRICE, $/ton	Revenue, $000
1. Egg noodles (Large)	49.5	3000	148.5
Egg noodles (Small)	49.5	3500	173.25
2. Spaghetti	54	2000	108
3. Salad pasta (Large)	32.5	3500	113.75
Salad pasta (Small)	32.5	4000	130
4. Short pasta (Large)	21	2500	52.5
Short pasta (Small)	21	2800	58.8
TOTAL	260		784.8

Table 12.23. Costs and profit, $000

Cost	Planned	Actual
Total sales	770.2	784.8
Fixed cost (60% from revenue,)	462.12	470.88
Labour cost	45.2	46.6
Inventory holding cost	0.56	0.95
Total cost	507.88	518.43
Taxable profit	262.32	266.37

planning. It is interesting to analyse how the production will be affected by using a single level planning system. In that case, the chase strategy would be implemented. The comparison of the results is given in Table 12.24. The results, of course, depend on the actual demand, but in the long run they will be approximately the same.

The optimum strategy left us with the safety stock 4 tonnes lower than expected because of overselling (the forecast was insufficient) of this volume. Due to heavy demand in the last weeks, there was not an opportunity to catch up with the proper level of safety stock. This will require an increase of the next month's production plan by the same 4 tonnes. If the demand in the first week of the next month is slack, this increase will cause no problem. Otherwise, we will have an overtime shift in the first week.

Table 12.24. Comparison of results from the three strategies

	Week 1	Week 2	Week 3	Week 4	Safety stock	Overtime shifts	Inventory
Actual demand, t	54	67	70	69			
Optimum strategy, t	58	64	66	68	-4	2	5
Chase strategy, t	58	60	66	66	-10	2	4
Level strategy, t	63.4	63.4	63.4	63.4	-6.4		16.2

The chase strategy, if implemented, would give drastic results. Not only does it have nearly the same overtime and inventory costs, but the extensive use of the safety stock gives a real danger of backlogs if the demand at the beginning of the next month is heavy. To catch up with proper levels of safety stock, we need at least two overtime shifts, which adds to the cost of this strategy.

The closest to the optimum is the level strategy, which shows that it is not extremely necessary to use complex software for aggregate planning. Of course, in the long run, it will pay off, but in its absence, the level aggregate planning is a good approximation.

In any case, whether the optimum or level strategy is chosen, it means that the production is working under control of aggregate capacity planning, and the company meets the demand variations with open eyes, and has the opportunity to react adequately. Without aggregate planning, the company blindly chases the demand, which always results in heavy losses in capacity, inventory costs, and backlogs.

Some Further Questions

The case provides the opportunity for further exercises for the keen reader and students. In all cases, the production planner must know the cost of the planning and capacity decisions. To this end, the following questions have been framed as typical of the type that the production planner at Tasty Pasta is dealing with.

1. Recently the engineer suggested a new regime for combined packing. It produces small packs in a much better ratio to large (3:2), and at the same time capacity loss is smaller than in Regime 2. Draw a Gantt chart for such a regime.

2. Would you recommend adding packing capacity to remove the bottleneck on small packing? Two new packing machines (current price is $200,000 each) will balance the line.

3. Would you recommend to extend the current warehouse to accommodate another weekly safety stock? The building cost is $250,000, depreciation rate is 0.05% per year, costs to run (wages, electricity, etc.) $3,000/ week.

Chapter XIII

Conclusion

Current Problems

The implementation of the Production Planning and Control (PP) module of the SAP system uncovered a need to provide an effective computer support to related managerial decisions not covered by typical SAP applications. Examples are given in subsequent paragraphs.

The manufacturing process requires an updated short-term forecast each week. Sales managers must produce the forecast, and then it is automatically processed within the master production scheduling. Sales figures for individual products have to be provided on a weekly basis for the current month and the next month. Actual sales made each week are captured and available for reporting on the following morning (after actual sales completion). Sales staff compare actual sales with long-term forecasts and, using judgment, make necessary adjustments. Currently forecasts are prepared manually and then put into the database. The process needs computer support to relieve sales personnel and to eliminate data entry.

Stock control of raw material and finished items needs double checking. Initially, the line manager puts the data about actual production and actual use of raw materials into the database, using the process "completion and confirmation of the production order." However, due to possible conflict of interests, this data is not absolutely reliable. The actual amounts of goods produced should be verified from the store of finished-goods entries. This data indicates the actual use of raw materials as well. Any variances must be investigated; hence, the necessary data must be kept in the database.

Based on the MRP process, the system can recommend requirements for purchasing of materials up to the planning horizon. These requirements can be reviewed, maintained, and automatically generated into purchase orders. Changes to the following week's forecast may require purchase orders to be maintained in order to update quantities of materials to be purchased.

More thought is required on the handling of rejects/seconds, as some are almost planned by-products. This will also have ramifications with stock control and sales analysis.

Epilogue and Lessons Learned

The implementation of the Production Planning and Control (PP) module of the SAP system was successful. The new planning system used only standard SAP software. However, it required agreeing to some difficult tradeoffs between the targeted efficiency and achieved efficiency.

The planning staff (the master scheduler) and line schedulers learned some lessons in computer support issues:

1.   The desired degree of automation in MPS and aggregate capacity planning is not achievable by the standard software. Moreover, it is not achievable even with individual programming, because it involves too much creative work that is difficult to formalise.

2.   The line scheduling could not be sufficiently computerised, because it is mostly informal. The rules for batching products and assigning crews are so complex that it is difficult to produce a working algorithm. It seems that the best computer support is given just by a well-run database.

3.   Because of the informality of production planning and scheduling, the difference between standard and individual computer support is insignificant. However, standard computer support is cheap and reliable.

Therefore, even as the typical software does not provide the desired efficiency, typical software currently is preferable, nevertheless, to individual programming. The additional changes in the production management can be summarised as follows:

1.   Development of a two-level sales forecasting system. The long-term rollover forecast is produced every quarter with a time horizon of 1 year, the short-term rollover forecast is performed weekly with a time horizon of 5 weeks.

2.   Development of a mid-level MPS procedure. Its main goal is to keep stock levels between the designed minimum and maximum. The minimum was defined with regard to necessary customer service.

3.   Introduction of proper feedback procedures; Establishment of necessary communications between planning levels.

There were more changes in management of the company than those described in this case study. They include product innovations, process improvements, changes in marketing strategy, and development of the most important parameters of the production planning system (i.e., cycle times, batch sizes, minimum balances [safety stock levels], capacity tables, etc.). Though such changes in the management of the company contributed to the increasing marketing success, changing the production strategy from MTO to MTS provided the main contribution.

Chapter XIV

References

Alexander, I. (2002, September 9-10). Modelling the interplay of conflicting goals with use and misuse cases. In *Proceedings Eighth International Workshop on Requirements Engineering: Foundation for Software Quality (REFSQ'02)* (pp. 145-152), Essen.

Al-Mashari, M. (2002). Business process management: Major challenges. *Business Process Management Journal, 8*(5), 411.

Al-Mashari, M., Al-Mudimigh, A., & Zairi, M. (2003). Enterprise resource planning: A taxonomy of critical factors. *European Journal of Operational Research, 146*(2), 352-364.

APQC's International Benchmark Clearinghouse & Arthur Andersen & Co. (1996). *Process classification framework*. Retrieved May 2004, from http://www.apqc.org/portal/authentication/html/downloadPCF.jsp?_requestid=88097

ARIS. (2001). ARIS software. *IDS Scheer*. Retrieved from http://www.ids-scheer@com/

Bancroft, N. H., Seip, H., & Sprengel, A. (1997). Implementing SAP R/3: How to introduce a large system into a large Organisation (2nd ed.). Upper Saddle River, NJ: Prentice Hall.

Beischel, M. E., & Smith, R. K. (1991, October). Linking the shop floor to the top floor. *Management Accounting, LXXIII*(4), 25-29.

Bhattacherjee, A. (1999). *ERP implementation at Geneva Pharmaceuticals*. Retrieved January 2005, from http://www.isworld.org/onlineteachingcases/cases/Geneva.pdf

Boehm, B. (1981). *Software engineering economics*. Englewood Cliffs, NJ: Prentice Hall.

Brady, J., Monk, E., & Wagner, B. (2001). Production and materials management information systems. In *Concepts in enterprise resource planning*. Course Technology.

Brehm, L., & Markus, M. L. (2000). The divided software life cycle of ERP packages. In *Proceeding of Global IT Management Conference*, Memphis, TN.

Brehm, L., Heinzl, A., & Markus, M. L. (2001, January 3-6). Tailoring ERP systems: A spectrum of choices and their implications. In *Proceedings of the 34th Annual Hawaii International Conference on Systems Sciences*, Hawaii.

Broadbent, M., Weill, P., & St.Clair, D. (1999). The implications of information technology infrastructure for business process redesign. *Management Information Systems Quarterly, 23*(2), 164.

Brown, C. V., & Vessey, I. (2000, December 16-19). NIBCO's big bang. *Best Teaching Case, International Conference on Information Systems*. Brisbane.

Buck-Emden, R. (2000). *The SAP R/3 system: An introduction to ERP and business software technology*. London: Addison-Wesley.

Callaway, E. (1999). *Enterprise resource planning: Integrating applications and business processes across the enterprise*. Charleston, South Carolina: Computer Technology Research Corporation.

Chen, I. J. (2001). Planning for ERP systems: Analysis and future trends. *Business Process Management Journal, 7*(5), 374-386.

Childe, S. J., Maull, R. S., & Bennett, J. (2001). Frameworks for understanding business process re-engineering. In D. Barnes (Ed.), *Understanding business: Processes*. London: Routledge.

Cole, G. A., (2001). Organisations as systems. In Barnes, D. (Ed.), *Understanding business: Processes*. London: Routledge.

Curran, T., Keller, G., & Ladd, A. (1998). The business blueprint. In *SAP R/3 business blueprint: Understanding business process reference model* (chap. 2). Upper Saddle River, NJ: Prentice Hall.

Davenport, T. H. (1993). *Process innovation*. Boston: Harvard Business School Press.

Davenport, T. H. (1998). Putting the enterprise into the enterprise system. *Harvard Business Review*. Boston: Harvard Business School Publication Corp.

Davenport, T. H. (2000). *Mission critical: Realizing the promise of enterprise systems* (pp. x, 333). Boston: Harvard Business School Press.

Davenport, T. H., Harris, J. G., & Cantrell, S. (2004). Enterprise systems and ongoing process change. *Business Process Management Journal, 10*(1), 16-26.

Davis, R. (2001). *Business process modelling with ARIS: A practical guide*. UK: Springer-Verlag.

Dhar, V., & Stein, R. (1997). *Intelligent decision support methods: The science of knowledge work*. Upper Saddle River, NJ: Prentice Hall.

El Sawy, O. A. (2001). *Redesigning enterprise processes for e-business*. Boston: McGraw-Hill.

Gartner IntraWeb, Magic Quadrants. (2001). Retrieved June 12, 2001, from http://80-www2.auckland.ac.nz.ezproxy.auckland.ac.nz/uaonly/gartner/index.html

Genovese, Y., Bond, B., Zrimsek, B., & Frey, N. (2001). *The transition to ERP II: Meeting the challenges* (pp. 1-34). Gartner Group.

Goodhue, D. L., Wixon, B. H., & Watson, H. J. (2002). Realising business benefits through CRM: Hitting the right target in the right way. *MIS Quarterly Executive, 1*(2), 74-94.

Hammer, M., & Champy, J. (1993). *Reengineering the corporation*. New York: HarperCollins.

Harwood, S. (2002). *Implementing ERP: Strategies, planning and solutions*. Burlington, MA: Butterworth Heinemann.

Hernandez, J. A. (2000). *SAP R/3 Handbook*. New York: McGraw-Hill.

Hoffer, J. A., George, J. F., & Valacich, J. S. (2002). *Modern systems analysis and design* (3rd ed.). Upper Saddle River, NJ: Prentice Hall.

Holtham, C. (2001). Business process re-engineering: Contrasting what it is with what it is not. In D. Barnes (Ed.), *Understanding business: Processes*. London: Routledge.

Hong, H. K., & Kim, Y. J. (2002). The critical success factors for ERP implementation: An organisational fit perspective. *Journal of Information and Management, 40*(1), 25-40.

IDS Scheer. (2000). *ARIS Methods.* Retrieved on January 2005 from the ARIS Software Environment.

Jacobs, F. R., & Whybark, D. C. (2000). *Why ERP? A primer on SAP implementation.* Boston: Irwin/McGraw-Hill.

Jacobs, F. R., & Bendoly, E. (2003). Enterprise resource planning: developments and directions for operations management research. *European Journal of Operational Research, 146,* 233-240.

Jang, W., & Lim, H. H. (2004). Integration of enterprise resource planning systems into a production and operations analysis course. *International Journal of Engineering Education, 20*(6), 1065-1073.

Kagermann, H., & Keller, G. (2001). *mySAP.com industry solutions: New strategies for success with SAP's industry business units.* Boston: Addison-Wesley Professional.

Kalakota, R., & Robinson, M. (2003). *Services blueprint: Roadmap for execution.* Boston: Addison-Wesley.

Keen, P. (1997). *The process edge: Creating value where it counts.* Boston: Harvard Business School Press.

Keller, G., & Teufel, T. (1998). *SAP R/3 process oriented implementation.* Harlow: Pearson Education Limited.

Kirchmer, M. (2002). *Business process oriented implementation of standard software* (2nd ed.). Berlin: Springer.

Ko, D-G., Kirsch, L. J., & King, W. R. (2005). Antecedents of knowledge transfer from consultants to clients in enterprise system implementations. *MIS Quarterly, 29*(1), 59-67.

Lapin, L., & Whisler, W. D. (2002). *Quantitative decision making with spreadsheet applications.* Belmont, CA: Duxbury/Thomson Learning.

Lea, B. R., Gupta, M. C., & Yu, W. B. (2005). A prototype multi-agent ERP system: An integrated architecture and a conceptual framework. *Technovation, 25*(4), 433-441.

Legare, T. L. (2002, Fall). The role of organizational factors in realizing ERP benefits. *Information Systems Management,* 21-42.

Lozinsky, S. (1998). *Enterprise-wide software solutions: Integration strategies and practices.* Reading, PA: Addison-Wesley Pub Co.

Mabert, V., Soni, A., & Venkataramanan, M. (2001, May-June). Enterprise resource planning survey of US manufacturing firms. *Business Horizon,* 69-76.

Markus, M. L., & Tannis, C. (2000). The enterprise systems experience: From adoption to success. In R. W. Zmud (Ed.), *Framing the domains of IT management: Projecting the future through the past.* Cincinnati, OH: Pinnaflex Education Resources, Inc.

Martin, E. W. (1999). *Managing information technology: What managers need to know* (3rd ed.). Englewood Cliffs, NJ: Prentice Hall.

Martin, M. H. (1998). An ERP strategy. *Fortune,* February 2, 95-97.

McCarthy, J. (1995). *Dynamics of software development.* Redmond, Washington: Microsoft Press.

McDermott, J., & Fox, C. (1999). Using abuse case models for security requirements analysis. In *Proceedings of the 15th Annual Computer Security Applications Conference* (pp. 55-66). Washington: IEEE.

McNair, C. J., & Vangermeersch, R. (1998). *Total capacity management: Optimizing at the operational, tactical, and strategic levels.* Boca Raton, FL: St. Lucie Press.

Meyr, H., Rohde, J., Schneeweiss, L., & Wagner, M. (2000). Architecture of selected APS. In H. Stadtler, & C. Kilger (Eds.), *Supply chain management and advanced planning: Concepts, models, software and case studies* (pp. 293-304). Berlin: Springer-Verlag.

Meyr, H., Rohde, J., Stadtler, H., & Surie, C. (2000). Supply chain analysis. In H. Stadtler, & C. Kilger (Eds), *Supply chain management and advanced planning: Concepts, models, software and case studies.* Berlin: Springer-Verlag.

Meyr, H., Rhode, J., & Wagner, M. (2000). Structure of advanced planning systems. In H. Stadtler, & C. Kilger (Eds), *Supply chain management and advanced planning: Concepts, models, software and case studies.* Berlin: Springer-Verlag.

New Shorter Oxford English Dictionary. (1997). Oxford: Oxford University Press.

Parr, A. N., & Shanks, G. (2000). A model of ERP project implementation. *Journal of Information Technology, 15*(4), 289-303.

Parr, A. N., Shanks, G., & Darke, P. (1999). Identification of necessary factors for successful implementation of ERP systems. In O. Ngwenyama,

L. D. Introna, M. D. Myers, & J. I. DeGross (Eds.), *New information technologies in organizational processes: Field studies and theoretical reflections on the future of work* (1ˢᵗ ed.) (pp. 99-119). Boston: Kluwer Academic.

Perez, J. (2003). *TDWI study reveals critical CRM success factors*. Retrieved on January 2003, from http://www.intelligententerprise.com/010629/news2.shtml

Porter, M. E. (1985). *Competitive advantages: Creating and sustaining superior performance*. New York: The Free Press.

Pressman, R. (1992). *Software engineering: A practitioner's approach* (3ʳᵈ ed.). New York: McGraw-Hill.

Robey D., Ross J. W., & Boudreau, M. (2002). Learning to implement enterprise systems: An exploratory study of the dialectics of change. *Journal of Management Information Systems, 19*(1), 17-46.

Robinson, A. G., & Dilts, D. M. (1999, June). OR & ERP. *OR/MS Today*, 30-37.

Robinson, B., & Wilson, F. (2001). Planning for the market? Enterprise resource planning systems and the contradictions of capital. *Database for Advances in Information Systems, 32*(4), 21-33.

Rosemann, M. (1999). ERP-software: Characteristics and consequences. In *Proceedings of the 7ᵗʰ European Conference on Information Systems (ECIS '99)*, Denmark (pp. 1038-1043).

Rosemann, M. (2001, March). *Business process lifecycle management* (pp. 1-29). Queensland University of Technology. Retrieved on February 20, 2003, from http://www.code.auckland.ac.nz/files%5CBusinessProcess Modelling.pdf

SAP. (2000). *ValueSAP*. Retrieved January 2005, from SAP Software Environment.

SAP. (2002). *The release strategy of mySAP.com components*. Retrieved January 2005, from http://uk.builder.com/whitepapers/0,39026692,60041703p-39000867q,00.htm

Scheer, A. W. (1998). Business process engineering: Reference models for industrial enterprises. Berlin: Springer-Verlag.

Scheer, A.-W. (1999). *ARIS-business process frameworks* (3rd ed.). Berlin: Springer.

Scheer, A.-W., & Kirchmer, M. (2004, April). Business process excellence & OR. *OR/MS Today*. Retrieved October 19, 2005, from http://www.lionhrtpub.com/orms/orms-4-04/business.html

Scholz-Reiter, B., & Stickel, S. (1996). *Business process modelling*. Berlin, NY: Springer.

Scott Morton, M. S. (Ed). (1991). *The corporation of the 1990s: Information technology and organisational transformation*. Oxford: Oxford University Press.

Scott, J., & Vessey, I. (2002, April). Enterprise systems implementation risks. *Communications of the ACM*, 74-81.

Shafiei, F., & Sundaram, D. (2004, January 5-8). Multi-enterprise collaborative enterprise resource planning and decision support systems. In *Proceedings of the 37th Hawaii International Conference on System Sciences* (CD/ROM).

Shang, S., & Seddon, P. (2000). A comprehensive framework for classifying the benefits of ERP systems. In *Proceeding of Americas Conference on Information Systems 2000 (II)* (pp. 1005-1014).

Sharp, A., & McDermott, P. (2001). *Workflow modeling: Tools for process improvement and application development*. Boston: Artech House.

Sherer, E. (1998). *Shop floor control: A systems perspective*. Berlin: Springer.

Sindre, G., & Opdahl, A. L. (2000, November 20-23). Eliciting security requirements by misuse cases. In *Proceedings of TOOLS Pacific 2000* (pp 120-131).

Starfield, A., Smith, K., & Bleloch, A. (1991). *How to model it: Problem solving for the computer age*. NY: McGraw-Hill.

Swanson, E. B., & Wang, P. (2005). Knowing why and how to innovate with packaged business software. *Journal of Information Technology, 20*(1), 20-31.

Vollmann, T. E., Berry, W. L., & Whybark, D. C. (1997). *Manufacturing planning and control systems* (4th ed.) Chicago, Ill.: Irwin.

Walters, D. (2002). *Operations strategy: A value chain approach*. Palgrave.

About the Authors

Victor Portougal (1941-2005) was associate professor in the Department of Information Systems and Operations Management, Business School, The University of Auckland, New Zealand. His research interests were in quantitative methods, both in management science and information systems. In information systems, his research specialised in security, information systems design and development, and ERP. Dr. Portougal's practical and consulting experience included information and ERP systems design and implementation for companies in Russia and New Zealand. He was the author of many articles in scholarly journals, practitioner magazines, and books. Dr. Portougal held degrees from University of Gorki, Russia (BSc, MSc, computer science), Academy of Sciences, Moscow (PhD, operations research), and Ukrainian Academy of Sciences, Kiev (Doctor of Economics).

David Sundaram is a senior lecturer in the Department of Information Systems and Operations Management, Business School, The University of Auckland, New Zealand. He has a varied academic (BE in electronics and communications, PG Dip in industrial engineering, and PhD in information systems) as well as work (systems analysis and design, consulting, teaching, and research) background. His primary research interests include the (1) design and implementation of flexible and evolvable information, decision, and knowledge systems, (2) process, information, and decision modeling, (3) triple bottom line modeling and reporting, and (4) enterprise application integration with a focus on ERP-DSS integration.

Index

releasing and implementation 74
reporting 118
requirements planning 195
requisition to payment 16
resource planning 211
resource-related data 234
risks 83
rolling plan concept 180
Rosemann's Categories of Improvement 26
RUP (rational unified process) 72, 75

S

sales and distribution (SD) module 86
SAP (Systems Applications and Products in data processing) x, 130, 223
SAP R/3 system 136
SAP-structured entity relationship model 64
SBU (strategic business unit) 17
scheduling x
screen masks 117
SD (sales and distribution) module 86
selling process 138
SEM (Strategic Enterprise Management) 135
"sense and respond" strategy 13
setup 90
shakedown phase 89
shift calendars 231
shop floor control level 230
shop floor level 174
shop floor scheduling 155, 163, 230
short-term shop level 158
SMART objectives 15
software development 72
software selection 100
sponsorship 102
standard software 154
statuses (events) 49
strategic business unit (SBU) 17
Strategic Enterprise Management (SEM) 135
strategic goals 10
strategic objective 12

success 123
super users 104
supply chain management 17, 136
supporting activities 9
system clock 278
system integration tests 120
systems 1
Systems Applications and Products in data processing (SAP) x, 130, 223

T

tactical 135
tailoring 118
test 90
testing 74
theoretical benchmarking 18
to-be models 45
transformations (functions) 49
transition 121

U

UI (user interfaces) 120

unique approach 111
user exits 118
user interfaces (UI) 120
utilities 140

V

value chain 8
ValueSAP 144
vector balancing 256
vendor lock-in 144
vendor selection xiii, 97

W

Waterfall Model of software development 73
work tasks 2
workflow programming 117
workflows 75, 117

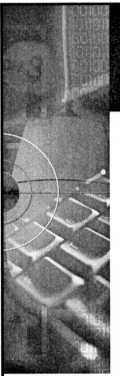